PRAEGER LIBRARY OF U.S. GOVERNMENT DEPARTMENTS
AND AGENCIES

The Internal Revenue Service

The Internal Revenue Service

John C. Chommie

Professor of Law
University of Miami

PRAEGER PUBLISHERS

New York · Washington · London

The passage on pages 137–38 is reprinted with
permission from *Journal of Forensic Sciences* (July, 1961),
published by Callaghan & Company, 6141 North Cicero Avenue,
Chicago, Illinois 60646.

PRAEGER PUBLISHERS
111 Fourth Avenue, New York, N.Y. 10003, U.S.A.
5, Cromwell Place, London S.W.7, England

Published in the United States of America in 1970
by Praeger Publishers, Inc.

Library of Congress Catalog Card Number: 74–95666

This book is No. 25 in the series
Praeger Library of U.S. Government Departments and Agencies

Printed in the United States of America

IRS
$9.50

THE INTERNAL REVENUE SERVICE

JOHN C. CHOMMIE

Who pays taxes in a democratic society?
What economic groups bear the burden?

Tax expert John Chommie asks these questions in the first chapter of this authoritative book. He does not answer them directly, but his succeeding chapters go a long way toward providing the information on which answers to these questions must be based.

THE INTERNAL REVENUE SERVICE does more than examine the tax structure of the United States—it is much more than a bare-bones account of what this U.S. Government agency is and what it does. Emphasis today is on the income tax, but it was not always so, and the book begins with a colorful history of U.S. tax administration in the long, hot summer of the Whisky Rebellion of 1794. It traces the story of taxes and tax-collecting through the subsequent years to the recent revolution in revenue-processing, precipitated by the high-speed digital computer.

Separate chapters are devoted to the organizational structure of the Internal Revenue Service, its field activities, and its management functions—in the course of which the reader is given a behind-the-scenes account of what actually happens to the millions of tax returns that are stuffed into U.S. mailboxes each year before midnight, April 15. Other chapters describe the work of the Intelligence Enforcement Division and the Alcohol, Tobacco, and Firearms Division (the "revenooers"), as well as the agency's complex international activities (overseas tax administration, the author asserts, involves "some of the most head-swimming rules ever devised").

Lastly, Professor Chommie glances briefly into the future and describes in detail the careers open today—and tomorrow—in an agency whose future is inextricably linked with that of the electronic computer. Along the way, the reader will encounter a collection of sometimes surprising anecdotes about such matters as

- The crisis that arose in President Jackson's Administration over how to spend the government's surplus revenue
- The Al Capone case, in which the Internal Revenue Service was able to do something no law-enforcement agency had ever been able to do before—indict and convict the gangster king of the 1920's
- The Civil War tax-collectors hired on a commission basis, some of whom simply made their way west, with their own—and the government's—money
- The 100,000 "squeal letters" written each year by jealous lovers, vengeful wives, disgruntled employees, and tattling neighbors, which produce no less than $20 million annually in taxes and penalties
- The Boston lawyer who claimed before the Supreme Court that the 1894 Income Tax Act was based "upon principles as communistic . . . as ever have been addressed to any political assembly in the world"

The appendixes include a vivid bit of Americana, printed here for the first time—a letter recounting the trials and tribulations of a tax-collector in 1866 in the Territory of Montana, "where nearly 200 murders have been committed but no man [has been] convicted [and] where every man takes his life into his own hands wherever he goes." The narrative is enlivened throughout with equally colorful sidelights that illuminate a subject usually smothered in debate and legal doubletalk—making this perhaps the most readable, comprehensive treatment ever published of the organization that administers the tax laws of the United States.

THE AUTHOR: John C. Chommie, born in Thief River Falls, Minnesota, has been a member of the Minnesota Bar since 1941. He is the author or a co-author of two books on taxation and has written more than a score of articles on various aspects of the subject. A member of the National Tax Association and the Inter-American Bar Association, he is Professor of Law at the University of Miami, Coral Gables, Florida.

PRAEGER PUBLISHERS
New York • Washington • London

Preface

General Andrew Jackson's victory over the British at New Orleans in 1815 is credited by some historians to the combined use of the traditional, the technological, and the innovative. Faced with a force more than twice the size of his, General Jackson invoked the *traditional* by throwing up a palisade on the banks of a dry canal lying athwart the line of march of Major General Sir Edward Pakenham. The *technological* aspect was the use of the recently developed rifled long-gun, with its increased range and accuracy over the smoothbore musket. This enabled the American defenders to reach the advancing British troops while they considered themselves out of range as they moved across the field of Chalmette. The *innovative* was General Jackson's order to fire in relays: When one defender had fired, he stepped back to reload, and his firing place was immediately taken by a second defender, ready to fire. In this manner General Jackson's collection of militiamen from Kentucky and Tennessee—his Creoles, Negroes, and pirates—thrice repulsed attacks by Wellington's veterans before the British withdrew.

The relevance here of these criteria of success in warfare is that, arguably, they can be applied to an evaluation of almost any cooperative endeavor, including an appraisal of the record of a public administrative agency such as the Internal Revenue Service. And measured by the criteria of the use of the traditional, the technological, and the innovative, the Internal Revenue Service comes out quite well, as this volume will reveal.

The Internal Revenue Service, of course, can and perhaps should be evaluated in more traditional terms—in terms of how well it serves the public interest. It is principally by this criterion that the agency is described and evaluated in this volume. Although tax administration as a discipline is a branch of public administration, in the political order it is a part of the taxing process, and its orderly development is a critical part of tax policy-making. The broad goal of tax policy-making is the public interest.

Evaluation in these terms, however, can never be wholly satisfactory if for no other reason than that the concept of public interest is so illusive and is subject to such fundamental conflicts as to what measures serve it best. In the case of tax administration, probably broad-based agreement can be found to exist only as to what must be measured or evaluated—in other words, only as to the proper line of inquiry that should be taken with respect to how well the agency is organized and managed and how well the fundamental taxing techniques of assessment, enforcement, and collection are carried out.

But, even without widespread agreement as to what measures in tax administration best serve the public interest, perhaps most would agree that this interest is served by any light that may be shed on how an administrative agency functions. If this volume contributes in any measure to this ideal, it will have been worth writing.

I have obligations that must be acknowledged. At the top of the list is the debt owed Joseph Rosapepe, Director of Public Information of the Internal Revenue Service, and his assistant, Philip Rothchild, who provided documents and data requested during the writing of this volume, and who arranged my itinerary during a visit to the agency's national office. I am also obligated to the numerous national office officials who gave so generously of their time in interviews and who provided a managerial viewpoint of Internal Revenue Service policies, practices, and problems, and to the agency's revenue agents, special agents, and revenue officers who provided insights with respect to field enforcement activities.

I am also indebted to a number of my students at the University of Miami—Joseph Young, Waldo Rothenberg, James Miggins, Michael Werner, Ridgely Scott, Stuart Gollinger, Martin Greenberg, William Fenton, Daniel Shepro, and Ronald Brodie, among others—who provided research memoranda, and especially to Sheldon Kurland, who provided draft material for Chapter XII as well as a critique of the form and substance of the manuscript. My wife, June Chommie, provided a reading and a portion of the typing; the typing of the final manuscript was the work of Mrs. Bert C. Kirby and Mrs. Henrietta H. Porterfield. I am also grateful for the encouragement provided by Dean Frederick Lewis of the University of Miami and by Mrs. Lois O'Neill, the publisher's Washington office director and editor. Finally, my thanks go to Fred S. Howard, associate editor, for his painstaking work in making this manuscript presentable.

JOHN C. CHOMMIE

Coral Gables, Florida
May, 1970

Contents

TABLES

CHARTS

A section of photographs follows page 84.

The Internal Revenue Service

I

From the Whisky Rebellion to the Computer Revolution: A Historical Survey

Under the date of August 4, 1794, Justice James Wilson of the United States Supreme Court wrote President Washington:

> SIR: From the evidence which has been laid before me, I hereby notify you that in the counties of Washington and Allegheny, laws of the United States are opposed, and the execution thereof obstructed by combinations too powerful to be suppressed by the ordinary course of judicial proceedings, or by the powers vested in the Marshall of that District.

Besides reports of general unrest in the four western counties of Pennsylvania, centering at the bustling village of Pittsburgh, with its 1,200 burghers, evidence of specific incidents was also available to Justice Wilson that indicated that more than normal law enforcement measures would be needed, not only to enforce the mild 1791 excise tax on whisky but also to restore law and order and to quash what became known as the Whisky Rebellion. The evidence of rebellion was clear. The month before, United States Marshal Lennox had served forty writs upon still-owners for nonpayment of the tax; for his efforts he had been seized and beaten by a band of thirty-six men, and his home had been burned to the ground. Elsewhere, two of Treasurer Alexander Hamilton's revenue agents had been tarred and feathered; others had been subjected to similar abuse and indignities. Although almost all western

Pennsylvania farmers owned stills, those who did comply with the tax law or refused to aid in repression of the tax often had their stills "mended" (destroyed) by a band of "tinkers"—all this in the spirit of an insurrection whose elected leaders openly defied enforcement of the excise tax in the name of the "virtuous principles of republican liberty."

Back of the high-sounding rallying cries of liberty and freedom lay the memory of the hated excise taxes imposed by the British Parliament. These western Pennsylvania farmers, many of them Revolutionary War veterans, had a pungent reason for their rebelliousness: the economics of transportation. Without roads and with only trails to market, a horse could carry only four bushels of grain, the principal money crop of the region; one horse could handle the equivalent of thirty-two bushels in the form of whisky. Furthermore, western Pennsylvania whisky—"Monongahela rye"—had already gained fame and commanded a premium. More, indeed, was felt to be at stake than liberty.

But, if President Washington was willing to overlook a pocket of tax resistance, neither he nor his cool and calculating Secretary of the Treasury, Alexander Hamilton, was willing to overlook this first test of survival for the republic under the 1787 Constitution. As the evidence of rebellion mounted during that hot summer of 1794 and reports of the disturbances flowed into the new nation's capital in Philadelphia, it became clear that more than revenue agents and writ-serving marshals was needed.

In September Washington acted. Calling up the Pennsylvania, New Jersey, Virginia, and Maryland militias, the President-General and his staff, including Hamilton and Secretary of War Henry Knox, left Philadelphia on September 30 for the West. Arriving at Carlisle in central Pennsylvania on October 4, Washington took command of some four thousand Pennsylvania and New Jersey troops. The troop movements had not been without effect. At Carlisle, Washington met with two emissaries from the western counties, who contended that peace could be maintained without arms. The President, however, informed them that the military orders had been issued but that additional conferences could be held in Bedford, farther west, where the Pennsylvania and New Jersey militia would rendezvous with the militiamen from Virginia and Maryland.

At Bedford, where some thirteen thousand militiamen had assembled, Washington met again with emissaries from the western counties, who convinced him that there would be no resistance. On October 28, after turning command over to General Henry ("Light-Horse Harry") Lee of Virginia, the President returned to Philadelphia. Although an accidental discharge of a pistol during a chase of the "whisky boys" near Carlisle had resulted in one death, the rebellion had been quashed without a skirmish. The occupation of the western counties and the arrest of the leaders of the rebellion were peaceful events. Although a score of the leaders were sent to Philadelphia for trial, only two were convicted, and both were pardoned by President Washington. Thus ended, for the time being, resistance to internal revenue tax measures. A critical milestone in the life of the young republic had been passed.

THE CUSTOMS DUTIES ERA

The Whisky Rebellion could not be attributed to a lack of experience of the colonists with internal revenue taxation—which, in one form or another, has been known to man during all of recorded history. The early American colonists had been subject to both internal tax levies and to customs duties. Internal levies imposed by the various colonies included taxes on property, a poll tax, taxes on commerce, and a "faculty tax," the forerunner of the modern income tax. The so-called faculty tax was enacted by a New Plymouth ordinance in 1643 and was based on assumed earnings and gains of New Plymouth colonists "according to their estates or faculties."

The colonists were also subject to taxes imposed by the

British Parliament, and those so imposed during the 1760's contributed substantially to the break with the mother country because of the lack of colonial representation in Parliament. These taxes included customs duties on sugar and molasses imported from the West Indies under the Sugar Act of 1764 and an internal revenue duty on newspapers, periodicals, marriage licenses, and legal documents, collected through the use of stamps under the Stamp Act of 1765. It was the Stamp Act, which was repealed the following year, that led to the colonial Stamp Act Congress in October, 1765, and a resolution voicing the colonial protest that "taxation without representation is tyranny."

During the Revolution, since the Continental Congress lacked power to tax, the responsibility of imposing taxes fell on the individual colonies. Many of them imposed a faculty tax; the Massachusetts form of this tax, authorized by an act of 1777, was in effect an income tax. However, in the main, the tax revenues of the colonies were inadequate, and they were forced to rely upon the issuance of paper money and upon domestic and foreign loans.

The deep-seated suspicion of central power that the colonists had developed in their struggle with England carried over to the Articles of Confederation after independence was assured. This quasi-political entity, like its predecessor, the Continental Congress, was also denied the power to tax. It could only borrow and requisition from the states. However, the states felt so little regard for the Confederation that requisitions were frequently ignored. This central government ended up bankrupt, its lack of power to tax being regarded as the principal cause of its failure.

The failure of the Articles of Confederation, however, had a singular compensating feature: the growth and emergence of Federalism as the dominant political theory of the day. This theory was subscribed to by most of the state representatives who were sent to Philadelphia in 1787. Although compromise between federal and state power was necessary, the written Constitution for the new government, which was adopted in 1789, did provide for a federal government rather than a league of states, and one with a central government with the power to impose taxes. In Article 1, the founding fathers granted the national Congress the power to "levy" and "collect" taxes, duties, imports, and excises. However, a direct tax, which was not defined and, as a result, rose to haunt the nation a century later, was required to be levied on the basis of apportioned state population, and duties, imports, and excise taxes were required to be uniform. Furthermore, taxes on exports were forbidden to the federal government, and the state governments were denied the right to tax imports and exports without the consent of Congress. (This consent has never been granted, and hence the distinction between internal and external revenue—custom duties—does not exist with respect to state and local taxation.)

An early order of business before the first federal Congress when it met on January 4, 1790, was the funding of the Revolutionary War debt of some $80 million, mostly unpaid state debts assumed by the federal government and foreign loans. Here Congress was met with the ambitious plan of Secretary of the Treasury Hamilton, the new nation's most ardent and articulate exponent of a Federalism dominated by a strong central government. Hamilton presented Congress with a fiscal plan designed both to provide some $2.4 million a year in revenue and to strengthen the central government's power as a political entity. In the Act of March 3, 1791, over some opposition, Congress gave Hamilton what he wanted: (1) a tariff system that provided for selected duties on imports; (2) excise taxes on whisky distilling and tobacco products, the former to be collected from both public and private distillers by supervisors of revenue; and (3) the delegation of congressional power to the Treasury Department to "collect," a power the Treasury has held ever since.

Other internal revenue duties were added by Congress during the Washington and Adams administrations, although revenue yields were small; these included excise taxes on carriages, salt, investments, sugar refining, and, in 1798, a direct tax, apportioned among the states as required by the Constitution, on slaves, houses, and land. This scheme of taxation required a collection system, and the office of Commissioner of Revenue was accordingly established in 1792.

However, federal taxation is, and has been, inherently a political matter, and the Federalist system of internal revenue, except for a tax on salt, was swept away by the Democrats, along with some four hundred tax collecting personnel, when Jefferson assumed the Presidency in 1801. Except for a brief revival of some excises during the War of 1812, when shipping was hazardous and revenue needs overriding, the federal government relied almost entirely on tariff duties for its revenue up to the commencement of the Civil War in 1861. Not even the Mexican War in 1846 or military operations against the Indian tribes generated a need for internal revenue during the early life of the republic. In spite of fluctuating economic conditions, the tariff and the sale of public land provided ample revenue for the expanding nation. Incredibly, they produced a surplus in some years. During Jackson's Administration, after the federal debt had been liquidated, a hotly debated political issue arose as to the means of disposing of such surplus. After a part of it had been returned to the states, an economic crisis intervened, and the nation has never been forced to face such a shattering experience again.

The reliance of the federal government upon customs duties during the formative years of the nation, a common phenomenon of developing countries, is revealed by some data on collections. In 1800, customs duties provided $5 million in receipts, and internal revenue provided only $400,000. In 1850, customs yields were $25.6 million, and internal revenue less than $50,000.

THE FORMATIVE DECADE

When the Confederate batteryman pulled the lanyard that sent the first shell screaming from the Charleston shore batteries toward Fort Sumter, it signaled more than the start of a bloody conflict between the states. Few persons could have foreseen that the Civil War would result in a fiscal revolution comparable to the political revolt then shaping up. Nor could anyone have foreseen that the collapse of the South could possibly be attributed as much to ineptitude with taxation as to the Northern armies.

On the other hand, taxation had played a part in the issues upon which the nation was sharply divided in 1861. During the decades preceding the outbreak of hostilities, the feelings between the North and South had been irritated more than once over the use of the tariff as a protection device for Northern industry. However, all this passed into history when Lincoln was elected in 1861 and he found himself faced with a falling off of customs duties and a mounting federal debt. When the war broke out, Congress was forced to take a new turn in the fiscal road, down which it was never to retreat. The Revenue Act of July 1, 1862, which superseded a prior, inadequate measure, provided for a broad-based excise system (all manufactured articles were taxed), death duties, and the prototype of the backbone of the present federal tax system— a net income tax.

Although it would not be until the turn of the century that internal revenue receipts would catch up to customs receipts, never again would the national government be able to rely upon customs receipts for its revenue needs. The era of customs duties as the federal government's principal revenue producer was passing into history; the era of internal revenue was already on the horizon. (See Charts B1 and B2 in Appendix B.)

The Revenue Act of 1862 also provided the structure for

the modern internal revenue collection system when it established the Office of the Commissioner of Internal Revenue in the Treasury Department and provided for 185 collection districts. In July, 1862, the first Commissioner, George S. Boutwell of Massachusetts, started with only three clerks in a single office in the Treasury Building. By January, 1863, he had built his force to almost 4,000. It was to remain at this level for the next fifty years.

From the beginning, the bulk of the work of the Internal Revenue Service has been in the field rather than at national headquarters. This was the case during the Civil War. The key salaried officers in the district offices, appointed by the President, were the district collectors, the assessors, and the assistant assessors. Revenue collectors were also employed and were paid a percentage commission of their collections. Revenue inspectors were paid on a fee basis by the manufacturers whose property was inspected. Commissioner Joseph J. Lewis, Boutwell's successor and a friend of Lincoln, hired private collectors for delinquent accounts on commissions ranging up to 50 per cent, an arrangement tailor-made for some unscrupulous collectors, who, after effecting collection, simply continued westward with both their own and the government's money.

Probably the most burdensome administrative tasks fell on the assessors, the workhorses of the collection staff. Their offices were kept open at all hours. They were required to issue a summons after notice to make returns had been issued, to hear appeals, examine taxable property, accept income tax returns, and audit returns for correctness. The four-page income tax return of those days did not approach the complexity of the current form 1040 used by individual taxpayers, but even President Lincoln was found to have overpaid $1,250 on his salary in 1864—a sum refunded to his estate in 1872. Other administrative difficulties stemmed from rulings issued by Commissioner Lewis that conflicted with interpretations in the field. These matters, however, were simply symptoms of the growing pains of an administrative agency dealing with the unprecedented task of collecting internal revenue fairly, a task which, events were to reveal, requires a high degree of sophistication, especially with respect to a progressive income tax.

In historical perspective, the over-all record of the Office of the Collector of Internal Revenue during the Civil War was an impressive one. Although 80 per cent of the costs of the war were met by loans, the four-year-old agency collected some $311 million in excise, income, and inheritance taxes for fiscal 1866. This mark, not to be reached again for forty-five years, should be compared with some $28.5 million of total federal revenue collected just fifteen years before. No small portion of this success may be attributed to a prosperous nation with a patriotic willingness to pay. If fiscal history teaches anything, it is that a successful collection system depends in large measure on the willingness of informed citizens to bear their fair share of governmental costs. With the end of the war in 1865 came a lessening of willingness and a mounting drive to reduce taxes, notwithstanding that the national debt had reached a record $3 billion. As a result, Congress established a three-man Revenue Commission to make recommendations for the future.

The commission's report recommended reductions in the rates of some taxes, the elimination of others, and the retention of the income tax. The commission had found that not all was as it should be with the new agency. Pay scales were lower than those prevailing in private industry; appointments were made on the basis of political patronage; and efforts were made to secure the discharge of Service personnel who, in carrying out their duties, had interfered with the private interests of influential persons. From this report and the recommendations of Commissioner John W. Douglass, Congress enacted legislation in 1872 that eliminated the office of assessor, dividing its function between the district collectors and the Commissioner. In 1874 Congress eliminated the use of private collectors on a commission basis, a practice which had given rise to much dissatisfaction on the part of the agency's salaried personnel.

POLITICAL SOURCES OF THE INCOME TAX

The case was styled *Pollock* v. *Farmers Loan & Trust Company*. The time was 1895. Mr. Joseph H. Choate was to address the Supreme Court for the taxpayer. In precise terms the issue was: Is an income tax a direct tax which requires apportionment among the states on the basis of population as required by Article I of the Constitution? If so, the 1894 Income Tax Act was unconstitutional because apportionment was not a feature of the new law. In a populous state where incomes were low, apportionment could have resulted in a taxpayer with a low income paying a higher tax than a wealthy taxpayer in a less populous state. In short, apportionment was a political impossibility.

The precedents on this point were against Mr. Choate, since the validity of the Civil War income tax had been upheld by the Supreme Court fifteen years before in *Springer* v. *United States*, and there were indications in other cases that only taxes on land and poll taxes were regarded by the founding fathers as direct taxes requiring apportionment. But the Boston lawyer was equal to the task and, while not ignoring the legal arguments, directed himself to the political argument in the following manner:

> The Act of Congress which we are impugning before you is communistic in its purposes and tendencies, and is defended here upon principles as communistic, socialistic—what shall I call them—populistic as ever have been addressed to any political assembly in the world. . . . No member of this court will live long enough to hear a case which will involve a question of the fundamental rights of private property and equality before the law, and the ability of the people of these United States to rely upon the guarantees of the Constitution.

Mr. Choate's argument carried the day. The Supreme Court, in a five to four decision, struck down the tax. The majority of the Court rationalized that a tax on income from property was the same as a tax on the property, and hence a direct tax, but it is clear from both majority and minority opinions that the judges had been moved by the political arguments. Justice Stephen J. Field saw the tax as the beginning of an assault upon capital and a steppingstone to other attacks "till our political contests will become a war of the poor against the rich." Conversely, Justice Henry B. Brown, for the minority, saw the defeat of the tax as "nothing less than a surrender of the taxing power to the moneyed class."

While the dire prediction of Mr. Justice Field has hardly come to pass, the background of fiscal affairs from the Civil War period to 1913 can only be understood in terms of the social and political considerations of the income tax. Although an income tax had been suggested by the Secretary of the Treasury in 1815, based perhaps on British experience during the Napoleonic Wars, it was not until Congress was faced with the task of financing the Civil War that political debate on the social desirability of the income tax reached the boiling point.

The overriding need for revenue made an income tax as a war measure inevitable, and the Civil War income taxes proved to be satisfactory revenue producers. The final Act of the war imposed rates of 5 per cent on incomes up to $5,000 and 10 per cent on incomes over $10,000. For the 1866 fiscal year, this provided $79 million, or about 25 per cent of the total internal revenue for that year.

Most members of Congress and the Administration seemed to have accepted the validity of the income tax at that time, regarding it as an indirect tax, an assumption later upheld by the Supreme Court. However, issue was joined on the progressive feature, and charges of confiscation and punishment of the rich were heard as well as counterarguments, such as that a progressive income tax reflected an "ability to pay." The progressive, or graduated, idea carried the day. The Civil War inheritance tax was also imposed on a progressive basis, the 1864 Act providing rates ranging from 1 to 6 per cent depending on the relationship of the recipient to the decedent. This Act was upheld by the Supreme Court on grounds it was not a direct tax but an excise tax or duty.

When the drive to repeal the various Civil War taxes opened in 1865, the progressive income tax was recognized as a proven revenue producer, but its peacetime acceptance was another matter. Notwithstanding the need for public revenue to retire a $3 billion public debt and to meet reconstruction costs, the immediate lessening of tax burdens was the order of the day. Burdens that were tolerable during the war now became, in the words of political opportunists, "crushing," and the businessman was now "groaning" under the "wrongs and anomalies" of the income tax. The pressure on Congress was severe, and Congress gave ground. The inheritance tax left the scene in 1870, and, after several rate reductions to a flat-rate proportional tax, the income tax was repealed in 1872.

The income tax, however, did not quit the scene without a struggle on the part of its supporters, mostly from the states west of the Alleghenies where payers of income tax were fewer in number. As the Southern states re-entered the union in the decades following the war, they joined with the Westerners in continued agitation for the re-establishment of an income tax—a tax that, with only a modest exemption, would fall mostly on the high-income earners concentrated in the Eastern states of New York, Massachusetts, Pennsylvania, and New Jersey. No less than fourteen income tax bills were introduced in Congress during the 1870's. During the 1880's, customs receipts and excise taxes on spirits, beer, and tobacco were adequate to meet current revenue needs, and re-establishment of the income tax was prevented.

However, when the expanionist era commenced in 1893 (expansionism necessitated a build-up of the navy), the proponents of an income tax were able to muster sufficient strength to secure an income tax amendment to the Tariff Act of 1894. This tax was a flat-rate 2 per cent levy on net income over $4,000. It met its fate on constitutional grounds in the *Pollock* case, described above, in which charges that the tax was "communistic, socialistic, and inquisitorial," were trotted out for the edification of the Supreme Court, along with the more refined and genteel direct-tax argument.

The social revolt then underway, of which the income tax issue was but one manifestation, was not to be denied. The income tax issue was kept alive by the political activists of both major political parties, by the leaders of such splinter groups as the Greenback, Populist, and Anti-Monopoly parties, and by a number of popular writers. Frequent demands were made to give the Supreme Court a chance to reverse itself with another income tax. In 1909, the opposing camp, consisting mostly of Eastern Republicans, and the income tax supporters in Congress hammered out a compromise. The opponents of the income tax believed this to be a shrewd political maneuver in that it would hopefully end the agitation for an individual and perhaps a corporate income tax. Working through Republican President William Howard Taft, who presented the plan to Congress in a Presidential message, the opponents supported a 1 per cent excise tax on corporations, measured by net income, and the initiation of an amendment to the Constitution that would empower Congress to tax incomes "without apportionment among the several States." The opponents of the income tax believed that there was a possibility the excise tax would be declared invalid as a disguised direct income tax under the *Pollock* case, and that there was more than a possibility that the requisite three-fourths of the states would not ratify the proposed amendment.

This political maneuvering backfired on both counts. Two years later, the 1909 Corporation Tax Act was upheld by the Supreme Court in *Flint* v. *Stone Tracy Company*; the Court distinguished this from the *Pollock* case and concluded that a tax on the privilege of doing business in the corporate form was an excise tax and hence did not require apportionment.

Two years later, the opponents of the income tax met their second disappointment when Wyoming became the thirty-sixth state to ratify the amendment. On February 25, 1913, Secretary of State Philander C. Knox certified that the amendment was part of the Constitution. In the same year, Congress enacted the first income tax act under the amendment, and the income tax became a permanent part of the federal tax structure.

The political events leading to the adoption of the Sixteenth Amendment reveal how complete a victory was won. The 1894 Act had stamped the Democratic Party as the income tax party because the Act had been enacted during Democratic President Grover Cleveland's second Administration, an event which one Republican predicted would constitute the signing of the party's own death warrant. However, during the following two decades, prominent Republicans one after another, especially those from the insurgent Western element of the party with progressive or liberal leanings, jumped on the bandwagon. Somewhat of a climax was reached when Republican President Theodore Roosevelt shocked his supporters in 1906 with an open espousal of both a progressive income tax and a progressive inheritance tax. This was followed, as related above, by the equivocal action of his Republican successor, President William Howard Taft, with the 1909 compromise. During the 1910 off-year elections, many candidates from both major parties made political capital in open support of the adoption of the proposed amendment. With the 1912 election of Woodrow Wilson, a Democrat, the Republican Party threw in the towel. From that point on, the social desirability of a progressive income tax has never been seriously questioned by either major political party.

Today the oft-heard charge of the post-Civil War period that a progressive income tax is a communistic device that fosters class warfare is heard only from extreme right wing groups. While these groups are quite vocal in their opposition to the income tax and frequently point out that Karl Marx listed a progressive income tax as one device to be used in wresting control from the *bourgeoisie* in a communistic march toward a classless society, their espousals have yet to be taken seriously by the general public or by Congress.

Less extreme groups, however, continue to make repeated attempts to eliminate or to soften the progressive features of the income tax and to limit the power of Congress in this area. During the past several decades, at least two distinct moves have been made to limit the power of Congress to tax income by imposing a top rate of 25 per cent by constitutional amendment. The first of these efforts was via the unused route of a call of a constitutional convention—under Article V of the Constitution—upon "application of the legislatures of two-thirds of the several states." This movement started in 1939, when the first state adopted such a resolution. Although in excess of thirty states (thirty-four are required) have adopted similar resolutions, they differ in terms. Malapportioned legislatures and the length of time that has elapsed since the early resolutions leaves considerable doubt as to their present viability. Additional debate was generated by the 1951 Reed-Dirksen proposal, which would also have limited the income tax to a 25 per cent top rate and which was timed to take advantage of the natural postwar reaction to the high World War II income tax rates. The proponents of this proposal in Congress have never been able to muster the necessary two-thirds vote required for initiation of a constitutional amendment.

The elimination of the issue of the desirability of a progressive income tax from the national political scene does not mean that the income tax has been shorn of its political trappings. It does mean that the battleground has been shifted from the open view of the general public to Capitol Hill, where the infighting, as a practical matter, is shielded from the view of the American public. The issues now relate to the content of the income tax and rarely generate such emotionally charged terms as "communistic," "class warfare," or "un-American." Debate now generates slightly more sophiscated terms, such as "taxing incentive," "loophole," and "preference."

Meanwhile, back on Constitution Avenue and in the field, what was happening at the Bureau of Internal Revenue (as the Internal Revenue Service was called before 1953)? During the 40-year period from 1872 to 1913, there was no complicated income tax to administer, and most Civil War excise taxes had been eliminated. The only significant remaining internal revenue duties were those on liquor and tobacco. Although these levies produced some 90 per cent of internal revenue, an amount equal to customs duties, a collection staff of 4,000 up to 1915 normally would not have been necessary for such functions. The answer to the continued need for this staff is to be found, in part, in new nonrevenue uses of the government's taxing power. Thus, in 1886 the dairy interests were successful in securing passage of a tax on oleomargarine because it competed with butter, and in 1890 a tax on opium manufactured in the United States was also passed. The administration of these and other regulatory tax measures was assigned to the Bureau of Internal Revenue.

It is worth special mention that these measures generated political and constitutional debates of considerable magnitude and that, historically, Congress has had variable success with the use of its taxing power to regulate. These early regulatory taxes were upheld, but a 1918 tax on industries employing child labor and a 1933 processing tax designed to control agricultural production were struck down by the Supreme Court. On the other hand, use of the federal taxing power to regulate interstate commerce has generally been upheld.

THE AGE OF INTERNAL REVENUE

"The fiscal year of 1918," said Commissioner of Internal Revenue Daniel C. Roper in his annual report, "marks the beginning of a new era of internal revenue taxation." This observation was the gross understatement of the year. At the turn of the century, internal revenue collections of $207 million had just passed collections of $185 million in customs duties (Chart B2, Appendix B). In 1925, when the dust had settled after the repeal and reduction of many World War I levies, internal revenue was producing $3.2 billion and customs a paltry $464 million. Thus, from World War I onward, it was no contest, and customs duties were never again to constitute anything other than a minor source of federal revenue.

German troops triggered World War I by marching into Belgium in 1914. Following American entry into the war in 1917, the new era in federal taxation began. The effect on the Bureau of Internal Revenue was dramatic. In 1913, Bureau personnel in Washington and in the field numbered 4,000 and collected $344 million in revenue; in 1920 the Bureau employed 15,800 persons, who collected $5.5 billion. War and more war was later to result in even more drastic increases during the following decades. By 1970 personnel numbered 70,000 (60,000 permanent), and collections totaled $200 billion.

Why the drastic increase in personnel from 1913 to 1920? Consider what Congress asked the Bureau of Internal Revenue to do during this period. In addition to the normal costs of government, World War I costs totaled some $35 billion. About one-third of this amount was paid for through a wide variety of taxes. These included the first income tax under the Sixteenth Amendment, increased excise levies in 1914, and in 1916 a new income tax, a new estate tax, and a new tax on munition profits. When the United States entered the war in 1917, still further levies were imposed. These included drastic increases in income and estate taxes, a new excess profits tax, admission and stamp taxes, special levies on public utilities and insurance companies, and a greatly expanded excise system. The 1918 Act provided still further rate increases and made additional technical changes.

The proliferation of internal revenue measures during the war period resulted not only in increases in Bureau personnel but in changes in programs and organization. For example, during this period the Bureau launched a wide-scale public relations program designed to educate the public, especially with respect to the income tax, and the Intelligence Division was established to combat tax fraud.

The election of Republican President Warren Harding in 1920 ushered in a new era in governmental fiscal theory, which was to last for a decade and which was personified by Secretary of the Treasury Andrew Mellon. Writing in 1924 in *Taxation: The People's Business*, at a time when collections were producing an annual surplus of $300 million, Mr. Mellon regarded a balanced budget as a national necessity and took the position that the maximum income surtax rate should be 25 per cent as against the then existing top rate of 58 per cent; he stated that, in general, a high tax rate adversely "affects the prosperity of the country." As a result, during the 1920's taxes were cut five times, notwithstanding a large outstanding funded debt, which amounted to $21.6 billion in 1924; by 1932 annual collections amounted to only $1.5 billion, the lowest figure in fifteen years.

The Mellon era ended with the crash of the stock market in 1929. This catastrophic event not only heralded the nation's worst economic depression, with unemployment reaching 13 million in 1933, but brought about a new approach to government spending for economic recovery and the general welfare. With the election of President Franklin Roosevelt in 1932 came deficit spending, required by a wide variety of New Deal legislative measures and programs, including the Social Security Act of 1935, a measure requiring additional taxes to be collected by the Bureau of Internal Revenue. In addition, Congress re-enacted a federal gift tax, complementary to the estate tax, and greatly increased the rates of the latter (automatically increasing the work of the Bureau). As a result, the number of Bureau personnel grew from 11,500 in 1933 to 27,230 in 1941. The Bureau of Internal Revenue had indeed come of age.

THE AGE OF THE INCOME TAX

Operation East Wind, launched by the Japanese High Command on December 7, 1941, constituted more than a declaration of war; as the bombs from the Japanese planes rained down on Pearl Harbor, more was to be destroyed than the United States Pacific fleet. For the American taxpaying public, the destruction and costs of World War II and its aftermath of more war—including a continuing cold war with the Communist bloc—meant a new age of consciousness in taxpaying. For the Bureau of Internal Revenue it meant a new dimension in tax administration, and for Congress and the courts new efforts to provide sound guiding policies, principles, and rules to ensure that the world's most complex tax structure would work equitably in history's most complex democratic society.

In the main, the principal tax device utilized to meet unprecedented World War II and postwar revenue needs was the income tax. The drastic changes brought about during the war period may be illustrated briefly. For the 1939 fiscal year, 6.5 million individuals provided $1 billion of income tax revenue and 550,000 corporations $1.1 billion. Excise taxes produced an additional $1.9 billion, almost as much as the income tax. Further, taxpayers with income under $5,000 accounted for only 10 per cent of income tax revenue. For example, a married taxpayer with two dependents and an income of $5,000 paid a federal income tax of approximately $75 (1.5 per cent).

These data for the immediate prewar period do not differ

substantially from those for all of the pre-1941 history of the income tax from the Civil War to the eve of World War II. Although rates were increased and exemptions lowered during World War I, the pre-1941 income taxes were essentially levies upon the more affluent of American society, a fact reflected by the bitter political struggle behind the income tax discussed above.

When the smoke had cleared after the war, all of the preceding was history. During the peak war year of 1945, 48 million individuals provided $19 billion of income tax revenue; 603,000 corporations provided $16 billion of income and excess profits taxes, and excise taxes yielded $6.3 billion. The base of the income tax had been so expanded that a married person with two dependents and a $2,000 income paid $45 in taxes. Rates were reduced in 1948, but, because of the Korean War (which commenced during 1950 and which turned a revenue bill that started out as a rate reduction bill into one which increased rates), the income tax rate structure did not become stabilized until 1954. In 1955, one decade after the end of World War II, 58 million individuals provided $31.6 billion of income tax revenue, 836,000 corporations $18 billion, and excise taxes yielded $9.2 billion. Further rate reductions were made in 1964, but, with an expanding economy and population, collections continued upward. For fiscal 1968, 73 million individuals provided $78 billion, 1.6 million corporations $30 billion, and excise taxes (including employment taxes and estate and gift taxes) yielded $45 billion. (See Chart B3 in Appendix B.)

One of the more critical questions asked in a democratic society is: Who pays the taxes? That is, what economic groups bear the burden? In the case of the individual income tax, this is not an easy question to answer. The scale of progressive rates has given rise to many misconceptions concerning tax burdens. A basic analysis, but still incomplete, is provided by Table 1, which shows federal income tax liability for earned income for 1973, (subject to a top rate of 50 per cent for post-

1971 years), when all the changes made by the 1969 Tax Reform Act will have come into effect.

TABLE 1

Federal Income Tax Liability, 1973,
for a Married Couple with Two Dependents and Average
Itemized Deductions of 18 Per Cent of Gross Income

Earned Income (dollars)	Amount of Tax (dollars)	Effective Rate (per cent)
3,500	0	0
5,000	140	2.8
10,000	848	8.5
25,000	3,680	14.7
100,000	31,560	31.6

The table does not reflect the exemptions from tax of interest received on state and local government bonds and the special treatment accorded capital gains, which are taken into account only to the extent of 50 per cent and are subject to a maximum tax rate for post-1971 years of 35 per cent (25 per cent on the first $50,000 and certain other transactions). Nor does it reflect a small minimum tax imposed on certain untaxed investment income (but not on state and local bond interest). Most tax-exempt interest and capital gains are realized by upper bracket taxpayers. When these amounts are taken into account, it has been estimated that, collectively, taxpayers in the $100,000-and-above bracket pay at an effective rate of 35 per cent.

The emergence of the progressive income tax as the mainstay of the federal tax structure has resulted in an extremely complex body of federal tax law. The basic legal document, the 1954 Internal Revenue Code as amended, has grown from a simple 16-page instrument in 1913 to a massive volume of some 250,000 words, which must be interpreted in the light of hundreds of volumes of court decisions and Internal Revenue

Service rulings. Only the salient features of the income tax can be portrayed here.

The broadening of the income tax base during the early years of World War II to embrace most of the nation's wage earners, necessitated the utilization of a number of new and innovative collection techniques. One such device was the withholding of tax on salaries and wages. This collection method had been used as early as 1862 and was used extensively with respect to dividends, interest, rent, salary, and wages in the 1913 Act. It was abandoned in 1917 but re-established with respect to salary and wages in 1943. Under the withholding system, an employee files a form W-4 with his employer, which indicates the number of exemptions claimed (himself, wife, dependents). As salary and wages are earned, the employer is required to withhold specified percentages on a progressive scale, which is correlated to the income rate scale, and to remit the amounts withheld to the Internal Revenue Service. Taxpayers not subject to withholding, corporations, and individuals with income other than salary and wages are required to estimate their income for the year and make payment in four installments. In this manner, most taxpayers keep current in their income tax obligation to the government.

A final self-assessment of tax liability is made at the end of a tax year by each taxpayer required to file a return. In the case of an individual, a return of form 1040 is required to be filed by April 15 for the preceding year.

As a further aid to administration, a short form return was adopted in 1941 (combined with the long form in 1970), and in 1944, permission was granted to taxpayers with income from wages of less than $5,000 (increased to $10,000 in 1969) to have their tax computed for them by the Internal Revenue Service. In all other instances the taxpayer must compute his own tax and pay any balance due in excess of amounts withheld or prepaid on estimated returns. If amounts withheld or prepaid are in excess of tax liability, the return functions as a claim for refund. This process, by which a taxpayer computes his own tax on his own return, has resulted in the characterization of the United States income tax as a self-assessed tax.

Corporations file their returns on form 1120, and trusts and estates on form 1041 (trusts and estates are allowed deductions for distributions to beneficiaries but otherwise compute tax as individuals). Special forms are provided for insurance companies, aliens, foreign entities, and certain others. Partnerships, charitable organizations and other tax-exempt entities file information returns only. A partnership is not a taxable entity, and each partner includes his share of partnership income and deductions on his own return.

Individual income tax rates range from 14% on income in the first taxable bracket ($500 for single persons and married persons filing separate returns and $1,000 for married couples and heads of households) to 70%, which is reached at $100,-000 ($200,000 in case of a married couple and $180,000 in case of heads of households). Thus, for post-1970 tax years, the statute prescribes four separate rate tables, all with the same rate range—a table for married couples, one for heads of households, another for unmarried individuals, and a fourth for married individuals filing separate returns (also applicable to trusts and estates). In general, a single person is subject to tax at rates 20% higher than a married couple filing a joint return, although two single persons with equal incomes will pay less tax than a married couple reporting the same total on a joint return.

Rates on corporations are 22% on the first $25,000 of taxable income and 48% on the balance. Capital gains—gain realized from the sale of capital assets (mostly securities, real property, and property used in business)—held more than six months and realized by individuals are taken into account, after deducting capital losses, if any, only to the extent of 50% of the gain. In effect, this is a 50% rate reduction, and, for post-1971 years, these gains are subject to a maximum rate of 35% (25% on the first $50,000 and certain other transactions) on the total amount of the gain. Corporations pay on capital gains at a 30% rate (for post-1970 years subject to certain limitations until 1975, when the older 25% rate fully expires) unless the 22% basic rate applicable to the first $25,000 of business income yields a lesser amount.

For 1968 and 1969 respectively, a 7.5 % and 10% surcharge on tax liability was imposed on individuals and 10% on corporations for both years. For 1970, there was an effective rate of 2.5% on both individuals and corporations. These surcharges were designed to cool down an inflated economy and to defray the military costs of the United States commitment in Vietnam.

The rates are applied to taxable income, called the tax base; this consists of gross income less allowable deductions, and, in the case of individuals, personal exemptions of $750 (for post-1972 years) for each family member. Deductions are allowed for gain-seeking expenses, losses, bad debts, depreciation and depletion on property used in gain-seeking, and for certain other expenditures. Individuals are also allowed certain personal deductions that need not be related to gain-seeking, including those for charitable contributions (also available to corporations), interest, certain taxes, extraordinary medical expenses, alimony, and child care. The personal deductions are not available if an individual elects the standard deduction. For post-1972 years this is 15 per cent of adjusted gross income (income less business expenses) up to a maximum of $2,000 ($1,000 on a married person's separate return) unless the low-income allowance of $1,000 (post-1971 years) yields a larger amount. The standard deduction was introduced in 1944 to aid in the administration of the broad-based tax and before 1970 was elected by some 58 per cent of individual taxpayers.

A number of receipts are exempt or excluded from income, such as one-half of capital gains, interest on state and local bonds, gifts and inheritances, certain meals and lodging provided by employers, and certain pay of military personnel.

However, dividends received by individuals are subject to tax (after a $100 exclusion), even though they constitute the residue of pretaxed income at the corporate level.

The preceding summary of exemptions, exclusions, and deductions cannot begin to record or portray the growth in complexity of the income tax laws since 1913. Nor can this be done simply by recording the tremendous growth in collections and expenditures of federal revenue. While expenditures have been primarily the product of military needs, the growth in complexity of the law has been the result of many factors. Outstanding among these have been rate increases on ordinary income coupled with low preferential rates on capital gains. This has required Congress, the courts, and the Internal Revenue Service to draw fine lines with complex rules in order to distinguish ordinary personal service and business income from realized gain on investments. Complexity is also generated by taxing part of corporate income at one level and then subjecting the balance to tax at the hands of the shareholders when it is received from the corporation as dividends. Additional complexity derives from special privileges accorded certain economic groups for one policy reason or another, and to special rules governing certain relationships, such as those between corporations and shareholders, partnerships and partners, and trusts and beneficiaries. Finally, the elimination of loopholes has often necessitated complex rules so that the loophole plugs will not operate unfairly.

The administration of all this and more—estate, gift, and excise taxes—is the mission of the Internal Revenue Service. It is no small task. (A typical present-day IRS work load is pictured graphically in Chart B4, Appendix B.)

The Electronic Age

Harper's Ferry, Virginia, lies at the junction of the Potomac and Shenandoah rivers. It was here in 1859 that John Brown attempted to precipitate a slave uprising with a raid on the federal arsenal. A few miles to the northwest, at the head of the peaceful Shenandoah Valley, lies the bustling city of Martinsburg, West Virginia. Here, some seventy miles from Washington, the Internal Revenue Service has located its National Computer Center, the heart of a different type of revolt—an ongoing revolution in tax administration precipitated by the high-speed electronic digital computer.

An extensive one-story brick and glass structure houses the "Martinsburg Monsters" (the IBM computers) and the 1,000 miles of master tapes containing the tax records of all U.S. taxpayers—both individuals and corporations—for three cumulative tax years.

When the National Computer Center at Martinsburg was opened officially in 1961, the Internal Revenue Service had been engaged for a number of years in attempts to catch up to private industry in the use of electronic data computers. As the mountain of paper forced upon the agency grew during the postwar years, it became evident that eventually only machines would be able to penetrate the thickening paper jungle. In 1930, the Internal Revenue Service was processing 6 million tax returns annually; by 1969 the number had risen to 110 million, plus some 350 million information returns, and the end was not in sight. As early as 1950, the agency had introduced automatic punched cards and other equipment into the processing of tax returns. In 1955 it opened the first of the three mechanized service centers in Kansas City. The really revolutionary stage of mechanical processing was reached in 1962 with the introduction on a nationwide basis of high-speed electronic computers capable of handling up to 680,000 characters a second. The tax return—processing system, which will be described in Chapter III, now embraces the National Computer Center at Martinsburg and seven regional service centers. Thus, when a taxpayer files his return with his regional service center, the data on the return are fed into a computer through a scanning machine, and the computer records the data on magnetic tape. Perfected tapes—each reel containing 15,000 returns—are forwarded to the National Computer Center, where they are posted by the computer to the taxpayer's master file, also on tape, and then returned to the regional center. The return tapes and output tapes from the National Computer Center are used to determine whether the taxpayer has reported all his income, whether more than one refund claim was filed, and whether a taxpayer owes other taxes, including those from other years. All this for a three-year period, kept current through weekly updating of the master file.

A less publicized segment of automatic data processing was the 1966 opening of the Internal Revenue Service Data Center in Detroit. The Data Center has a management support mission in that it processes all data not related to the maintenance of the taxpayer master files at Martinsburg. This includes the preparation of payrolls, information retrieval printouts, and statistical and related data. In short, automatic data processing not only has resulted in the consolidation of the major field functions of processing returns, accounting for collections, and enforcement, but promises to provide almost unlimited aid in carrying out the management function. As described in more detail in Chapter XII, the potential of the electronic computer for tax administration and for tax policy-making is indeed bright, limited perhaps only by man's imagination.

II

Organization

During the early post–World War II period, a number of events led Congress to believe that all was not well with the Bureau of Internal Revenue. These events led to the formation of the King committee (named after Representative Cecil R. King of California), a subcommittee of the House Committee on Ways and Means, for the purpose of investigating the Bureau's organizational structure and its functions. Although a number of studies looking toward change were then underway, the disclosures of the King committee served in large measure as a catalyst in bringing about a major reorganization in 1952, a reorganization that provided the basic pattern of the present structure of the Internal Revenue Service (IRS).

Probably the most important underlying factor leading to the initiation of congressional investigations and resultant reorganization was the fact that the income tax had reached full maturity during the war. As the IRS struggled with the work load of an expanded and broad-based income tax, it became apparent that measures such as the withholding of tax at source, the short-form return, and the standard deduction were not going to be enough. When a backlog of unprocessed returns built up, it became clear that the collection organization, which had remained structurally unchanged since the organic Act of 1862, was not adequate to meet modern ad-

30

ministrative needs. The IRS organizational structure had developed over the years largely on a patchwork basis as new taxes were introduced into the internal revenue system. For example, when the income tax was introduced in 1913, the Bureau of Internal Revenue simply established a new administrative unit, the income tax unit; and when the Social Security Act became law in 1935, an employment tax unit was created. By mid-century, the Bureau, as stated in the King committee report, was a collection organization that "was exposed not only to the hazards of duplication of authority and effort but also to underdiffusion of responsibility."

Compounding the over-all problem of efficient tax management was a patronage system, headed by sixty-four politically appointed collectors of internal revenue. These islands of power in the field resulted in interorganizational relationships that frequently led to friction between the collectors and the Washington staff with civil service status.

Another factor leading to the 1952 reorganization, which probably provided immediate impetus to the reorganization, was the series of revelations of the King committee, made in public hearings, that certain top agency personnel, including some politically appointed collectors, had participated in numerous corrupt transactions. As a result, prior to proposing a structural reorganization in 1952, the Commissioner of Internal Revenue had engaged in some housecleaning of his own, which resulted in the dismissal or forced resignation of 103 employees on charges ranging from inefficiency to acceptance of bribes. Some of these employees were subsequently prosecuted successfully for violations of United States criminal statutes.

The reorganization plan of 1952, however, should not be attributed solely to the King committee disclosures. Postwar studies of federal government administration by the Hoover Commission, headed by former President Herbert Hoover, and other studies, including one on internal management conducted by the Bureau in 1946, also played important roles.

Historically, Congress has never exercised its full constitutional powers over the collection of taxes or in structuring the collection agency. In the main, it has legislated only to establish specific offices, such as Commissioner and collector, and has otherwise delegated its collection authority to the Department of the Treasury. Since 1932, it has pursued a policy, through enabling legislation, of leaving the initiation of the reorganization of the executive branch of the government to the chief executive. Thus, when President Truman submitted to Congress Reorganization Plan 1 of 1952, dealing with the Internal Revenue Service, reorganization was virtually effected, unless disapproved by either the Senate or the House—and motions to disapprove were defeated in both houses.

The 1952 reorganization plan provided for the organization of the agency on a decentralized, functional basis rather than on the basis of the type of tax administered. The change in name—from Bureau of Internal Revenue to Internal Revenue Service—was intended to emphasize the taxpayer-service aspect of the agency's administration of the internal revenue laws. In addition, the plan provided more meaningful career opportunities for IRS personnel, as well as more effective checks on their conduct. Both the functional aspect and decentralization were effected by concentrating all return-processing, auditing, billing, refunding, and intelligence work at what is now the district level under district directors, and by delegating supervisory functions to regional commissioners (district commissioners in the original plan), presently seven in number. This left basic policy-making to the national office, a function which is now divided between six assistant commissioners and a chief counsel, all of whom are responsible to the Commissioner of Internal Revenue (the chief executive of the IRS).

In order to further the career objectives of the plan, all political offices other than that of Commissioner were abolished (the chief counsel was later restored as a Presidential appointee). This meant the elimination of the field offices of collector and of revenue agent in charge and their replacement by a district director. In order to provide for more effective surveillance of IRS personnel, the agency's inspection function was restructured under an assistant commissioner (Inspection) in Washington, who maintains a staff at each of the seven regional offices.

THE NATIONAL OFFICE

The organization of the national office of the Internal Revenue Service with its 3,700 employees reflects its over-all managerial control functions, including its coordination of the supervisory functions of the regional offices. The work of the national office embraces such matters as departmental planning, budgeting, research, field support, and statistics. These managerial functions must be distinguished from both the supervisory functions performed at the regional level and the field functions of auditing and collecting, which are performed primarily at some 1,000 district and local offices.

The basic IRS organizational structure at the national level consists of the Office of the Commissioner, six assistant commissioners, and a chief counsel (Chart I).

The *Commissioner of Internal Revenue*, who reports to the Secretary of the Treasury, is the primary policy-maker and administrator for IRS activities. He is assisted in his immediate office by a deputy commissioner—the agency's "general manager"—who is responsible for the supervision of the seven regional commissioners, and a Foreign Tax Assistance Staff, which, as described in Chapter VI, assists other countries in improving the administration of their tax laws.

The assistant commissioner organizational structure at the national office level consists of six managerial offices, each of which is organized on a divisional basis. In most cases, each division is divided into branches. This office-division-branch nomenclature is reflected in the field at the regional and district levels.

CHART I
The Internal Revenue Service Organization

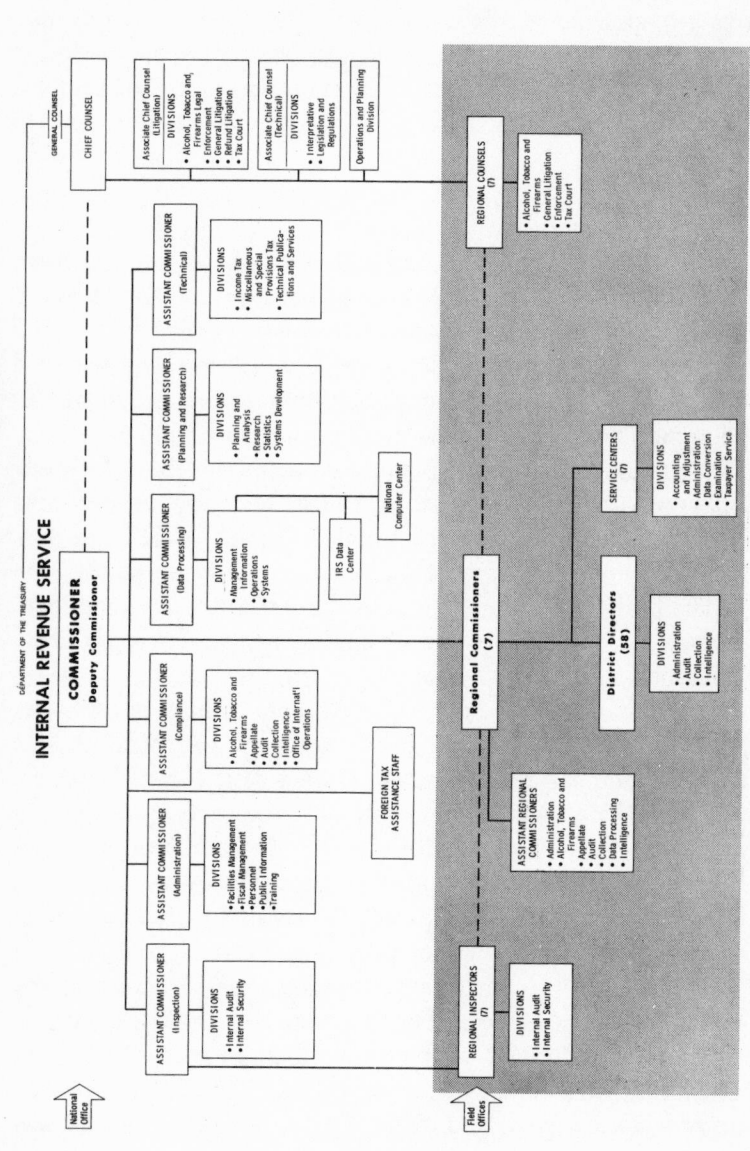

The office of the *assistant commissioner* (*Administration*) provides a wide variety of support functions for the national office and is responsible for functional supervision of similar administration activities in the field. In addition, the assistant commissioner (Administration) represents the Commissioner on general matters of administration in the agency's relationships with Congress, other Treasury Department offices, the Bureau of the Budget, the Civil Service Commission, and the General Services Administration. The office functions through five divisions: Facilities Management, Fiscal Management, Personnel, Public Information, and Training.

The *assistant commissioner* (*Compliance*) is the Commissioner's chief enforcement officer. In private industry, he would be the "production manager." His office provides the managerial guidance for the core operational activities in the field; it is the most heavily structured of all the assistant commissioner offices. Each of its five divisions (and its Office of International Operations) has from five to fifteen branches, staffs, or other separate units. Their work is programed through five divisions (Alcohol, Tobacco, and Firearms; Appellate; Audit; Collection; Intelligence) and the Office of International Operations, which has four divisions of its own (Collection; Audit; Foreign Operations; Research, Tax Treaty, and Technical Services). Three of the first five divisions (Intelligence; International Operations; Alcohol, Tobacco, and Firearms) are treated in detail in Chapters V, VI, and VII.

The *assistant commissioner* (*Data Processing*) can be broadly characterized as the Internal Revenue Service's comptroller or chief accountant. He is charged with the development and implementation of the various automatic data processing programs and with the accounting for the internal revenue collected by the IRS. He also has national office responsibility for the National Computer Center and the IRS Data Center at Detroit and, in addition, exercises a functional supervision over processing activities in the field, including those at the seven regional service centers. The national office structure is divided into three divisions: the Operations Division (which has authority over the National Computer Center), the Management Information Division (which has authority over the IRS Data Center), and the Systems Division.

The office of the *assistant commissioner* (*Inspection*) reflects an operating entity found in most large government agencies: a special unit designed to protect them from what one writer has termed the "internal enemy." About this IRS organizational unit the general public hears but little. It is responsible for carrying out an independent review of all IRS activity to assist management to maintain what is described by the Internal Revenue Service itself as "the highest standards of honesty and integrity among its employees." There are two divisions: Internal Audit and Internal Security. The review work of the Internal Audit Division relates mainly to the formulation of policies and practices for the protection of the revenue; that of the Internal Security Division to the developing of programs designed to preserve the integrity of the IRS.

The office of *assistant commissioner* (*Planning and Research*) was established in 1958; it grew out of a long-felt need for centralized over-all planning in order to maximize the resources of the entire IRS in administering the Internal Revenue Code. Its planning and research responsibilities are discharged in cooperation with other assistant commissioners and officials who are charged with planning and research within their own functional areas. The work is carried out in four divisions: Planning and Analysis, Research, Statistics, and Systems Development.

The *assistant commissioner* (*Technical*) might be regarded as one of the Commissioner's "office lawyers." This office, together with two divisions in the chief counsel's office, is responsible for the administrative interpretation of the federal tax laws. Functionally, this includes the issuance of taxpayer rulings, the providing of technical advice to the field, and a publications program. The office also develops the tax return forms and the accompanying instructions to taxpayers. It consists of three divisions: Income Tax, Miscellaneous and Special Provisions, and Technical Publications and Services.

The *chief counsel* is also an assistant general counsel in the Treasury Department. His office has a threefold responsibility: Its first responsibility is the supervision of litigation work, carried out in four divisions (Tax Court, Enforcement, General Litigation, and Alcohol, Tobacco, and Firearms), under the direction of the associate chief counsel (Litigation). Its second function, which is technical, is the responsibility of two divisions (the Legislation and Regulations Division and the Interpretative Division), under the direction of the associate chief counsel (Technical). An Operations and Planning Division is responsible for its third function—supervision of miscellaneous legal matters, personnel administration, and other administrative work of the chief counsel's office.

REGIONAL OFFICES

Probably the most revolutionary of the changes made by the 1952 reorganization of the Internal Revenue Service was the decentralization of supervision that was effected by the establishment of the office of regional commissioner. This shift in locus of the supervisory function from the national office to the field has been credited with providing one of the principal means by which the IRS has managed to cope with the increasing complexities of federal tax administration; it ranks in importance with the adaptation, a decade later, of the electronic computer to the many mechanical tasks now required in modern tax administration.

As can be seen in the map (Chart II) the regional commissioners are seven in number, and each regional office supervises the work of from six to eleven district offices. Although the principal mission of the regional offices consists in supervision, they have two main operating functions: the carrying

CHART II
Internal Revenue Regions and Districts

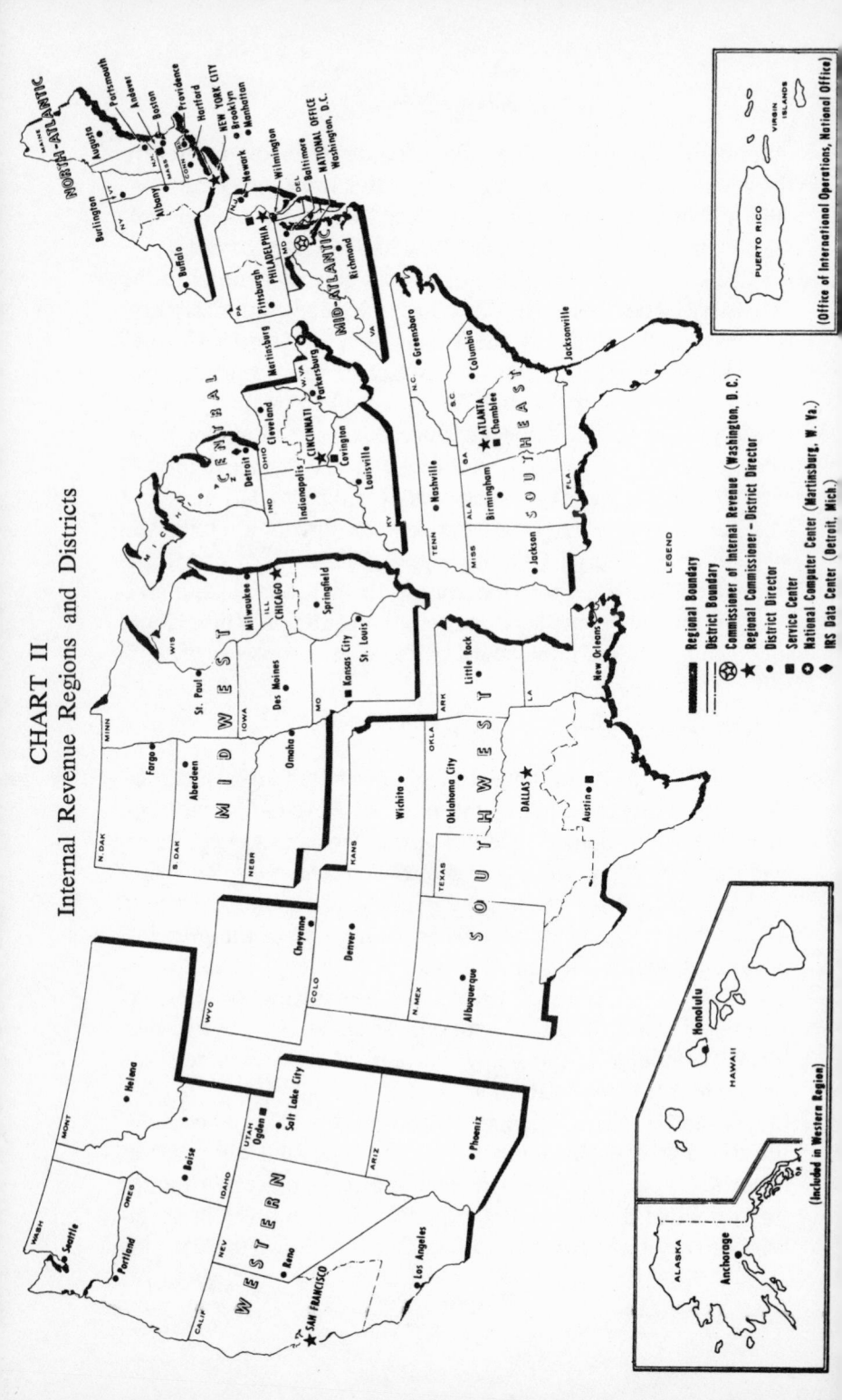

LEGEND

━━━ Regional Boundary
─── District Boundary
⊛ Commissioner of Internal Revenue (Washington, D.C.)
★ Regional Commissioner – District Director
● District Director
■ Service Center
○ National Computer Center (Martinsburg, W. Va.)
◆ IRS Data Center (Detroit, Mich.)

(Included in Western Region)

(Office of International Operations, National Office)

out of the appellate program and the alcohol, tobacco, and firearms program. These two functions have no district office counterparts, although both programs are effected through branch offices located outside of regional headquarters. In addition, each regional office is the locus for two field units— the offices of the regional inspector and the regional counsel— which report directly to Washington and are not subject to the authority of the regional commissioner.

The organizational structure of a regional office is substantially similar in all regions. It consists of the *regional commissioner*, who carries out his supervisory mission through seven assistant regional commissioners, each heading up a separate division (Alcohol, Tobacco, and Firearms; Appellate; Data Processing; Audit; Collection; Intelligence; and Administration).

Each of the seven *regional service centers* is headed by a director who is responsible to his regional commissioner. The director of a service center has a status comparable to that of a district director but is responsible for servicing all the districts in the region with respect to return-processing and related documents and for maintaining records for revenue collected in the region. Each service center consists of the office of the director, an audit staff, a program staff, and five divisions (Accounting and Adjustment, Administration, Data Conversion, Examination, and Taxpayer Service).

DISTRICT OFFICES

The fifty-eight district offices and their suboffices constitute the operational heart of the Internal Revenue Service. Here the bulk of the agency's 70,000 employees, working in and out of some 1,000 offices, provide the basic enforcement of the federal internal revenue laws other than those relating to alcohol and tobacco taxes. Each district office is headed by a district director, who is subject to functional supervision by his regional commissioner. While the organizational structure of a district office varies to some extent, the principal organizational divisions are four in number: Administration, Audit, Collection, and Intelligence.

The *district director* is provided with delegated authority to administer the four operating functions of these divisions, which, in general, consist in the determination and assessment of tax liability, the scheduling and certification of refunds, and the investigation of criminal and civil violations of the revenue laws. This work is carried out by revenue agents, revenue officers, special agents, and other personnel attached to the district office and its suboffices.

As its name indicates, the *Administration Division* provides the office management services for a district office.

The district *Audit Division* is one of three basic types of enforcement units in the Internal Revenue Service. It participates in the selection of returns for audit examination, conducts examinations of all types of federal tax returns (other than those involving alcohol, tobacco, and firearms taxes), provides technical aid to the taxpayer assistance program, and participates with the Intelligence Division in the conduct of tax fraud investigations. The Audit Division has six distinct functions: classification of tax returns, district conference, review, field audit, office audit, and service. The work of this division and the interrelationship of its branches are described in Chapter III.

The district *Collection Division* has recently been subject to a structural change, which reduced its four branches to two: Office and Field. The Office Branch effects collection of delinquent accounts and secures delinquent returns through correspondence, telephone, or office visit by the taxpayer; it also processes certain returns, deposits collected revenue, and carries out the taxpayer assistance program at the headquarters office. The Field Branch, functioning through groups of five or more revenue officers, is responsible for the more difficult collection activities, including the filing of liens and the seizure of property; it also handles certain offers-in-compromise and provides taxpayer assistance outside the district headquarters area.

The district *Intelligence Division* (Branch in some districts) is responsible for the investigation of alleged violations of the criminal laws pertaining to federal taxes other than those on alcohol, tobacco, narcotics, and certain firearms. As described in more detail in Chapter V, this work consists of the development of information by special agents, who make recommendations with respect to prosecution; these agents also assist other government agents in special drives on crime and assist United States attorneys and regional counsel in processing and preparing cases for trial.

A district division, as described above, may be responsible for the work of one or more *area, zone,* or *local offices,* which are subject to the over-all control of a district director. Administrative supervision of these subdistrict offices, which bring the Internal Revenue Service closer to the American taxpayer, may be vested in a senior employee in a functional category, who then acts as the district director's representative for public functions and for the coordination of the activities of the particular office.

III

Field Administration

When revenue agent Tom Jones informed the girl at the information desk that he had an appointment with Mr. Johnson, the office manager, the odds were better than two to one that Smith Company had underpaid its income taxes on the tax returns Jones carried in his brief bag. Jones had made his initial contact by phone; he was now ready to begin his field audit examination of Smith Company's books.

Jones is one of some 13,000 revenue agents, the largest single category of IRS employees; his work is critical in the enforcement of the federal revenue laws. Even so, the performance of his audit is only one of many functions and operations involved in the field enforcement mission of the Internal Revenue Service. Before Smith Company's income tax returns came full circle in Jones' brief bag, they had been subjected to some of the most complex processes known to modern tax administration. Nor would they necessarily be laid to rest when Jones completed his audit and bowed out. Conceivably, they could continue on an even more tortuous course and wind up subject to the scrutiny of the Supreme Court of the United States.

This chapter will describe these basic field enforcement functions in the context of the income tax—the levy that absorbs most of the energies of IRS personnel at all levels of administration—although Jones could find deficiencies in excise and employment taxes during the course of his examination, since these are subject to substantially similar administrative processes. This chapter, however, will not treat the areas of enforcement discussed in Chapters V through VII. Thus, if Jones' audit revealed what appeared to be an intentional omission of income by Smith Company, a special agent from the Intelligence Division of the district office would soon join Jones in a search for fraud (Intelligence work is described in Chapter V). If Jones was not satisfied with Smith Company's accounting for its large-scale sales of sugar, it is possible that an investigator from the Alcohol, Tobacco, and Firearms Division would soon be pursuing the matter further (as described in Chapter VII). Finally, if Smith Company was a foreign corporation, instead of agent Jones from the district office, the knock on the Smith Company door would be that of agent Dawson from the Office of International Operations (enforcement activities in the international area are discussed in Chapter VI).

CURRENT PAYMENT

The permeating character in American economic life of the federal income tax, including its enforcement features, may be revealed by an example. Suppose John Larson, Washington High School graduate, decides to take a job. His entry into the nation's labor force will be preceded by the execution of documents that are vital to the functioning of one of the most important of IRS enforcement devices: current payment of tax through withholding. Before John has earned his first day's pay, he will be brought within the sweep of the tax collection system when his employer requires him to sign an Employee Exemption Certificate (form W-4). This form will reveal the number of personal ($750) and dependency ($750 each) exemptions claimed and will enable the employer to determine the amount of tax to be withheld from John's wages.

When payday arrives, John will discover that some amount of income tax (and Social Security tax) has been deducted from his check. The amount will depend upon the number of exemptions claimed and where John's wages fit on a graduated scale of withholding rates, which range from 14 per cent to 30 per cent. This scale is designed to yield an annual withholding amount (taken proportionately each payday), substantially equivalent to tax payable on annual incomes up to $12,000 earned by single persons and $24,000 earned by married couples. A more affluent salary earner can arrange for additional withholding by his employer. Otherwise he will be required to file installment returns and pay amounts based on his estimated income for the year. The withholding device brings the employer into the initial stage of enforcement, since it obligates him to act as a United States tax collector, an obligation sanctioned by personal liability for the tax if there is a failure to withhold and pay over to the Internal Revenue Service.

Justification for placing this burden on the employer may be found in the history of the withholding system, which, in the United States, dates back as far as the Civil War Act of 1862; the system was also utilized extensively in the 1913 income tax act under the Sixteenth Amendment. Except for withholding made on payments to foreign corporations and nonresident aliens, the device was abandoned in 1917 and was not revived until World War II, when its revival was dictated by the necessities of a broad-based wartime income tax. It was a wartime measure, the Current Tax Payment Act of 1943, that provided the statutory framework for the present system of wage withholding, which results in the collection of some 70 per cent of total individual tax liability each year. Postwar events and a steady rise in the number of taxpayers have increased rather than lessened the need for the system as an enforcement mechanism.

The current payment system does not neglect nonwage earners who are not subject to withholding. Professionals, businessmen, corporations, taxpayers with investment income, and others must make installment returns and payments on the basis of estimated tax liability. Although this complement to the withholding system adds to the administrative burden, since it requires the annual processing of some 6 million additional documents, it not only equalizes the current payment obligation of all taxpayers but undoubtedly reduces the IRS's over-all burden of ensuring compliance.

TAX RETURNS

The tax return is the basic document upon which the Internal Revenue Service depends for carrying out its enforcement mission. The return is prepared on a form provided by the IRS. In essence, this form is a truncated profit-and-loss statement of the taxpayer for the year, although, in the case of an individual, it will not reflect most of his personal expenditures.

The federal income tax system is frequently referred to as a voluntary self-assessment system. This simply means that the taxpayer computes the amount of his own tax liability on his return instead of providing data from which a tax official may assess the tax. For an individual, this means that he must secure a form 1040 (if he filed in the previous year it will be mailed to him), fill it out, and mail it to his IRS service center. If he has overpaid because of excess withholding or excess payment of estimated tax, the return serves as a claim for refund; if additional tax is due, it must be included with the return. Variants of form 1040 are prescribed for nonresident aliens.

All tax entities must file returns. A trust or an estate must file (form 1041) on much the same terms as an individual, as must a corporation (form 1120), whether or not it has taxable income. An affiliated group of corporations may file a single consolidated return for all corporations in the group. A partnership, although not a taxable entity, must file (form

1065) in order to provide a detailed check on its members, who pick up their individual shares of the partnership's income and deductions on their own returns.

The some 110 million tax returns (many of the large corporate returns with supporting schedules measure several feet in thickness) are joined annually at the service centers by some 350 million information returns. This additional mountain of paper and tape (10 per cent of these returns are on computer tapes) is a much needed backstop to enforcement. Two-thirds of the information returns are those required from employers on compensation paid to employees (form W-2's, a copy of which is given each employee for filing with his return). Another 100 million consist of form 1099's, on which corporations and financial institutions report payments of dividends and interest totaling $10 or more made to any person during the year. Employers must also report withholding taxes and Social Security taxes quarterly on form 941. The housewife employing a maid once a week will probably find it mandatory to file form 942 quarterly and to pay Social Security (employment) tax. The informational reach of the collector is a broad one.

SERVICE CENTER PROCESSING

Each regional service center, as described in Chapter II, services from six to eleven district offices and is the original recipient of most returns. What do they do with the returns they receive? How do they manage, control, and record the data? To put the processing of returns in perspective it is necessary to trace the flow of work through the IRS automated processing system.

The processing at each of the seven regional centers (three more are planned for the early 1970's) follows essentially the same procedures, and automation takes over early. The tied bundles of envelopes are removed from mailbags, untied, and fed into an automated mail processor (SCAMP), a small monster controlled through an operating console.

SCAMP processing (30,000 envelopes per hour) includes sorting the envelopes for machine size, opening them with high-speed milling knives, coding their edges, and, after the contents have been removed manually, candling the empty envelopes to ensure that all documents have been removed. The coding, which is both made and read by the sorter, is designed to permit the separation of the returns into five basic categories by each district in the region.

After the mail-sorting, the returns are batched together on the basis of similarities (1,000 to 6,000 in each batch, depending on type of return), and a control card is made for each batch, designating the operations to be performed. The batches of returns are then sent to the Documents Analysis Branch for editing and perfecting. Returns containing discrepancies are referred to a special correspondence unit, which contacts the taxpayer for any needed missing information.

After document analysis, the returns are numbered and subjected to a scanning process by a machine with a keyboard and a TV-like screen. The keyboard operator enters the data from the return, which is displayed on the screen, directly into a process control computer. These data include the taxpayer's account number, types of income and deductions, and related information. The computer in turn performs certain arithmetic and validity checks, identifies any error detected, and signals the operator so it can be corrected immediately. The verified data are then written by the computer onto magnetic tape.

This Direct Data Entry System (DDES) was installed in the various service centers during 1968–70 to replace a keypunching operation, in which data from returns were reduced to computer-readable form through card-punching, and which required separate verification and error-resolution operations.

The new system eliminated the need for the punching and processing of some 400 million cards a year and resulted in savings of several millions of dollars annually in return-processing costs.

Each of the final tapes produced by the service center computers is a 2,400-foot reel containing the essential data from 15,000 returns. These tapes are forwarded to the National Computer Center in Martinsburg, West Virginia, for weekly posting to the master files, and the tax returns are returned to the taxpayer's district office for filing.

The master files maintained at the National Computer Center on some 14,000 reels constitute the heart of the taxpayer accounts control system. They are maintained in two parts on a three-year running basis, one part for business entities (BMF) and the other for individual taxpayers (IMF). Business entities are identified by their assigned employer identification number, and most individuals by their Social Security number.

The weekly posting of regional service center tapes at Martinsburg results in a number of output tapes. These include updated master tapes, tapes containing bills and other taxpayer notices, and refund tapes. Refund tapes are sent to regional disbursing offices of the Treasury Department, where refund checks are prepared from the tapes and mailed to taxpayers (about 50 million refunds are made annually). In addition, the Martinsburg output includes the production of microfilm containing such data as taxpayer directories, return indexes, and settlement registers. For use in enforcement, these films are forwarded to the regional service centers and district offices, where microfilm readers make specific data available in a matter of minutes.

Except for the refund tapes sent the Treasury disbursing offices and the microfilm sent to the district offices, the Martinsburg output is forwarded to the regional service centers, together with the tapes that were originally produced by the service centers. Thus, the basic relationship between the regional service centers and the National Computer Center is based on the exchange of tapes rather than of paper documents.

SELECTION FOR AUDIT

From the magnitude of the document processing task (80 million income tax returns alone, annually), it is clear that each taxpayer cannot anticipate the dubious benefit of having his return examined in detail to determine whether he has complied with all relevant aspects of the law in reporting his taxable income. Yet it is equally clear, in the interest of fairness to taxpayers, that some auditing must be done. Without the examination of returns, enforcement could quickly become a shambles.

The Internal Revenue Service has traditionally rejected random selection as the basic mode of selection of returns for audit. Although a small number of returns are selected on a random basis, the IRS has pursued a policy of selecting those returns that experience indicates will be most fruitful of error. This experience must first be translated into criteria of selection. What are these criteria? For obvious reasons the IRS does not publicly announce such standards. They may be gleaned only from the experiences of taxpayers whose returns have been audited and from past selection practices. In general, income tax returns with the following characteristics are likely candidates for selection for audit:

(1) Returns reporting large amounts of income, those of gamblers and known members of the underworld—the "automatics";

(2) Returns claiming substantial deductions or deductions exceeding norms;

(3) Returns with a formal claim for refund (other than a claim for excess withholding or estimated payments);

(4) Returns revealing discrepancies between income reported and that reported on information returns;

(5) Returns selected for inclusion in special audit projects, such as those involving an occupational group or a geographic area;

(6) Returns that local district experience indicates require special attention; and

(7) Business returns indicating deviation from rationorms, such as "gross profits–gross receipts–net profits," "bad debts–receivables," and "bad debts–sales."

There are other criteria. Information received from a variety of sources (informers, news stories, tax returns of related persons or business entities) may also result in the selection of a return for examination.

Prior to 1963 and the installation of the pilot regional service center in the Southeast Region, screening and selecting tax returns for audit was essentially a manual operation, which meant that a number of revenue agents in each district were taken off their auditing jobs temporarily for the purpose of screening about 25 per cent of the returns for audit potential. Following guidelines established in Washington but using their own judgment, these "classifiers" would select the returns they believed to have audit potential.

The introduction of the computer has changed much of the foregoing. Today, using tapes returned from the National Computer Center, each regional center effects a computerized screening of all returns on the basis of programed selection criteria. But although this initial screening—Discriminant Function System (DFS)—identifies a quantity of returns that are ready for assignment and audit, the number of returns so selected greatly exceeds the agency's audit capacity. As a result, a secondary, manual classification is needed to determine the scope of the audit, the type of examination, and the geographic distribution of the work load. This selection, performed by classifiers in the district Audit Division, reduces total annual audit examinations to some 2.5 million, or 3 per cent of the individual, fiduciary, corporation, and estate-and-gift tax returns filed.

As we shall see in Chapter XII, there is every evidence that this machine-manual process will be subject to still further refinement, directed toward a substantial reduction in—if not complete elimination of—all manual screening and selection.

THE AUDIT PROCESS

Although the computer has had a revolutionary impact on tax administration, it cannot perform the really critical field enforcement functions. Auditing, collecting, and the conducting of conferences and litigation still require people. These functions bring into play some of the agency's most skilled professionals and technicians—men and women who have received training in accounting, law, and engineering before entering the Internal Revenue Service. Consider revenue agent Tom Jones who, as noted at the beginning of this chapter, is about to embark upon a field audit of Smith Company's returns. Tom graduated from college as an accounting major with a BBA degree and entered the Internal Revenue Service shortly thereafter. He has been further trained in special in-service courses of study as well as by experience. He has the status and skills of a professional accountant, a knowledge of tax law, and the ability to work effectively with business executives and tax practitioners.

Tom, who works under a group supervisor (who supervises from twelve to eighteen agents) in the Field Audit Branch, is starting on a field audit. However, some 80 per cent of income tax examinations are conducted by tax auditors (formerly tax technicians) in the Office Audit Branch by correspondence or by office audit—that is, by writing the taxpayer or by asking him to bring his records to the local IRS office to verify the data on his return. The remaining 20 per cent of returns examined are subject to field audit, an examination undertaken at the taxpayer's home or place of business by one or more revenue agents.

What type of problems is a revenue agent likely to encounter during a field audit? Who will provide him with the verifying documents he asks for? How long will it take to conclude the audit? These are all variables. In the case of an individual wage or salary earner, the audit examination will usually be conducted in the living room or dining room with the cooperative taxpayer in attendance (and perhaps his apprehensive wife). The verifying documents, spilled out of a shoebox, will consist of canceled checks, conditional sales contracts, and a variety of receipts. The items the agent has noted for verification may include a dependency exemption claimed for a relative not living with the taxpayer (and occasionally for the family pet, simply designated "Rosie" on the return), or deductions in excess of norms claimed for charitable contributions (how often does the taxpayer go to church?) and for sales taxes. The whole unpleasant business —from the taxpayer's point of view—may be over in an hour and may result in a small deficiency, agreed to by the taxpayer, who regards himself as getting off easy.

Suppose the taxpayer is not cooperative and refuses to talk or to produce his records. What can the agent do? He is not without power. Congress has provided him with a number of legal devices that enable him to proceed with his audit. Although a taxpayer may not be subjected to "unreasonable examination," a revenue agent is expressly authorized by law to examine all books, records, or data relevant to his audit, including records (other than those to which a legal privilege attaches) held by other persons. He may summon any person to produce relevant records and may administer oaths and take sworn testimony subject to the penalties of perjury. If this is not enough, his summons may be enforced by an order of a United States District Court, which, if not obeyed, will subject the person summoned to the penalties of contempt of court.

Moving up the economic ladder, if the taxpayer is a professional (lawyer, doctor, accountant, or businessman), the examination might be conducted in the office of the taxpayer's representative (lawyer or accountant), and the records available for verification (daily journal, ledger, vouchers) will be more sophisticated. The issues or unusual items may be similar to those noted above, and, in addition, the agent may be concerned with whether the real value of a painting contributed to a charity was that claimed on the return, or whether the taxpayer has reported all his cash income. If there are indications he has not, the agent may recommend an investigation by the Intelligence Division and suspend his audit until a special agent has concluded the fraud issue. The time involved? Perhaps a day if all goes well; this would be the case, for example, if the taxpayer had a written appraisal report on the painting that was acceptable to the agent.

At the top of the ladder of affluent taxpayers are the giant corporations, who provide 90 per cent or more of the $30 billion of corporate income tax. Here, instead of a single agent, there will be a team of top-grade (GS-12 and GS-13) agents, headed by a case manager and working under the large-case program. The problems here involve multistate and related corporations and each agent is assigned to a specific portion of a programed audit under the over-all supervision of the Coordinated Examination Branch in the national office Audit Division. The actual audit work may require the use of the Auditape System (developed by the accounting firm of Haskins and Sells) which is available in each region. This system consists of a reel of magnetic tape with specification sheets and enables the examining agent to retrieve specific data from the taxpayer's own computer.

The issues faced in the audit of these industrial giants are complex and involve such matters as consolidated returns, multicorporations, foreign transactions, and reorganizations. The time involved may be considerable. One survey of 400 large companies for the 1956–60 tax years revealed that the average lapsed time from commencement of multiple-year audits to the submission of the agent's report was ten months, and that the average revenue agent time devoted to each audit was three months.

Team audits, however, are the exception. The bulk of business firm audits, including those of small and medium-sized corporations, are conducted by a single agent at the journeyman level (GS-11), although the legal and fact issues may be just as complex as in the case of the industrial giants. These may include questions of the rules pertaining to the accumulated earnings tax, constructive dividends, personal holding companies, stock redemptions, and reasonableness of salary payments. The time involved may range from one day to several months, with perhaps an average time expenditure of one to two weeks.

If a valuation issue arises during an audit, the examining agent may find it necessary to ask for assistance from a field engineer (such assistance will also be provided, if requested, by the taxpayer, and if the chief of the Audit Division approves). Field engineers are located at some forty district offices. Their services will often be required on such complex issues as the basis of property in claims for depreciation deductions, determinations of useful life of property, mine exploration costs, and depletion problems of oil and gas and other natural resources. In the same manner, technical advice may also be sought from the national office on unusually complex legal issues or where there has been a lack of uniformity in interpretation.

At the conclusion of an audit, the taxpayer will have an opportunity to discuss the agent's findings with him. Can the agent and the taxpayer compromise at this point? Theoretically, the agent lacks this authority, but he is a human being and is encouraged to secure the taxpayer's consent to findings of additional tax. Further, some findings may be weak and questionable, others clear and convincing. Some practical compromise may be inevitable.

In any event, upon completion of the audit, the revenue agent will inform the taxpayer whether the audit resulted in a tax deficiency, an overassessment, or no change. If the taxpayer agrees to a proposed deficiency, the mechanics in effecting the settlement will depend upon the type of case. If the audit involves an individual or a small corporation, the agent, under a procedure established in 1969, will prepare a short report (made up in four-part carbon interleaved snap-out assemblies) and leave one copy with the taxpayer or his representative before submitting his report for review. If the case involves a large corporation (and in all cases where the taxpayer does not agree to a proposed deficiency), the agent will first submit a more detailed report to his group supervisor who, if he approves, will transmit the report to the Review Staff in the Audit Division.

Ordinarily the revenue agent's recommendations in his report will be approved on review, but in some instances the agent may be required to rewrite his report or seek additional data from the taxpayer. (In the Central Region, review of agents' recommendations is centralized in the regional office). These initial reviews, together with selected postaudit reviews at the regional level—which normally do not result in upsetting settlements—are designed to provide a measure of national uniformity in audit policy and procedures.

Following initial review in an agreed large-corporation case, the taxpayer will be sent a copy of the part of the agent's report designed for this purpose, which contains a brief statement of the proposed adjustments and the reasons for them. However, in all agreed cases at the termination of the audit, the agent will ask the taxpayer to sign a form 870 (Waiver of Restrictions on Assessment and Collection of Deficiency in Tax and Acceptance of Proposed Overassessment). The execution of form 870 by the taxpayer and the IRS—in form a contract, although technically this does not have a binding legal effect on either party—ordinarily will be the end of the matter where an audit has revealed either a deficiency or an overpayment, but it does not prevent a taxpayer from paying a deficiency and later suing for a refund, nor does it prevent the IRS from asserting a further deficiency. It does, however, permit the Internal Revenue Service to assess and collect the deficiency without sending the taxpayer a required statutory notice (90-day letter) which in turn precludes the taxpayer from litigating the proposed deficiency in the Tax Court. This will be discussed more fully below.

REFUNDS

Suppose that the revenue agent's audit reveals that, instead of being responsible for a tax deficiency, the taxpayer has overpaid—a not infrequent occurrence. Or suppose the taxpayer discovers his own error in overpaying. In such cases, the taxpayer has a claim for refund (plus 6 per cent interest) against the United States; the revenue laws and the Commissioner's regulations dictate how he must proceed in order to collect.

Overpayment is essential to a valid claim. Most overpayments result from excess amounts withheld on wages and from overpayments on estimated income. On these overpayments, the tax return serves as a claim, and the IRS makes these refunds, which amount to some 80 per cent of the $10 billion refunded annually, within an average period of thirty-five days through refund output tapes from the National Computer Center. Before the refund tapes are forwarded to the Treasury disbursing offices, they are subjected to computer verification to ensure that the tapes do not contain more than one refund claim. (Multiple refund claims—some fraudulent but most unintentional because of lack of knowledge that earnings from more than one employer belong on a single return—were an early casualty of the automatic data processing system.) The tapes are also checked to determine whether the taxpayer owes the government other taxes or taxes from other years. Such claims are deducted from the refund.

The processing of return claims described above does not

mean that these returns are treated as closed; they could still be selected for audit and subject to a deficiency assessment.

Claims other than return claims, and overassessments disclosed upon audit examination, require a formal claim for refund (form 843). In a nonaudit situation, the filing of the claim will frequently trigger an audit, even if one was not scheduled, and often the audit will include all years on which the statute of limitations (three years) has not run out. A critical question for the taxpayer who discovers his own overpayment is whether he can stand an audit of all open years. Even if the claim is approved, it will not be paid until it has been checked against outstanding liabilities of the taxpayer for other taxes or other tax years. If such liabilities exist, they will be deducted from the refund due the taxpayer.

In case an audit of a return after a claim for refund reveals an excessive claim, the revenue agent will attempt to close the matter through a form 870 in a manner similar to a proposed deficiency.

Refunds in excess of $100,000 are subject to special handling and ultimately require approval in Washington by Congress's Joint Committee on Internal Revenue Taxation. These so-called joint committee claims (about 500 annually) are first reviewed by the group supervisor and the review staff in the district office under special guidelines and then are forwarded to a staff of joint committee coordinators at the district office located at regional headquarters. From here, the file and a report go to Washington—through the assistant commissioner (Compliance), except in cases in which no agreement has been reached, in which case the file is forwarded by the regional commissioner (Appellate)—to the assistant to the Commissioner and thence to the joint committee, whose staff subjects the claim to a final review.

In filing a refund claim, a taxpayer, in addition to seeking a return of his money, may be motivated by a choice of courts. If a revenue agent has recommended a disputed deficiency, as described below, the taxpayer may be interested in litigating in a federal District Court or the Court of Claims rather than in the Tax Court of the United States. If this is the case, he will pay the deficiency and file a claim for refund (even though he knows it will be rejected), because a claim for refund is a necessary prerequisite for a refund suit in the District Court or the Court of Claims.

APPEAL PROCEDURE

Suppose the audited taxpayer disagrees with the revenue agent's findings of a tax deficiency, or that a claim for refund is rejected after an audit. For these cases, highly developed administrative appeal procedures are available, designed to dispose of these controversies without resort to litigation in the courts (Chart III). These procedures, which function at both the district and regional level, result in agreement in some 80 per cent of the disputes prior to the issuance of a formal notice of deficiency.

In brief, the mechanics are these: After an audit (or rejected claim), the agent's group supervisor sends the case to the review staff. If the review staff agrees with the agent's findings, it informs the taxpayer by mail (30-day letter) of the proposed deficiency, repeats the offer to settle with a form 870, and states that he has thirty days to file a written protest with the district director and request a district conference; as an alternative, the letter informs him that he may go directly to an Appellate Division conference, a procedure that is encouraged in complex cases, especially those involving large deficiencies. A copy of the revenue agent's report, reciting the basis for the proposed adjustments, is enclosed with the letter. A written protest is not required for a district conference if the proposed deficiency does not exceed $2,500 for a tax year.

After the protest and request for a conference is received (a request for a conference may be made after an interview in case of an office audit), the case is handled by the con-

CHART III
Income Tax Appeal Procedure

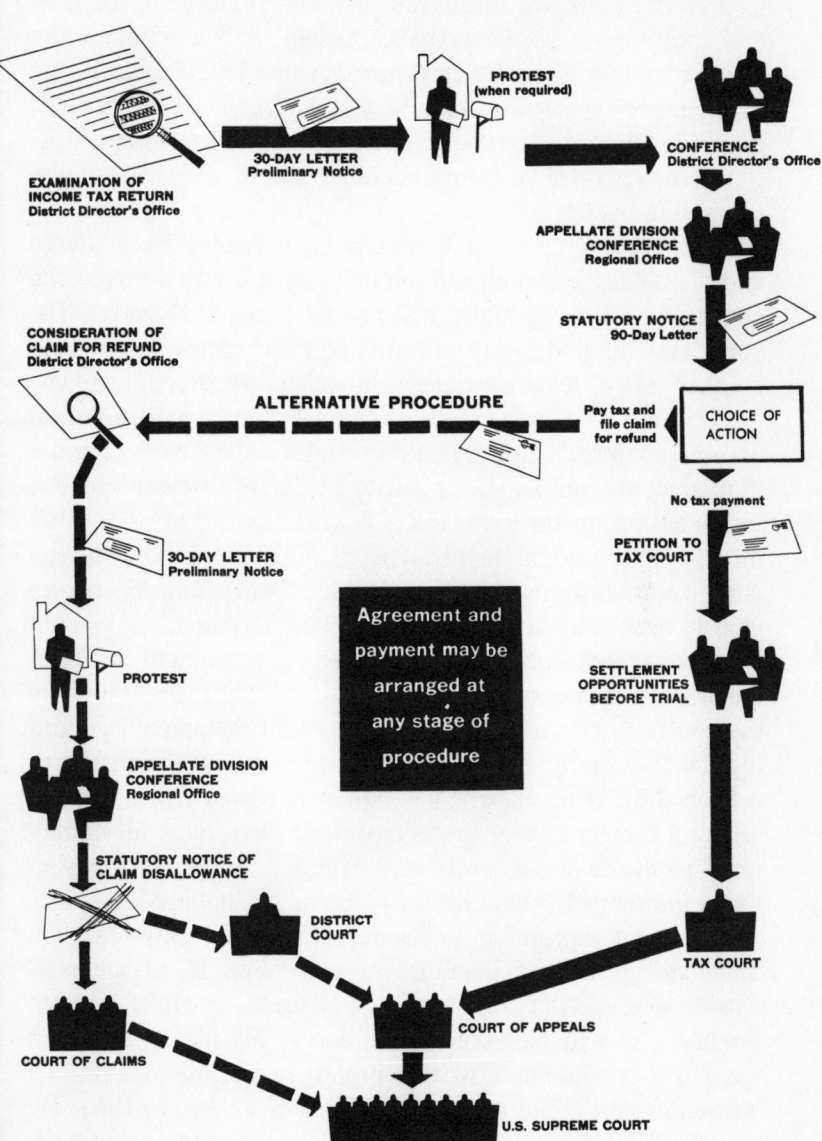

ference staff, a branch of the Audit Division. The chief of the Conference Staff will assign the case to a conferee in the general location where the taxpayer resides, and a time for the conference will be set by agreement. A district conferee is one of the more experienced members of the Audit Division staff; normally he does not have auditing duties to perform. His mission is to conduct an independent review of the work of the examining agent.

At the conference, or conferences, between the conferee and the taxpayer (who need not be present if represented) the examining agent normally will not be present. However, the conferee is limited in his authority to settle issues in the same manner as a revenue agent; in other words, agreements reached must be based upon the concession of whole issues, and the conferee's conclusion constitutes only a recommendation, since he, unlike the appellate conferees discussed below, lacks authority to bind the Commissioner. On the other hand, if the amount involved is $2,500 or less, the district conferee is authorized to compromise issues that have previously been ruled upon by the Appellate Division.

At the conclusion of the conference, if agreement has been reached (as it is in 65 per cent of some 40,000 cases annually) the conferee will issue a Conference Audit Statement containing the data on the conference and will close out the case with a form 870. If agreement has not been reached, the stage is set for a further appeal to the Appellate Division, which functions at the regional level; each regional Appellate Division has a number of branches, forty-one in all, nationally.

In case of a proposed deficiency, a taxpayer may reach an appellate conference in either of two ways. If, at the conclusion of a district conference, he requests an appellate conference (he will be asked if he does), his file will be forwarded if it contains a written protest or he provides one (a written protest is not required for cases of $2,500 or less). He will then be given a conference; if no agreement is reached, he will be issued a statutory notice of deficiency (90-day letter) which provides him the means of petitioning the Tax Court for a redetermination suit. If this is done, his case is docketed and he is then given a further opportunity for an additional conference. In the alternative, he can skip either or both conferences at the nondocketed stage and go into conference after his petition to the Tax Court has been filed. In a similar manner, in case of a rejected refund claim, a taxpayer may also follow the conference procedures.

Appellate conferences normally are conducted at a local district or Appellate Division branch office by an appellate conferee, who is a lawyer or an accountant or both and who has had considerable experience in tax administration. Appellate conferees are vested with authority to settle cases. This authority stems directly from the Commissioner, and, unlike that of the district conferee and revenue agent, permits appellate conferees to take practical considerations, such as the hazards of litigation, into account in effecting settlements. In preparing for conferences, they have two computer information retrieval systems available. The first enables them to keep up with cases pending in the branches of the regional counsels' offices (the Reports and Information Retrieval Activity, RIRA, described below) and the second with cases in other Appellate Division branches through the country (Appellate Reports and Information Retrieval Activity, or ARIRA). The conferees function effectively in that, of some 30,000 cases disposed of annually by the Appellate Division, only 3 per cent are left for actual trial in the courts.

If agreement is reached with the conferee (approval of the regional counsel's office is required in docketed cases and settlement is effected by stipulation in the Tax Court), the case will be reviewed by the Appellate Branch chief. If the case is not approved, the taxpayer will be offered a further conference. Upon final approval, and if the agreement involves concessions by either side, as is usually the case, the taxpayer will be asked to join in signing a form 870-AD (AD for Appellate Division). This waiver differs from the usual form 870 in that, in terms, it constitutes a final settlement in absence of fraud or misrepresentation. As a practical matter, the form 870-AD settlement has proved to be just that, although the courts have refused to regard it as final on grounds that the Internal Revenue Code itself provides the only means of settling tax liabilities by contract. These Code provisions are those pertaining to closing agreements—agreements on the interpretation of the law with respect to a specific item or a specific tax liability—and to offers-in-compromise, which constitute a compromise of liability where there is doubt as to liability or collectibility. The latter agreements must be made public and other safeguards established by the law must be met.

JUDICIAL REVIEW

If no agreement is reached at the appellate conference, the way is open for judicial review. Thus, in an unagreed case involving a proposed deficiency, as distinguished from a claim for refund, if the taxpayer has not previously received a statutory notice (90-day letter) from the district director, the notice will be issued at this time by the Appellate Division. Following the issuance of this letter, the taxpayer has ninety days (150 days if he lives outside the United States) to file a petition with the Tax Court for a redetermination of the deficiency, during which time the IRS is precluded from assessing or collecting; if the petition is filed on time, no assessment or collection may be made until the judgment of the court becomes final.

In the alternative, the taxpayer may elect to litigate in a United States District Court or the Court of Claims by paying the deficiency and filing a claim for refund, which, upon formal rejection or the lapse of six months, will provide him the jurisdictional basis for a refund suit.

If the appellate conference was on a refund claim that remains unsettled, the taxpayer, of course, can only sue for refund in the District Court or Court of Claims. It is worth noting that it is the taxpayer, rather than the Internal Revenue Service, who has a choice of courts in seeking judicial review. The widest choice occurs when he is faced with a proposed deficiency. All three courts, however, are courts of original jurisdiction, and trial of a tax dispute is *de novo* of any district or appellate conference.

A number of factors may bear on a taxpayer's choice of courts, including his ability to pay a proposed deficiency. If this is lacking, litigation in the Tax Court is the only answer. Another factor is that of interest. If he loses in the Tax Court, interest at 6 per cent runs on any deficiency found to be due (unless payment is made after a statutory notice is sent), whereas, if the taxpayer sues on a refund claim and wins, interest at the same rate runs in his favor. A third factor is that the District Court is the only court where either party may have a jury trial.

Appeals may be taken by either party from both the Tax Court and the District Court to one of eleven Courts of Appeal and thence, in rare cases, to the Supreme Court of the United States upon petition. However, under recently established procedures, a taxpayer subject to a $1,000 deficiency or less may elect to litigate in the Tax Court under more informal small claims procedures, and in such event no appeal is allowed to either the taxpayer or the government. The Supreme Court hears only ten or twelve tax cases a year and will accept a tax case only if it regards it as being of prime importance to the revenue, or if the case will resolve a conflict in law between two or more lower courts. The only appeal from the Court of Claims is to the U.S. Supreme Court on petition.

The field enforcement activities of the Internal Revenue Service continue into the judicial review area only if the taxpayer elects to litigate in the Tax Court. In such cases, as soon as he files his petition in the Tax Court, the Tax Court Division of the chief counsel's office at the regional level is brought into the picture. Although the chief counsel's office has other litigation functions (refund, collection, enforcement) in which it participates with the Department of Justice, only lawyers from the Tax Court Division actually try cases as the Commissioner's representative, and then only in the Tax Court. In all other cases in the District Court, Court of Claims, Courts of Appeal, and the Supreme Court, the Commissioner or the government is represented by attorneys from the Department of Justice or the solicitor general's office.

At the regional level, the regional counsel's office functions in a manner similar to the Appellate Division, through branches in thirty-five major United States cities, and an attorney from one of these branches will be assigned to defend the Commissioner's position in the Tax Court.

Although the Tax Court functions as a court, it did not acquire its present name until 1942 and did not become part of the federal court system until 1969. Before that it was an independent agency in the executive branch, established in 1924 as the Board of Tax Appeals in order to provide the taxpayer with an independent review of asserted deficiencies by the collection agency, a review that would be available without prior payment of tax. Thus the very basis of the Tax Court's jurisdiction is the statutory notice of a deficiency (90-day letter) for income, estate, or gift taxes, although the court can find an overpayment so long as the requisite asserted deficiency is present.

The Tax Court, organized on a national basis, has its main office in Washington. Its sixteen members, headed by a chief judge, may sit in any city, and, in practice, cases are heard by single judges in some fifty cities (as requested by the taxpayer) throughout the United States. Its annual case load runs to some 7,000 petitions (as compared to 1,500 suits filed in the District Courts and the Court of Claims), more than 6,000 of which are settled before trial.

The Tax Court regards as one of its missions the providing

of a body of interpretative case law (through published reports of the cases) that is uniform throughout the United States. The chief counsel adheres to a similar policy with respect to the position of the IRS on legal issues. To this end, he has established a computerized legal information retrieval system (Reports and Information Retrieval Activity—RIRA), designed to solve three interrelated management problems: the maintenance of consistency on legal issues, the gathering of work load and legal statistics, and the location of published precedents for legal research.

The first problem merits additional attention at this point. In addition to legislative and regulations projects, the chief counsel's office handles some 30,000 tax matters each year. Prior to RIRA, much of this information was buried in closed files in the national office. How, for example, was an attorney in the Los Angeles or Houston branch office to know the IRS position with respect to the case on his desk? Published judicial opinions and administrative regulations and rulings were far from adequate for this purpose. The answer was found in the computer—through the formulation of a communications language, a Uniform Issue List; this required the design of a form—in a keypunching format—upon which the various branches could report their cases. The result was the establishment of statistical control and, even more important, a printout of an inventory index of current cases as well as abstracts of each case. The abstracts provide more detail about each case than does the index, and include the issues and position taken by the Commissioner and by the taxpayer.

Both the index and abstracts are updated monthly, the latter on microfilm, and are sent to the field branch offices. Thus, a field attorney can now check the index for the index terms in his case, and with these he can search for similar pending case abstracts; if inconsistent positions are found, he can contact the other office or offices involved in order to resolve the inconsistencies.

COLLECTION

As described earlier, the collection process may start as soon as the detection of a mathematical error (taxpayers favor themselves two to one), while a return is being processed at the service center. In these cases, if the taxpayer does not pay up after his correspondence with the computer, the government's claim will end up in the Collection Division of the taxpayer's district office. Here, along with other taxpayers in debt to the United States who have waived or exhausted their review remedies, he will be faced with the formal assessment process—not to be confused with the so-called self-assessment made by a taxpayer in filing a return—and the collection power of the revenue officer.

The collection process starts with an assessment by the district director and a recording of tax liability on an assessment list; assessment is a prerequisite to collection. However, it will be recalled that assessment and collection are stayed for ninety days after the issuance of a notice of a proposed deficiency in order to give the taxpayer time to petition the Tax Court for a redetermination. Does this mean that the taxpayer also has ninety days to remove himself and his goods from the reach of the collector? Not necessarily. Congress has provided the collector with two collection devices designed to frustrate such efforts. If the collection officer believes that assessment or collection will be frustrated by delay, he may make an immediate, so-called jeopardy assessment and a demand for payment (which may be lifted by the posting of bond), or he may order an immediate closing of the taxpayer's tax year and make a demand for payment.

Once assessment has been effected, the Internal Revenue Service has been given substantial powers to effect collection. These powers, in effect, place the tax debtor in substantially the same position as a judgment debtor. Thus, the collector is given the power (1) to bring a law suit against the delinquent taxpayer in any federal or state court, (2) to seize the taxpayer's nonexempt property and sell it to satisfy the tax debt (the power normally used), and (3) to proceed by court action to foreclose its lien. The IRS may also charge the amount of the assessment against any money owed the taxpayer and, in some instances, against property the taxpayer has transferred to another person. Finally, except in rare cases, the taxpayer is expressly prohibited from bringing a law suit to enjoin the collection of federal taxes.

Most of the preceding powers come within the purview of some 6,000 revenue officers (collectors) who work out of the field office branch of the district office Collection Division. Their main job is twofold: to seek out taxpayers who have failed to file returns and to collect tax obligations owed the United States. With the aid of the service center computer they turn up some 800,000 delinquent returns annually, yielding almost $300 million in revenue, and close out approximately 2.4 million delinquent accounts, yielding $2 billion. They have been likened to hard-boiled, sophisticated collection agency collectors (but for a really determined collector, see Appendix A). Actually, these college-trained revenue officers use their powers sparingly, and, if an account appears uncollectible, they will utilize the "offer-in-compromise" or other means of ensuring that the government collects at least a portion of its claim. The Internal Revenue Service thinks highly of its revenue officers.

IV

The Management Functions

From high in the air, the building appears to be square with an enclosed center courtyard; closer examination reveals that the Tenth Street side of the structure has the appearance of a long, neck-like appendage with an inward, head-like wing, which does not quite close in the courtyard. From ground level, the front of the building—the bottom of the square—extends 410 feet along Constitution Avenue, and the Twelfth Street side extends 452 feet back to C Street. The three arches at the main entrance at 1111 Constitution Avenue rise two stories to the architrave. This seven-story concrete, limestone, and marble structure is IRS's national office building in the Federal Triangle complex of government buildings in Washington, D.C., built in 1930 at a cost of some $10 million. Its design was inspired by Somerset House on London's Strand, the structure housing Britain's tax collection agency—Inland Revenue.

The IRS Building (the Tax Court occupies the second story) houses most of the national office staff of some 3,700. Here and at the seven regional offices and fifty-eight district offices scattered throughout the country, the IRS managers direct the activities of the Internal Revenue Service. What do these managers do? How do they provide the needed supervision of the field force? What problems do they encounter in making policy in carrying out the mission of the IRS to ensure compliance with the statutory rules enacted by Congress? While these questions do not admit of easy answers, in this and in succeeding chapters, an attempt will be made to shed some light on the agency's various management functions.

SUPERVISION

It is the lot of organization man that his work be subject to supervision, in one form or another, by others. So it is in the Internal Revenue Service, from the Commissioner on down to the newly hired mail clerk. And, as in case of most large organizations, the IRS employs what are perhaps standard techniques in discharging this management function at all levels. Staff meetings, employee appraisals, operating manuals, periodic reports, field visitations—all are utilized. The detailed supervision to which certain categories of employees are subjected, especially those who play a critical role in the tax liability adversary process, merits special attention. Most numerous here are the 13,000 revenue agents, whose tax return examination work puts them in the front line of this process.

Recall, for a moment, our description in Chapter III of the machinery that exists for review of a revenue agent's audit examination. This review starts with a scrutiny of his proposed report by his immediate superior, the group supervisor and may call for a discussion between the supervisor and the agent. The discussion may be a continuation of one or more discussions at the planning stage of the audit and during its conduct, especially in case of prolonged team audits of large accounts. At this stage, the evaluation of the agent's work by the supervisor will be primarily in terms of how well the agent has performed from the standpoint of issue recognition and in his oral and written presentation. This is, in effect, a challenge to the agent's professional competency.

But this is only the beginning of the review process. After the supervisor's review, an agent's proposed findings are subject to review by the Review Staff of the Audit Division. If the review staff questions the findings—in a survey in one district office approximately two hundred items were questioned during a 3-month period—the case is returned to the group supervisor for further consideration.

A further review of the revenue agent's report will be conducted by the Conference Staff in unagreed protest cases. These unsettled cases are subjected to a screening process, consisting of a comparison of the revenue agent's report with the taxpayer's written protest, and can result in a return of the case for further development. A still further review of the report will be made in the district conference by the conferee prior to and during the conference with the taxpayer.

Nor can an agent rest content that the evidence of his efforts will remain buried in his own Audit Division. If, during the course of his audit, the district audit chief has approved a request for technical advice, the national office will subject his efforts to scrutiny for technical accuracy, and, if the case is an unagreed one and the statutory notice is about to be issued, it will be reviewed by the regional counsel's office. Further, the revenue agent's report may be subject to the sampling process of postaudit review by the assistant regional commissioner (Audit). And, if the taxpayer appeals an adverse finding of a district conferee, the appellate conferee may find defects that will result in a return of the case to the district office. If Tax Court litigation ensues, a lawyer from the regional counsel's staff will give the report still further critical scrutiny and, in addition, the agent may be subject to a rigid cross-examination by the taxpayer's counsel concerning the agent's findings and conduct during the course of his audit. Finally, the quality of revenue agent performance is subjected to examination during regular scheduled meetings of representatives of the audit, appellate, and regional counsel's offices.

FIELD SUPPORT

Recall again what happened (in Chapter III) when revenue agent Tom Jones ran into a difficult valuation problem or legal issue during the course of his field audit examination of Smith Company. In such a case, Tom was able to call on a field engineer for aid with the valuation problem and on the national office for technical advice on the legal issue.

Field support services in the Internal Revenue Service are extensive and varied and are provided by both national and regional offices. However, this management function in scope and frequency has its greatest relevancy to the core field operating functions of return-processing, auditing, appeals, and collections. Support functions with respect to these activities will be considered here; other support functions will be described below in connection with the discussion of personnel, training, rule-making, and inspection.

Because the field function of return-processing has been completely revamped in recent years with the advent of the electronic data computer, return-processing is now centered at seven regional centers, with the National Computer Center at Martinsburg, West Virginia, serving the regional centers. In the wake of this automatic data processing revolution, top IRS management has been concerned with such problems as determining what processing should be retained at the district level, employee redeployment, procedures and techniques involved in taxpayer contacts, handling of payments and refund checks, taxpayer use of magnetic tapes instead of paper documents, and the use and procurement of new and modified automatic equipment.

Return operating processes also receive direct management support. Thus, the national office Systems Division provides significant field support in a number of ways. It is responsible for the testing and debugging of program routines, and its

Service Center Branch prepares machine instructions, keeps them up to date, contributes the schematic diagrams, and prepares the logic and block diagrams for service center processing.

Management support for the various auditing programs has always been a center of management attention in the Internal Revenue Service. Activities in recent years have included aid in the adaptation of the computer for the mathematical verification of tax returns and the development of computer programs for the selection of returns for audit. In the latter case, statistical and operations research has resulted in the development of formulas ("discriminate function") for classifying tax returns on the basis of the frequency and magnitude of potential error. However, the effect of machine selection of returns for audit, with its emphasis on the magnitude of error, remains to be evaluated in terms of the tax audit guidelines program initiated in the early 1960's. This "quality audit" program, which has required the utilization of a broad spectrum of management functions, was commenced when management realized that there was a lack of functional guidelines for conducting audit examinations. New revenue agents received limited classroom training and some guidance from experienced agents, but they were free for the most part to work out their own methods. As a result, there was often a lack of balance. Significant issues were not adequately pursued, or audits were too elaborate and time-consuming.

Further, there was increasing management awareness that field agents labored under the delusion that evaluation of their efficiency was based upon a quota system of cases closed and dollars assessed as additional taxes, since their monthly reports called for these statistics. In order to eliminate this barrier to quality, group supervisors in 1961 were prohibited from keeping data of this type, and monthly reports henceforth reflected and emphasized the more significant data with respect to legal and factual issues encountered.

The foregoing paved the way for the promulgation of new audit guidelines. These were developed by a task force of experienced agents who were called to Washington, where they recorded and discussed the actual techniques they used in conducting quality audits. The implementation of the guidelines—which are designed to aid an agent by telling him how to proceed with an audit rather than what to do—is an ongoing task.

The early response to the basic quality audit program has encouraged IRS management to provide further field aids in specialized areas. These include audit technique guidelines for a number of major industries and for tax-exempt organizations, supplemented with special classroom courses, conferences, and seminars.

Audit (and other) field support is also provided by the chief counsel's office in a number of ways. Technical assistance is provided through publication of "action on decisions" (periodic reports announcing the position of IRS on court decisions), and recommendations are given at a final stage in the handling of taxpayer refund claims. Here, the Refund Litigation Division in the national office, in conjunction with the Department of Justice, upon receipt of a taxpayer's complaint after denial of a refund claim, determines the legal position of the IRS and recommends defense or other action in the case.

The appellate program in the field—the hearing of taxpayer appeals from determinations by district directors—is also supported in a number of ways by management activities. One program was mentioned in Chapter III—the Appellate Reports and Information Activity (ARIRA). Patterned after a similar retrieval system available to attorneys in the field branch offices of the chief counsel's office, ARIRA provides machine printout data in document form on pending cases to all appellate branch offices. The program, which is designed to aid in the uniform interpretation of the revenue laws in settling cases at appellate conferences, is conducted by the Operation Analysis Branch of the Appellate Division in the national office.

Other management assistance provided to appellate work in the field includes aid (from the Operations and Analysis Branch) in preparing statistical reports and aid on technical and administrative problems (from the national office Coordination and Management Staff of the Appellate Division). The Appellate Division's Special Services Branch is charged with the development of the valuation assistance program, which includes the valuation aid available to revenue agents from field engineers and the providing of expert witnesses to testify at trials involving complex valuation issues.

In January, 1965, sóme 300,000 individuals in the Southeast Region received politely worded, printed requests from the service center, seeking their aid in correcting service center records. In essence, the recipients were informed that service center records revealed that they had filed tax returns for 1962 but not for 1963 and requested them to please explain why or, if a return was due, to file without delay. In this manner, the computer had been harnessed to aid the hard pressed district office collection divisions in their efforts to ferret out delinquent filers. The requests had been compiled (from 7.5 million returns), printed, separated, folded, and stuffed into envelopes entirely by machine.

Although the use of such aids creates other problems, the Internal Revenue Service believes it is only on the threshold of possible uses of the computer and other electronic and mechanical devices in aiding field collection activity. It has, for example, experimented in a similar manner with business entities through the Business Master File, in which the selection process takes into consideration the taxpayer's compliance history; this permits the setting aside of normal processing procedures in cases of flagrant violators and proceeding with immediate delinquency notices.

The national office Collection Division also provides substantial support to field collection activity. Its Analytical Services Staff disseminates information on methods and techniques for presenting statistical data; the Centralized Activities Office advises district directors with respect to the provisions of the revenue laws relating to assessment and collection; and the Delinquent Accounts Branch, Delinquent Returns Branch, and Taxpayer Assistance Branch provide aid by developing techniques and providing training guides.

Finally, field collection support is provided by the chief counsel's office from both regional and national offices. The Collection Litigation Division handles some 12,000 cases annually of tax debts due the United States, although actual litigation is conducted by attorneys from the Justice Department.

MANAGEMENT SUPPORT

In George Orwell's novel of the future, *1984*, man is depicted as engaged in an uneven and unsuccessful struggle against dictatorial government control, through mechanical means, of his everyday actions and thoughts. More than a few concerned citizens have equated such automated control over democratic man's existence with the government's use of computer systems similar to that of the IRS—especially its master file system at Martinsburg, West Virginia. However, government organizations and agencies have yet to harness the computer to their own entities. In more realistic terms of management control functions, computer science at best is still in the process of moving from integrated data processing—the use of common computer input data for a variety of separate applications—toward a total, over-all information system that will permit the monitoring of all facets of an organization by a computer or a group of interconnected computers.

Thus, although the Internal Revenue Service has adapted the computer to its principal production activity—the processing of tax returns—and has made some progress in the use of the computer in support of other field activities, its utilization as a management support device might be regarded as only in an incipient stage of development. In this area, IRS is still struggling with various applications of integrated data, and a "total systems" is still but a vision.

The organizational unit in the national office concerned almost exclusively with over-all management functions is Planning and Research, a unit that was raised to the assistant commissioner level in 1958. Although planning and research is by no means the exclusive province of this office, which grew out of a Management Staff established in 1948, it deserves special attention since it is responsible for the direction to be taken by the Internal Revenue Service and for serving the Commissioner in his responsibility of keeping the IRS, in the words of one Commissioner, "under critical and restless appraisal." In short, members of this unit regard themselves as the "guardians of the future" of the IRS.

The unit's four-division Washington staff of some 300 employees (250 in statistics) is responsible for IRS planning, research, statistics, and systems development. The unit's effectiveness is dependent upon the fullest cooperation from other national office units, especially the office of assistant commissioner (Data Processing), whose Management Information Division is responsible for an agency-wide management reports program and whose IRS Data Center at Detroit provides the "hardware" or "job shop" for much of the research and statistical work of Planning and Research.

The genesis of the present-day Planning and Research organization is to be found in the annual *Statistics of Income* series, the first of which was issued as a 391-page volume in 1916, as required by statute. This series, whose data are extracted from tax and information returns, is the responsibility of the organization's Statistics Division. The series now includes separate annual volumes on individuals, corporations, and unincorporated businesses as well as periodic reports on fiduciary returns (estates and trusts), and other special reports. Such data are used by the IRS in tax administration, but these statistical reports are also designed to aid Congress and the Treasury in tax policy formulation and are of use to other government agencies and departments and to private groups, such as trade associations, marketing and advertising agencies, universities, and charitable and research organizations.

It is only in recent years, and especially since the advent of the computer, that these statistical records have been designed for utilization as vital tools in planning and meeting the overall goals of tax administration. Many of the statistical records in current use were not designed for tax administration purposes, and the IRS still looks forward to a more perfect integrated statistical system. On the other hand, this has not prevented planning efforts to delineate the size and nature of the total tax administration task, the portion of the total task being carried out, evaluation of the scope of the tax administration gap (the gap between what is and what is not being done), and the determination of the type of research needed to improve the present system. This type of planning falls within the province of the Planning and Analysis Division.

One of the early tasks of the office of assistant commissioner (Planning and Research), when it was established in 1958, was the formulation of a 10-year, long-range master plan for the 1961–71 period—a plan which is subject to periodic modification and updating. The master plan, however, did not constitute a break from the past or from the over-all planning and research work of the unit's predecessor, the Management Staff. Rather, it is a catalog of projects that need doing—an "action plan," in the agency's own terms—to meet certain well articulated objectives.

What are some of these projects and objectives? As originally conceived in 1961, the plan contemplated a constantly increasing work load, measured in terms of the annual increase in tax returns; it aimed to expand audit coverage, increase enforcement in the tax fraud area, modernize return-processing through automatic data processing installations, improve the system for detecting delinquent returns, reduce the delinquent accounts inventory, bring all enforcement programs (including those of the Appellate Division and the chief counsel's office) into balance, modernize equipment and improve space allocation, and effect both the functional and geographic reorganizations needed to carry the plan into effect.

In 1965, the long-range master plan was integrated into a broad-based executive branch Planning-Programing-Budgeting (PPB) system. In the case of the Internal Revenue Service, implementation meant a Program and Financial Plan, with supporting "program memoranda," consisting of annual documents that spell out specific program objectives for the years ahead.

In terms of the involvement of the Planning and Research organization (and its predecessor, the Management Staff) with other IRS units and outside groups, these action projects have included: the installation of the automatic data processing system—which began with the experimental use of punched card equipment in a few offices in 1950 and reached a final phase in 1967—in all regional service centers and in the IRS Data Center at Detroit, which opened that year; an ongoing series of taxpayer compliance studies, among them studies designed to determine the scope of nonreporting of dividend and interest income, which led to legislation requiring information reporting; studies of business depreciation practices, which led to promulgation of new depreciation guidelines; interview surveys, including one to determine the type of assistance needed by taxpayers in preparing their tax returns; organization studies, which led to a number of consolidations; negotiations with most state tax agencies for the mutual disclosure of information; the development of tax models to provide a quick and accurate method of determining the effects of proposed legislative measures on both taxpayer groups and the revenue; the development of information retrieval systems in cooperation with the affected units and the

International Business Machines Corporation; and the formulation of a graduated tax-withholding scale, which was enacted into law by Congress.

Most of the foregoing "action projects" have been concluded; others of a current and ongoing nature include the continued updating of forecasts on the number and type of tax returns; statistical studies designed for tax management control purposes; a long-range study, already well under way, of a new automatic data processing system for the 1970's, carried out in cooperation with its potential users—the Audit, Collection, and Intelligence divisions and the office of the assistant commissioner (Data Processing); and experimentation with a direct data entry system to replace keypunching operations in service center return-processing, currently being phased in on a nationwide basis. In short, the tasks of Planning and Research are those of keeping ahead of a growing institution.

Much management support work in the Internal Revenue Service goes unheralded; not a little of this is performed by the five divisions of the office of assistant commissioner (Administration). This major unit, with some 600 employees in the national office and 3,500 in the field, is responsible for certain key portions of the Master Plan as well as for important short-range repetitive programs. Thus, its Fiscal Management Division is responsible for the development of the IRS annual budget of approximately $800 million and for establishing and maintaining adequate accounting controls over funds appropriated by Congress. The magnitude of the work of the Facilities Management Division is revealed by the need to provide working space for 70,000 people (77,000 at the peak of the season) in some 1,300 buildings located in upward of 1,100 cities across the nation. The work of the Personnel and Training divisions is highlighted in the following section, the work of the Public Information Division in Chapter X.

Finally, there is the management function of the annual accounting for $200 billion of collected revenue, in which the computer is utilized in large measure. This unmatched task is accomplished by the Collection Division in the office of the assistant commissioner (Compliance); the Systems Division in the office of the assistant commissioner (Data Processing) is responsible for the development of procedures pertaining to handling the receipt and processing of tax payments.

PERSONNEL

In a moment of candor, the late Judge Learned Hand, one of the nation's most distinguished jurists, observed:

> In my own case the words of such an act as the Income Tax, for example, merely dance before my eyes in a meaningless procession: cross-reference to cross-reference, exception upon exception—couched in abstract terms that offer no handle to seize hold of—leave in my mind only a confused sense of some vitally important, but successfully concealed, purport, which it is my duty to extract, but which is within my power, if at all, only after the most inordinate expenditure of time.

The implications of Judge Hand's revelation for tax administration are patent. How, for example, can IRS management expect its 13,000 revenue agents, 3,000 tax auditors, 1,700 special agents, 800 estate tax attorneys and examiners, and its other specialists such as conferees and attorneys, who are on the firing line of tax controversy constantly, to be reasonably conversant with the rules of the tax laws and their application to the thousands of transactions that dominate American business and family life? To state the problem of personnel administration in the IRS in this manner is simply to indicate one of its many dimensions—technical competency in tax law. It has others, but all are the principal concern of two divisions (Personnel and Training) in the office of the assistant commissioner (Administration) and the field counterparts of these divisions.

Entry into the Internal Revenue Service, position classification, establishment of occupation standards, and like matters are subject to the usual civil service rules and regulations. The more important specialist categories are filled from eligibles who have passed the Federal Service Entrance Examination, but there are exceptions. No written test, for example, is required by applicants for revenue agent, internal auditor, in-service appointment to special agent, and attorney, if applicants meet minimum educational requirements—although an attorney must pass a state bar examination within fourteen months after entry.

The dropping of these competitive examination bars has been necessitated in large measure by the postwar demands by both government and private industry for workers in many categories, particularly those requiring training in accounting, but this has not been sufficient to fill IRS needs for qualified personnel. (IRS work categories total about 110.) Organized recruiting has been necessary for most of the dozen or so unique IRS professional and semiprofessional occupations that constitute in excess of 60 per cent of its total work force.

Service recruiting is directed mainly at college graduates, both men and women. The programs utilize brochures, direct mailings, campus visits by trained recruiting teams from regional and district offices, and direct recruiting by district and other field offices. Most of the nation's colleges and universities are visited, and recruiting is supported in some instances by top IRS officials on speaking engagements. Recruiting has been aided in no small measure by the federal salary comparability legislation of 1962 and 1967, which permits the Civil Service Commission to set government salaries on a basis comparable to salaries paid similar workers in private industry.

The IRS is the largest single user of the nation's accounting talent. Indicative of recruiting success is its ability to add more than 2,000 accountants annually as revenue agents out of a national graduating class of some 17,000. Annual requirements in other large categories include 1,000 revenue officers, 600 tax auditors, and 250 special agents. Some IRS units recruit in-service (the Appellate Division, for example, recruits largely from the Audit Division). High-level management positions are rarely filled from the outside.

Unlike most government agencies, IRS has a "season," namely, from January 1 to April 15, the last date for filing individual tax returns. This requires the hiring and training of about 15,000 temporary employees. Most of this burden falls on the service centers, although increased numbers of "taxpayer service representatives" are also needed during the season in the district offices to meet the needs of the taxpayer assistance program described in Chapter X. Some of these temporary employees are college students.

IRS recruiting and retention policies and practices are not limited to filling immediate needs. In anticipation of future manpower requirements, a brochure, "Careers in Tax Work," describing opportunities in tax work, primarily in accounting, is widely distributed to high school counselors and the accounting industry, and a college student trainee program has been launched in cooperation with more than 130 colleges and universities. A fully established staff redeployment program has been particularly effective in recent years in utilizing manpower that would otherwise be lost as a result of organizational changes, particularly those resulting from the transfer of tax return–processing from district offices to the regional service centers (some 10,000 employees were affected by this change), and from a number of regional and district mergers.

TRAINING

Man, including Internal Revenue Service employees, does not live by bread alone. This is evident from the results of the attitude surveys conducted in different IRS districts each year. These surveys report that field workers are, in general, satisfied with their lot and that steps have been taken to correct certain dissatisfactions. Indicative of the growing professionalism in tax administration is the report that field employees regarded the actual work they do as "the most significant aspect of their job satisfaction." Job satisfaction on the part of revenue agents, revenue officers, and other IRS specialists may be attributed in no small measure to opportunities to grow and advance in meaningful ways, thanks to well-marked career ladders and in-service training programs.

The IRS training programs have been compared, in scope and depth of material and skills covered, to the training received in a school of business administration of a major university, supplemented with clinical on-the-job training. The size of the programs is truly enormous and reflects significant changes in attitude by both IRS management and Congress during the past half century. Although formal training in the Internal Revenue Service dates back to 1917, it was dominated at that time by off-the-job correspondence courses. It was not until after the 1952 reorganization that training assumed its present form.

Today, the national office Training Division provides guidance for a decentralized operating structure, consisting of a National Training Center, which occupies three floors of a large building in Arlington, Virginia, and seven regional training centers at each of the regional offices (a new center has been recently established on the campus of a major university). The National Training Center, in cooperation with the affected field organizations, has conceived and programed more than one hundred courses and is constantly engaged in the preparation of new courses and materials and in updating existing courses. Instruction at the various centers is provided by a faculty (twenty or more at the National Training Center) of experienced revenue agents and officers and others, relieved of their regular duties for specific periods. Outside instructors are used for some courses, such as data processing. Teaching methods range widely and are most innovative; they include texts, programed instruction, an automated audiovisual teaching system, closed-circuit television for testing interviewing skills and polishing lecture techniques, task analysis (behavioral job analysis), and the use of decision tables (algorithms) for organizing factual information into a series of steps to reach a decision.

Is all this elaborate training necessary? Consider the training received by the newly recruited revenue agent trainee, fresh out of business school. As an accounting major, he will have completed at least twenty-four semester hours in accounting, but he may or may not have received tax training. If he has, it is likely to be no more than a 3-6–semester-hour, over-the-top survey of the revenue laws, with emphasis on the preparation of tax returns for taxpayers. (A similar deficiency exists in legal education, except for the few law students who elect a fourth year of specialized tax training, available at ten or twelve of the nation's law centers.) From the IRS point of view, this is at best only a beginning. As reorganized in 1967, the training program for the new revenue agent is a three-part career training program designed to coordinate his development with the level of his case assignments; in other words, as his competency increases, so does the complexity of his audits and the depth of his training. The first part of this program—the basic revenue agent course—is a 7-month program, which includes classroom training in income tax law, auditing techniques, taxpayer relations, report writing, and fraud awareness, interspersed with periods of on-the-job supervision by experienced agents.

Similar basic recruit training is provided for revenue officers, estate tax attorneys, special agents, tax auditors, internal auditors, economists, statisticians, computer systems operators, alcohol, tobacco, and firearms inspectors, and other professional categories, but basic training is not limited to these levels. Particularly burdensome has been the need to train thousands of new employees for regional service center positions as a result of the shift in return-processing from the district offices to the service centers.

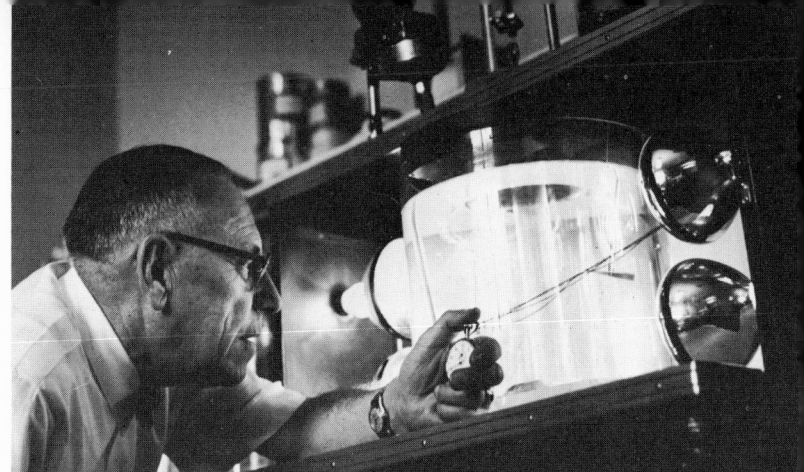

At the IRS National Laboratory, Washington, the age of a brandy sample is verified by determining the deuterium content.

Left: A special investigator of the Alcohol, Tobacco, and Firearms Division examines a sawed-off shotgun of the type used by gangsters. *Below:* IRS investigators test the destructiveness of two seized weapons.

United States Internal Revenue,
Assessor's Office, District of Columbia.

Washington, *April 27th*, 1872.

I hereby certify that Abraham Lincoln made *two* returns of income for the year ending, Dec. 31, 1863, *one* for his tax on income outside of his salary, amounting to 17.75 being a tax of 1½ ¢ on $1183; the *second* was for the tax as levied by the joint resolution of July 4. 1864, and known as the Special income tax, which embraced the above amount and his salary of $25.000 as President of the United States, amounting in the aggregate to $25.583 on which he paid tax of 5 ¢ amount of tax $1279 .15 Both of these returns appear on Form 58 for Dec. 1864, and are the only returns he made to this office.

Walter. S. Burr.

Assessor

STATEMENT OF THE AMOUNTS
OF INTERNAL DUTIES,
Imposed by the United States, (except those on Stamps,)
paid by each person in the first Collection District of
Kentucky, during the year 1819.

		Bot Forward.	$43.33
Moses Adams,	$ 13.37	Spencer Adkin,	$ 15.00
Caleb Asberry,	143.92	William Davis,	34.00
David Finley,	138.70	James French,	26.37
William Galt,	173.15	William Huckley,	141.82
Daniel Harrah,	79.40	Michael Hedrick,	248.78
William Johnson,	2.92	Matthew M'Clure,	79.70
Eli Metcalfe,	156.08	*William Martin,*	4.50
Thomas Pickett, (for a person unknown,)	} 20.00	Joseph Power,	34.36
		Edmund Ragland,	73.32
Oliver Saunders,	50.27	John Snider,	18.25
Cornelius Summers,	66.92		$1579.49
	$43.33		

I certify that the foregoing statement exhibits the full amounts of the duties aforesaid, paid in the first collection district of Kentucky, during the year 1819.

GEO. W. BOTTS,
Collector of the Revenue for the first Collection
District of Kentucky.

September 30, 1819.

Flemingsburg.—Printed at the STAR Office.

Reproduced here is an Internal Revenue assessor's statement regarding the claim for a $1,250 refund made by Lincoln's estate in 1872.

Tax-collecting was simpler in 1819 than today. George Botts of the first collection district of Kentucky had only twenty returns to report.

A moonshiner at work: More than 40 million gallons of illicit liquor, much of it containing poisonous lead salts, are consumed annually in the United States.

A still captured by "revenooers": Moonshine whisky is often distilled through automobile radiators with lead-soldered joints. The unsanitary conditions under which "white lightning" is manufactured are shown below.

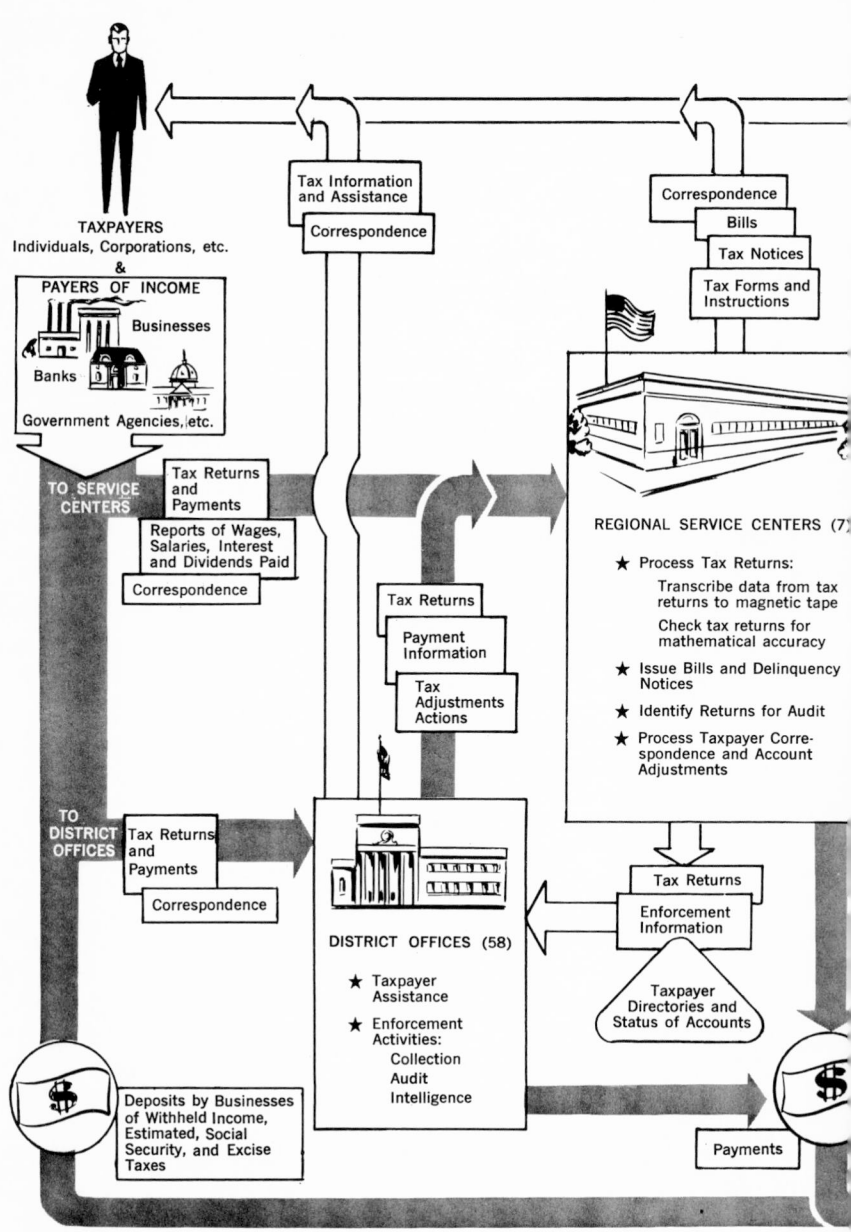

TAXPAYERS
Individuals, Corporations, etc.
&
PAYERS OF INCOME
Businesses
Banks
Government Agencies, etc.

TO SERVICE CENTERS

Tax Returns and Payments

Reports of Wages, Salaries, Interest and Dividends Paid

Correspondence

Tax Information and Assistance

Correspondence

Tax Returns

Payment Information

Tax Adjustments Actions

Correspondence

Bills

Tax Notices

Tax Forms and Instructions

REGIONAL SERVICE CENTERS (7)

★ Process Tax Returns:
   Transcribe data from tax returns to magnetic tape
   Check tax returns for mathematical accuracy
★ Issue Bills and Delinquency Notices
★ Identify Returns for Audit
★ Process Taxpayer Correspondence and Account Adjustments

TO DISTRICT OFFICES

Tax Returns and Payments

Correspondence

DISTRICT OFFICES (58)

★ Taxpayer Assistance
★ Enforcement Activities:
   Collection
   Audit
   Intelligence

Tax Returns

Enforcement Information

Taxpayer Directories and Status of Accounts

Deposits by Businesses of Withheld Income, Estimated, Social Security, and Excise Taxes

Payments

AUTOMATED FEDERAL TAX SYSTEM

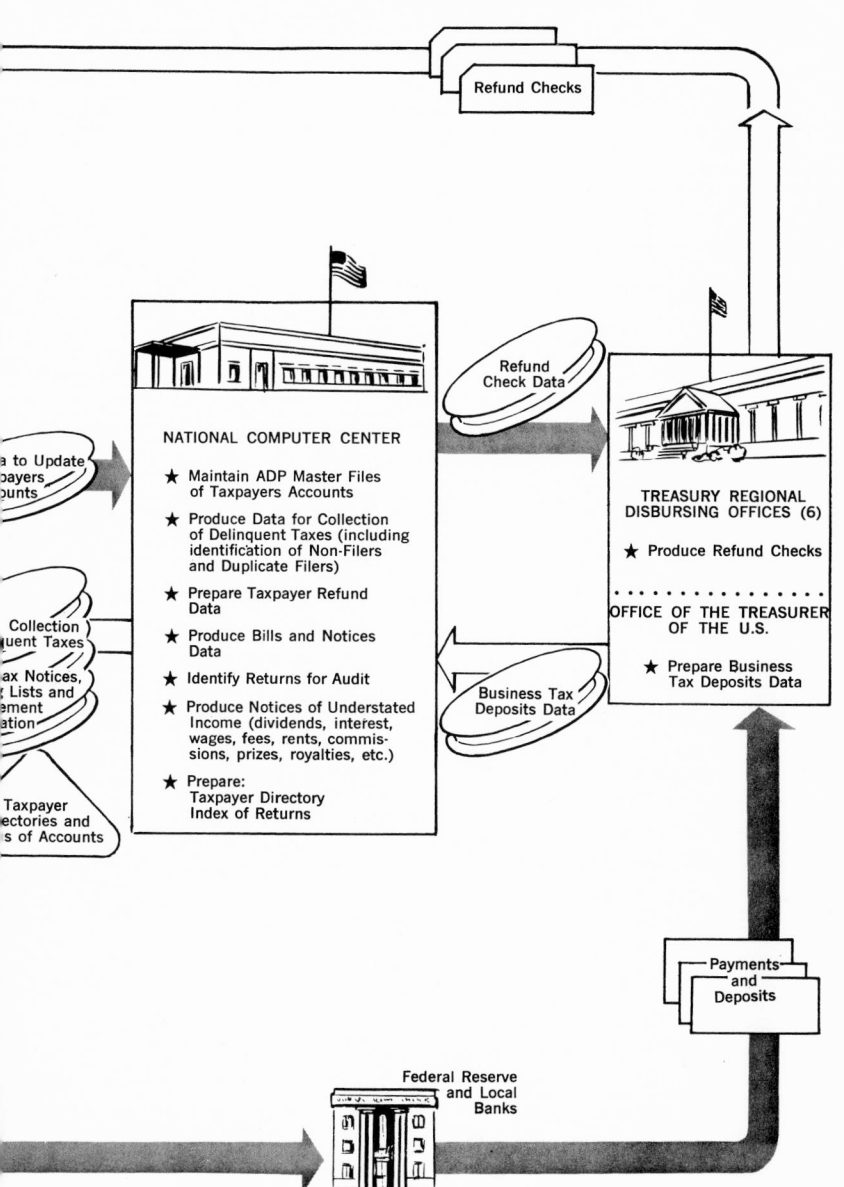

Refund Checks

Refund Check Data

NATIONAL COMPUTER CENTER

★ Maintain ADP Master Files of Taxpayers Accounts

★ Produce Data for Collection of Delinquent Taxes (including identification of Non-Filers and Duplicate Filers)

★ Prepare Taxpayer Refund Data

★ Produce Bills and Notices Data

★ Identify Returns for Audit

★ Produce Notices of Understated Income (dividends, interest, wages, fees, rents, commissions, prizes, royalties, etc.)

★ Prepare:
Taxpayer Directory
Index of Returns

a to Update ⟩ payers ⟩ ounts ⟩

Collection ⟩ quent Taxes ⟩

ax Notices, ⟩ Lists and ⟩ ement ⟩ ation ⟩

Taxpayer ⟩ ectories and ⟩ s of Accounts ⟩

TREASURY REGIONAL DISBURSING OFFICES (6)

★ Produce Refund Checks

. . . .

OFFICE OF THE TREASURER OF THE U.S.

★ Prepare Business Tax Deposits Data

Business Tax Deposits Data

Payments and Deposits

Federal Reserve and Local Banks

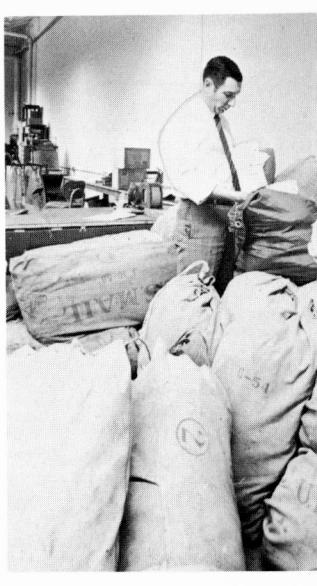

PROCESSING TAX RETURNS

Above left: The Mid-Atlantic Service Center, Philadelphia, is one of seven service centers processing taxpaper returns. *Above right:* The service center receiving room looks like this during the "season" (January–April). *Below left:* The Tingle Table, designed by James Tingle, is used for sorting returns; built-in light facilitates candling of envelopes. *Below right:* Returns are physically examined and coded to make keypunch operations more accurate.

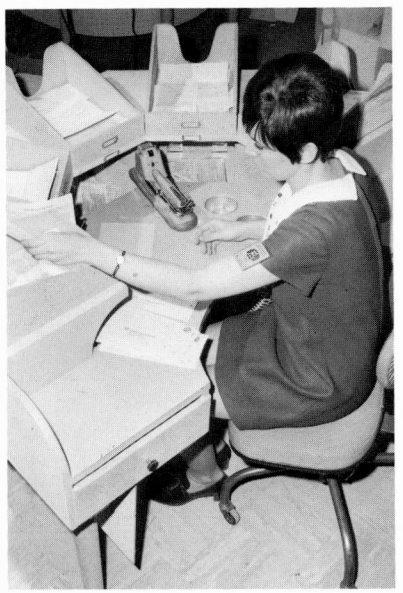

Above: Keypunching information from tax returns is essential to feeding the facts to the computer. *Right:* Notices to Taxpayers are prepared by the readout printer; it would take a typist five hours to do what the printer does in sixty seconds. *Below:* Returns must be retrieved manually for responding to taxpayer correspondence for a claim filed or for audit.

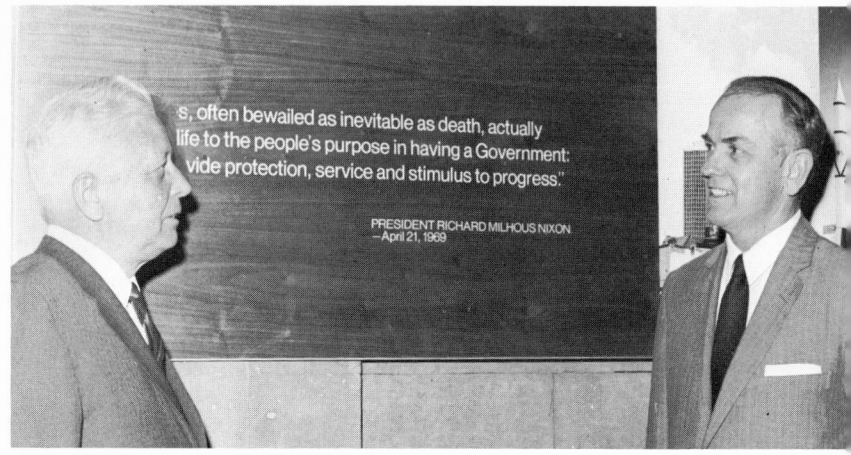

Secretary of the Treasury David M. Kennedy and Commissioner of Internal Revenue Randolph W. Thrower attend the dedication of the tax museum in the IRS Building, May 12, 1969.

This is the Internal Revenue Service Building, Washington, D.C.

Harold Moss, Director of the Foreign Tax Assistance Staff, meets with tax officials from the Caribbean area.

In addition to basic "boot training," the IRS provides a continuing stream of short courses, seminars, and workshops designed to meet particular problems and to keep enforcement personnel up to date on new legislation and new technological developments. These include, for field personnel, annual technical review institutes, institutes for special groups —engineers, for instance—and the use of publications such as *Tax Briefs* (a monthly review of technical developments for revenue agents), updated training manuals, a *Legal Handbook for Revenue Officers,* and a *Tobacco Tax Guide.*

There is, almost literally, something for everyone in IRS training programs. Supervisors and other middle management groups have been given increased attention in recent years, through service-wide equal employment seminars, special managerial training (for attorney-managers in the chief counsel's office), and supervisory training on delinquent accounts problems.

Finally, there is the training that leads to top-level management positions—a particular pride and joy of the IRS. At the starting level is a 12-year-old, 3-phase intern program, which provides a wide choice of career ladders leading to middle management administrative positions. At the top level is the Executive Selection and Development Program, the agency's version of training for its "senior civil service," designed to assure a continuing source of top executives and at the same time to provide effective career opportunities for IRS employees. The program, first announced in 1956, grew out of the 1952 reorganization and the difficulties encountered in finding competent executives through publicly announced competitive civil service examinations.

The selection process for the annual course (fifteen to twenty students depending on forecasted needs) is thorough. From three to four hundred applications are received each year from Internal Revenue Service employees and (as a guard against inbreeding) from a small number of career servants from other departments with significant management experience. District and service center division chiefs and assistant division chiefs are automatically considered. Thereafter, an initial nominating phase is conducted at the national, regional, and district offices and at the regional service centers for candidates from these offices. This is followed by an intermediate screening, conducted by regional screening committees. The final selection is made by a national selection board (the deputy commissioner and assistant commissioners with field jurisdiction).

The 6-month program commences with an orientation course of several weeks in Washington, continues in the field —where each member is assigned for short periods to regional, service center, and district offices—and concludes with a final session of several weeks at the national office, where outside experts meet and address the group.

Upon completion of the course, the graduate enters the elite Corps of General Executives—the 250 or so top IRS managers appointed by the Commissioner. Although completion of the course does not guarantee appointment to an executive position, few graduates fail to ultimately attain executive status, and the corps is now the sole source of new appointments to assistant district and assistant service center director.

The effectiveness of IRS training programs and personnel policies may be measured to some extent by the agency's turnover rates. Although it has substantial annual manpower needs (10,000–11,000), its separation rates are low in most categories. The 1969 turnover rates, for example, were: revenue agent, 8.9%; revenue officer, 7.1%; special agent, 6.2%; and tax auditor, 7.5%.

RULE-MAKING

The forty-five members of the delegation were all dressed in black suits; all wore wide-brimmed, round-crowned black hats. Although their dress was somewhat out of the ordinary

as they entered the outer office of Commissioner Mortimer
Caplin, they were dead serious as to their mission, and they
were certain that an interview with the Commissioner would
see it accomplished. They were Amish bishops. Congress
had recently expanded Social Security coverage to farmers
and others through a self-employment tax. In this form, the
bishops told the Commissioner, the tax was contrary to their
basic religious beliefs. Could the Commissioner please suspend its application as to them? The Commissioner was sorry
but he could not do this. The power of the Internal Revenue
Service, he informed his visitors, was limited to the interpretation of the revenue laws enacted by Congress. All the Commissioner could do would be to suspend collection of the
tax to allow time for a test of the constitutionality of the law.

The plight of the Amish bishops illustrates a common misunderstanding concerning the status of an executive agency of
the federal government with delegated regulatory power, as
compared to that of an enforcement agency, such as the IRS,
charged with implementing basic statutory rules enacted by
Congress. While the IRS has a regulatory function in a few
areas (with respect to the alcohol and tobacco industries, for
example, as described in Chapter VII), in most respects its
rule-making role is basically one of interpretation; it is this
image that the Internal Revenue Service fosters in its public
relations.

In one sense, the interpretative work of the Internal Revenue Service, which, in scope, has few if any equals in federal
government agencies, permeates most of its field enforcement efforts. It is part of the everyday work of the revenue
agent, in tax appeals and, in some measure, in collection
work. At the management level, however, rule-making is
shared by the assistant commissioner (Technical) and the
chief counsel.

The chief counsel's office, the world's largest "law firm,"
is staffed with some 1,300 persons; half of these are lawyers,
of whom 250 are located in Washington and the remaining

400 in the field. The work of the office is divided between lit-igation (about two-thirds) and technical work. Litigation is directed from Washington and carried out through seven re-gional offices. It is the technical work that gives the national office the main rule-making role of the IRS—a role shared by the chief counsel's Legislation and Regulations Division and Interpretative Division.

One of the two functions of the Legislature and Regulations Divisions is the preparation of drafts of proposed regulations. The importance of the regulations in the basic mission of the Internal Revenue Service cannot be overemphasized—the basic mission being, of course, the administration of the re-venue laws (the Internal Revenue Code) enacted by Congress. Although the Code is a detailed and complex document of approximately 250,000 words, it does not and cannot pro-vide the tax consequences for the myriad business and family transactions entered into daily in history's most developed industrial society. This, Congress has recognized. Hence, it has directed that the Secretary of the Treasury or his delegate (the Commissioner of Internal Revenue) shall implement the legislation with regulations.

Congress has also recognized that the power to interpret the revenue laws in this manner vests the Commissioner (and other agencies with similar rule-making authority) with a power that may be abused. Consequently, the federal Admin-istrative Procedure Act requires, subject to certain exceptions, that proposed regulations to new legislation and amendments to existing regulations be first published in the *Federal Regis-ter*. This is to provide interested taxpayers an opportunity to comment on them or to request a public hearing for present-ing their objections. After all comments and objections have been received, the final regulations, each of which covers a limited area of the Code, are published in the *Federal Register* in final form as a Treasury Decision, signed by the Commis-sioner and the Secretary of the Treasury. A typical year's output will result in the promulgation of twenty to thirty final

Treasury Decisions (after ten to twelve public hearings) and a similar number of notices of proposed regulations.

This process is a critical one, and the preparation of regulations requires that the attorneys from the Legislation and Regulations Division resort to more than just the terms of the statute. Regard must be had to the lawmaking processes, including the terms of the original proposals and the position of the Treasury on what the statute was designed to accomplish, and to the legislative committee hearings and discussions of the two tax-writing committees of Congress: the House Ways and Means Committee and the Senate Finance Committee. Of primary importance in determining what the content of the regulations should be and what examples should be used are the basic documents of the law's legislative history, consisting of the written reports of the congressional committees that accompany the legislation as proposed to the two houses of Congress. Not infrequently, the regulations, when first promulgated, simply paraphrase these committee reports.

A second level of IRS rule-making consists of published revenue rulings. Unlike regulations that are interpretations of particular sections of the Internal Revenue Code, a ruling is an interpretation of the tax law as applied to a particular situation not covered in the regulations, although the regulations are sometimes later amended to include them. Revenue rulings often are issued as a result of a taxpayer's request for a private letter ruling—a taxpayer service institution described in Chapter X—because such requests and the IRS position thereon have more general application. In form, a revenue ruling is a short legal opinion based on a specific fact situation and usually contains a brief explicit rationale. Rulings are published in the IRS's weekly *Internal Revenue Bulletin* (as are the regulations and other technical matter), and IRS personnel are required to follow them as precedents; they are regarded as important statements of IRS position by the courts and taxpayers.

Revenue rulings have their origins in the Income Tax Division or the Miscellaneous and Special Tax Division of the office of assistant commissioner (Technical), which administers the taxpayer rulings program. Under this program, some 30,000 private rulings are issued annually. However, only about 300 are proposed for publication, and these are reviewed (researched and opinion prepared) by the Interpretative Division of the chief counsel's office, which also reviews technical memoranda issued to the field and legal questions submitted to it by the litigation divisions of the chief counsel's office. These legal questions are the so-called formal referrals, totaling an average of 750 cases annually. In addition, the Interpretative Division reviews certain proposed taxpayer rulings on an informal basis.

INSPECTION

The only audible sound in the courtroom was a metallic click as the machine was turned on. Then, the voices of defendant German S. Lopez and revenue agent Roger Davis came through clearly:

LOPEZ: I've got a couple hundred more dollars here. As we go along there'll be a couple of hundred for you every time you drop in, but don't drop in too often.

DAVIS: Well, you gave me $420 the other day.

LOPEZ: Yes.

DAVIS: That makes a total of $620.

LOPEZ: Yes. Every so often I'll take care of you.

DAVIS: What do you expect me to do for this money?

LOPEZ: Well, you don't have to look at the books and you don't have to report any back taxes.

DAVIS: Is there anything else?

LOPEZ: No. You just drop in in another couple of months and I'll take care of you. I want to protect you as well as protect myself.

The jury was convinced. Lopez was convicted of attempting to bribe a federal officer and sentenced to one year in the penitentiary. The conviction was subsequently affirmed by the Supreme Court and the use of the challenged recording was upheld on grounds that it was simply a more accurate reporting of a conversation for which oral testimony could otherwise have been given. Davis had testified that during two prior visits to the defendant's lounge bar (he had reported to his superior after the first one) it had appeared that Lopez was not collecting and reporting the required federal cabaret tax. On Davis's second visit, Lopez had given him $420, which he turned over to his superior and the regional inspector. He had returned to Lopez's office with a concealed wire recorder (a concealed transmitter failed to function) at the directions of his superior and the regional inspector and had recorded the preceding conversation.

What about bribes that are not reported? Or taxpayer remittances that are converted by collection employees to their own use? Or tax practitioners who shake down their clients, contending that a revenue agent is demanding a payoff? What about distorted records and reports? Or failure to collect taxes due the United States? As long as man must labor in reasonably close proximity to large amounts of money, such practices will exist. Thus, these questions are more relevant: How extensive are negligent and corrupt practices in the IRS? What measures are taken to detect, eliminate, and prevent their occurrence? How effective are the management control measures that are taken?

While an internal inspection program existed prior to the 1952 reorganization, it functioned under the supervision of several operating units without over-all control or direction. For the most part, it was carried out only when complaints were made against individual IRS employees.

As a result, during 1951–52, a number of administrative steps were taken to strengthen the inspection program. Besides the basic reorganization plan of 1952, these included a specific recommendation of the King committee that all officials and key enforcement personnel be subject to annual tax audits and that they file annual net worth statements. (Today an audit is made and a net worth statement is required upon entry into the IRS; all annual returns are scrutinized, but not all are audited.) In addition, a final reform order in November, 1953, restructured the office of assistant administrator (Inspection) in the manner in which that office functions today.

Inspection is now an autonomous organization of some 800 persons, 90 of whom are assigned to the national office. It is independent of the rest of the Internal Revenue Service. The assistant commissioner (Inspection) reports directly to the deputy commissioner and the Commissioner. The seven regional inspectors are also independent of the regional commissioners and report directly to the assistant commissioner in Washington.

Functionally, Inspection is divided at both the national level and in the field into two divisions (Internal Security and Internal Audit) with a dual mission: (1) the investigation of IRS personnel, in order to assure the highest possible standards of honesty and integrity and (2) the independent review of all agency operations as a management support service. Although, conceptually, Inspection is an integral part of the IRS management control system, it is strictly an investigative service; any action on its reports and recommendations must be taken by national, regional, or district officials of the affected operating units.

Although the two missions of Inspection are interrelated, it is the exposure of the misconduct of IRS personnel—the work largely of Internal Security Division inspectors—that makes the best newspaper copy and affects the public image of the Internal Revenue Service. The Internal Security Division is charged with conducting character and background investigations of applicants for technical and high-grade positions and of employees handling funds, with investigating complaints and following up on information indicating criminal acts or improprieties on the part of IRS personnel and attempts of outsiders to corrupt agency employees, and with special investigations, including those based on complaints of unethical practices of tax lawyers and others admitted to practice before the Treasury Department and complaints of racial discrimination in the Internal Revenue Service.

The Internal Security Division employs the usual police techniques in carrying out investigative assignments, and many of its officials and inspectors have had FBI, special agent, or other investigative experience. Some of its cases involve strictly "inside jobs," such as cases in which employees have ready access to cash and where the "controlled mail" technique may be called for (an envelope with cash routed along a known path), or in which an officer-employee has access to undelivered refund checks (which may be readdressed to himself or an accomplice), or in which an employee files a refund return for a nonexistent taxpayer (a more difficult trick today, thanks to the computer and the master file system).

In some instances, it "takes two to tango"—the corrupt employee and the corrupt outsider. In recent years, the IRS has made special efforts to root out not only the bribe-taking employee (the maximum penalty for bribery was recently increased to fifteen years and a $20,000 fine) but the taxpayer or taxpayer's representative who is seeking the soft spots in the Internal Revenue Service. The standards here are high, and the sanctions on both taxpayers and employee are substantial. The mere offer of a bribe is a separate federal crime, as is the actual payment. Service employees have lost their jobs for taking small gratuities—for example, a suit of clothes in one case and $45 worth of fishing tackle in another.

As in all police investigative work, successful prosecution may require the testimony of one of the parties to the crime. In the 1965 New York scandals, discussed below, the testimony of four former examining agents was needed for the conviction of a single taxpayer. In some instances, chance events have resulted in the needed disclosures—in the case of the IRS employer who was detected because he cashed several different refund checks at the same bank and the case in which a plumber discovered that torn-up tax returns were the cause of the stoppage of the toilet in the ladies room in an Internal Revenue Service office.

Perhaps some nature of the success of Internal Security's efforts may be gathered from the data on actions taken for the 1964–68 period (Table 2). While the data appears to indicate an increasing effectiveness and control of the integrity problem, IRS officials are the first to admit that internal criminal activity has by no means been wiped out. They are periodically plagued with pockets of corruption which have

TABLE 2

Nondisciplinary and Disciplinary Action Taken Against IRS Employees, 1964–68

	1964	1965	1966	1967	1968
Nondisciplinary action	6,137	5,365	6,570	9,370	9,386
Disciplinary action	791	797	770	657	534
Separations	271	340	239	225	195
Bribery, extortion	40	62	22	7	25
Embezzlement	15	15	11	5	7
Failure to pay tax	14	21	20	17	9
Falsification of records	121	130	94	98	89
Unauthorized activity	9	10	8	8	5
Acceptance of gratuities	7	8	22	12	2
Personal misconduct	59	78	55	65	44
Other	6	16	7	13	14
Suspensions	53	35	58	48	27
Reprimands, transfers, demotions	467	422	473	384	312
Employees on rolls at close of year	59,000	60,000	62,000	65,000	65,000

existed for a number of years such as those uncovered in 1964 in the large Manhattan and Brooklyn district offices, which led to 124 arrests, equally divided between IRS personnel and non-IRS accountants, lawyers, and taxpayers. These arrests, followed by still others in subsequent years, involved crimes that ranged from embezzlement by a large embezzlement ring to repeated taking of bribes.

On the other hand, IRS officials can point to a survey by a national bonding company that reveals a favorable ratio of four to one for Service employees over private industry with respect to embezzlements. The task of keeping on top of the integrity problem in the Internal Revenue Service as compared to private industry is compounded not only by the size of IRS's fiscal operations—by any standard the largest in the world—but by the fact that the daily work of many key employees exposes them to opportunities for graft. Their work calls for the constant exercise of value judgments. A revenue agent examining the records of a corporate taxpayer may be required to determine whether the taxpayer has sufficiently "substantiated" claimed deductions for travel and entertainment expenses, whether the compensation paid its corporate officers was "reasonable" in amount, whether the "principal" purpose of a transaction was the avoidance of tax. There is no ready way to determine whether a gratuity from a grateful taxpayer might have influenced an agent's determination on these questions.

The initiation of an investigation normally has its source in a complaint. These come from many sources. A neighbor may question an IRS employee's apparent affluence. A tax practitioner may interpret an agent's remark as an invitation to a bribe offer. More often, a disgruntled taxpayer simply objects to the thoroughness of an agent's examination and not only complains of harassment but also levies charges of a personal nature. All such complaints must be checked out (a complaint against an IRS field inspector in the Internal Security Division is checked out by a special group working out of the national office). As a result, as indicated in Table 2, the vast majority of cases result in complete clearance of the employee, since the investigation is thorough. In one case, for example, after a witness at a trial testified that the agent did not destroy the moonshine seized at a still but sold it, IRS inspectors were able to dig out of a swamp the broken necks of 148 out of 150 jugs.

All of this, however, does not mean that operating personnel as a group relish the idea of a visit from an inspector. Reaction at times has gone beyond the to-be-expected grumbling of "gestapo methods." For example, a group of Newark employees sought legal aid in an effort to reduce what they described as police-state working conditions, and a complaint was registered by an American Legion post (composed largely of IRS employees) on the grounds that public disclosure of corrupt activities in the agency was damaging to morale. On the whole, however, most IRS employees probably regard the activities of the Internal Security Division as a disagreeable working condition, but one necessary to the preservation of the public image, free of widespread corruption, that the IRS now enjoys.

The less-heralded work of the Internal Audit Division is equally as important from a management control point of view. The internal audit program is carried out by a corps of accountants, whose methods are not unlike those pursued by the auditors of a large commercial auditing concern, except that the tasks are compounded in size.

Just as the Internal Security Division seeks to eliminate personal corruption, so the Internal Audit Division seeks to eliminate errors, mistakes, and inefficiency in all IRS operations. Some 10–15 per cent of its time is spent on integrity matters in cooperation with the Internal Security Division, but the bulk of its efforts consists of annual audits of about 350 field facilities; these include all the units in the regional, service center, and district offices. In recent years, the Internal Audit Division has been involved in a continuous examination of service center tax return–processing in an effort to correct errors in computer programs and systems. Improvements that have been made in this area as a result of this activity have been many and varied.

As in the case of the Internal Security Division, the Internal Audit Division cannot order the remedy for the deficiencies it finds; it can only investigate, report, and recommend. This it does to all levels of management, and the savings have been substantial (to say nothing of improved taxpayer relations). The resulting annual savings in 1968 were $48 million, including savings on specific cases, on interest, and on penalties not properly assessed.

One senator has likened the agency's investigations of its own activities to putting the fox in the hen house and locking up the hen house for the night. This raises a final question: Who audits and inspects the Internal Revenue Service?

The answer is the General Accounting Office, an independent agency of the federal government. The General Accounting Office, in accordance with federal law, must report to Congress, the Secretary of the Treasury, and appropriate Internal Revenue Service officials. In one year as many as six reports were made pertaining to the IRS, all calling for corrective action.

V

The Intelligence
Enforcement Mission

As the slow-moving excursion launch moves along the shore of Miami's Biscayne Bay, the guide's monotone voice takes on a vibrant note as one of the pocket-sized islands comes into view. The house off the port bow, the tourist is informed, was once the winter home of the notorious Alphonse "Scarface" Capone.

The saga of Al Capone, his rise to gangland power in the 1920's, his fabulous income from illicit liquor, gambling, and prostitution, and his eventual downfall is one of the most dramatic in the history of crime in America. A sly, clever, and ruthless ganglord, he ran his empire with unmatched cunning. Keeping no bank accounts, paying for everything he purchased in cash, including a $175,000 estate and a $40,000 yacht, Capone feared no one. But he made two mistakes. He failed to report and pay tax on his income, and he underestimated the investigative powers of the Internal Revenue Service's Intelligence Division.

Thoroughly and relentlessly, for more than two years, the IRS Intelligence Unit dogged Capone's financial trail with as many as a hundred agents on the job at a time. They posed as Eastern gunmen, looking for a connection. They followed leads to California, Michigan, Florida, and New York. Almost a thousand inquiries met fear-engendered silence. Finally, in the center of Capone's empire in Cicero, Illinois, a Chicago suburb, after months of painstaking examination of bank accounts, they struck pay dirt. The records of a Cicero bank revealed a succession of opened and closed accounts—of which bank officials professed ignorance, although they had honored large overdrafts on the same accounts—all using the first name "James." This lead took them to the depositors —Cicero speakeasy owners—and hence to the owner of the accounts, Ralph Capone, Al's brother. The heat generated by this discovery caused other gang members to talk. By 1931, the government's case had tied Capone to over $1 million of unreported income for the years 1925–29 (a small fraction of his estimated total take). Indictment and conviction followed, and Capone was sentenced to eleven years in prison and fined $50,000.

The Capone case soon became a symbol of the investigative power of the IRS Intelligence Unit, involving as it did, the kingpin of the country's then most notorious criminal syndicate. Intelligence found enough evidence to convict Al's brother, Ralph, and other gang members, including Frank Netti and Jack and Sam Guzik, and to secure guilty pleas from a number of local politicians, among others. Nor was this work a flash-in-the-pan effort. It has continued down to the present time. In fact, a *Who's Who in Crime* would more than likely include references to convictions or guilty pleas, on a federal income tax or wagering tax charge, of Frank Costello, "Johnny Dio" Dioguardi, Frank "Screw" Andrews, Tony Grosso, Joseph "Doc" Stacher, Mickey Cohen, "Waxey" Gordon, Moe Annenberg, "Dutch" Schultz, Johnny Torrio, Albert Anastasia, Paul "the Waiter" Ricca, Peter Licavoli, Elmer "Bones" Remmer and Joseph "Newsboy" Moriarty.

Nor has Intelligence slighted other big names outside the racket area. Its program has been well balanced and many taxpayers from other, more legitimate walks of life have faced prosecution. A partial listing would include Bernard Goldfine, industrialist; William Downey, former Illinois state official; Woodrow Wilson Bean, former Texas judge; Goose Tatum, professional basketball player; Jesse Owens, Olympic star; Le Vere Redfield, millionaire investor; Grant Foster, construction executive; Raymond C. Deering, banker; Morris Goldberg, laundry tycoon; Harold Turk, former mayor; James M. Landis, former law school dean and Presidential adviser; Fred B. Bland, public relations consultant; William H. Sermon, former mayor; Nelson S. Corn and Earl Welch, Oklahoma Supreme Court justices; F. Lee Welch, attorney; Percy Magnus, former president of the New York Board of Trade; George Raft, actor; Huey Long, politician; Henry Lustig, restaurant owner; Tom Pendergast, politician; Eleanor Patenotre, former newspaper owner; Bennett E. Meyers, retired army major general; Fred M. Saigh, Jr., former baseball club owner; Harold Adonis, politician; Poncet Davis, rubber company executive; Thomas J. Lane, congressman; Frank Keenan, politician; and Dave Beck, former Teamsters Union president. All of this may seem to indicate that Americans do a lot of cheating. It doesn't. Most Americans do not cheat —although the work of the Intelligence Division undoubtedly has helped to keep them honest in reporting their income in full and on time.

Although these more notorious cases have involved income tax violations, it is worth noting that the work of Intelligence is not limited to policing the income tax. It extends to the payment of estate and gift taxes, employment taxes, and certain excise and occupational taxes (other than those on alcohol, tobacco, and firearms, which, as described in Chapter VII, are enforced by the Alcohol, Tobacco, and Firearms Division). Further, a violator need not be a taxpayer; penal sanctions extend to persons who aid or who conspire to tax evasion. The basic mission of Intelligence is revenue enforcement, but in some areas the underlying purpose of the tax is regulatory. For example, the objective of federal taxes on wagering is to aid state and local governments in enforcing their gambling laws. On the whole, however, the major enforcement work of Intelligence is ferreting out income tax evaders. Evasion—a willful act—is to be distinguished from avoidance, which implies only that the taxpayer has utilized legal means of reducing or eliminating his tax liability. In common parlance, avoidance includes the finding or use of loopholes in the law to achieve this purpose.

However, it is not evasion alone that is penalized. Congress has almost literally cast a dragnet in the form of penalties for income taxpayers who cut corners too closely. These offenses are of two basic types—civil and criminal.

Civil penalties include: (1) a 5 per cent per month (up to 25 per cent) addition to tax liability for failure to file a timely return, unless the taxpayer can show that the late filing resulted from reasonable cause; (2) a 5 per cent addition for negligence or intentional disregard of the rules and regulations; and (3) a 50 per cent addition when the taxpayer has perpetrated a fraud with the intent to evade tax.

Criminal penalties are even more onerous. They consist of fines and imprisonment and may be imposed in addition to civil penalties. The major crimes, which require proof of willfulness, include: (1) the willful attempt to evade or defeat, in any manner, any tax or payment; (2) the willful failure to collect, to account for, or to pay taxes due the government (as in the case of an employer required to withhold tax on employees); and (3) the willful failure to pay tax when due, to file a timely return (other than a declaration of estimated tax), to keep proper records, or to supply required information. Other crimes pertain to false withholding, supplying of false information to an employer, preparing or assisting in the preparation of a false return or other document, and crimes relating to conspiracy, perjury, and bribery. The maximum penalties prescribed for felonies are five years' imprisonment and a $10,000 fine—in the case of (1) and (2) above.

While these sanctions constitute some rather serious matters for a taxpayer charged with a tax violation, he is not without rights. The government, for example, has to establish

proof that the taxpayer has been guilty of the claimed violations, including civil fraud with its 50 per cent penalty. Also,
the taxpayer may assert his constitutional rights, such as the
privilege not to incriminate himself, a right that extends to
producing documents (but not workpapers owned by the accountant) and to the making of wagering tax returns (but not
income tax returns). Also, when a taxpayer is in custody, he
is entitled to the so-called Miranda warnings that he may
remain silent, that any statement made be used against him,
that he has the right to the presence of counsel and to the
appointment of counsel if he is unable to hire one. As a matter
of practice, when a special agent enters a case, the taxpayer's
full constitutional rights are explained to him.

These guidelines however, were not established overnight,
nor did the Intelligence Division arrive at its present stage of
development in this manner. Its history is worth examining.

HISTORY

During the hustle and bustle of preparing new revenue
legislation in the early Civil War days, Congress overlooked
one matter: the need for specific administrative attention to
fraud. This was remedied in 1863 when it authorized the
Secretary of the Treasury to "appoint not exceeding three
revenue agents . . . to aid in the prevention, detection, and
punishment of frauds upon the revenue."

From this humble beginning, three fraud detection units
have developed in the Internal Revenue Service: the Intelligence Division, Security Inspection Division, and the enforcement branch of the Alcohol, Tobacco, and Firearms Division
(to be discussed in Chapter VII). Intelligence, as a separate
unit, traces its origins to the period shortly after the income
tax was re-established as a permanent part of the federal tax
structure under the Sixteenth Amendment in 1913. The
growth of the Bureau of Internal Revenue as a result of World
War I taxes, especially the new income tax with its high pro-

gressive rates, brought with it a need to bring fraud "upon the revenue" under control. In a 1919 order, Commissioner Daniel Roper, a former assistant postmaster general, established a special Intelligence Unit and made arrangements to staff it by transferring six experienced Post Office inspectors.

With the advent of Prohibition at this time and the establishment of the IRS Prohibition Unit, the major task of the Intelligence Unit during the first decade of its life was the investigation of cases involving collusion between personnel in the Prohibition Unit and outsiders. This activity contributed to such innovations as pre-employment investigations of IRS personnel, and, as fraudulent tax returns started to appear in substantial numbers, pre-enrollment investigations of tax practitioners.

By the early 1930's, when the number of special agents was approaching two hundred, the public image of the Intelligence Unit as a hard-hitting, antiracketeering force began to emerge. With the conviction of Al Capone and other gangland lords during the 1930's, its reputation grew. During this period, in addition to racketeering work, the Intelligence Unit was also utilized for a number of nonrevenue tasks, including investigations involving the supply of silver bullion, the Embargo Act, vice conditions in New York, and the Lindbergh kidnaping case. During the early World War II days, it also assisted in the roundup of Japanese aliens and their property.

The expansion of tax measures during the war resulted in an increase in the field force to 465 by 1945; but even this proved insufficient to control the flow of tax evasion cases resulting from large wartime profits. The result was an increase in staff to 1,335 special agents and a tripling of investigations and convictions for the 1946–50 period over those of the previous five years.

The 1950's saw the Intelligence Unit take its present organizational form—as a division under the assistant commissioner (Compliance) in the 1952 reorganization of the Service. There were changes as well in its work assignments. The establishment of the two Inspection divisions at this time relieved the Intelligence Division of making applicant and employee misconduct investigations. Another change, which worked in the opposite direction, was a renewed federal campaign against organized crime, which included the enactment of occupation and excise taxes on wagering. This legislation was used effectively until 1968 as a major weapon by the Intelligence Division in its aid to state and local government efforts to choke off organized crime's principal source of funds. Enforcement help during this period was also provided in the form of a Supreme Court decision, which upheld the use of the net worth method of proving taxable income, and the administrative use of "wanted" circulars, seeking tax violators on a nationwide basis.

The 1960's were ushered in with the establishment of a formal training program for special agents and the inauguration of the Kennedy Administration's drive on organized crime. Other developments included aid to the Foreign Tax Assistance Staff and the formation of a nationwide Intelligence Career Program in 1965. Of major importance during this period was the advent of the computer—making possible the automatic data processing of tax returns—and its utilization by the Intelligence Division in its various enforcement programs. For example, it was instrumental in coordinating data needed to indict eighty-six bookmakers in 1965 and has been repeatedly used to combat the multiple filing of fraudulent refund claims.

Toward the end of this decade, there was one disconcerting enforcement development. In 1968, the Supreme Court, in the *Marchetti* and *Grosso* cases, upheld the right of two taxpayers, who were convicted of failing to pay the occupational and excise taxes on wagering, to assert their privilege against self-incrimination under the Fifth Amendment, because the returns on these taxes were not restricted as to disclosure, and the extensive information contained therein was available to state and local prosecutors. Although these decisions halted criminal enforcement in regard to these taxes, legislation introduced in 1969 called for amendments to the statute, not only to increase the rate of the occupational wagering tax but to prohibit disclosure and thereby correct the defect that the Supreme Court found was in violation of the taxpayer's constitutional rights.

ORGANIZATION

The ink was hardly dry on Commissioner Roper's 1919 order that brought the Intelligence Unit into being when it had its first case: an investigation of a conspiracy between two certified public accountants and an IRS employee. The only special agent then on the job, a former postal inspector, was dispatched to New York to handle the matter.

Today, the Intelligence Division has about 1,800 special agents, working out of 58 district offices and 164 other posts of duty. The Washington staff, which is headed by a director who reports to the assistant commissioner (Compliance), includes some fifty technicians and officials. They perform management functions at the national level, supervise operations in the field, and coordinate and direct cases that have been centralized.

At each of the seven IRS regional offices is an assistant regional commissioner (Intelligence), who is responsible for the functional supervision of the intelligence mission in the region. The regional structure includes a Review and Conference Staff, which reviews the reports of special agents coming in from the district offices.

The Intelligence Division, at the district level, may consist of a chief, an assistant chief, a staff assistant, and one or more group supervisors, who head up ten to twelve-man teams of special agents. In addition to the district offices, special agents are posted at some 164 branch offices, which are responsible to their respective district offices.

The Intelligence Division—the major criminal enforcement arm of the Internal Revenue Service—is thus organized in the same basic decentralized manner as its sister units, the Audit and Collection divisions. This structure was not established without some opposition. Prior to 1952, the Intelligence field organization consisted of fourteen offices, headed by agents who reported directly to the national office. The decision to decentralize was taken with some misgivings. Today, however, IRS management regards the decision as sound. It not only has provided a more uniform organizational structure but has provided the district director with a criminal enforcement unit whose work can be coordinated with the audit and collection functions that are so critical in the over-all enforcement activities of the agency.

A description of the organizational structure of IRS intelligence activities would not be complete without some reference to the Enforcement Division, one of the five divisions of the office of the associate chief counsel (Litigation) in Washington. Each regional counsel's office contains a regional Enforcement Division, which handles field matters involving criminal cases and, in general, reviews recommendations of prosecution made by special agents, forwards such recommendations to the Justice Department, and closes nonprosecution cases with the concurrences of the assistant regional commissioner (Intelligence). Enforcement thus provides critical services in the administration of the criminal provisions of the tax laws.

A criminal prosecution for tax fraud is a serious matter to the suspect taxpayer, as well as the general public, and the Internal Revenue Service is not unmindful of the need to make sure that the case has received adequate administrative review before the evidence is laid before a grand jury and an indictment requested. The extreme care exercised in this area is due, in part, to the unique position of the special agent as a criminal investigator. Unlike most criminal investigators, who normally seek to establish only the identity of the criminal, the special agent seeks to establish that a crime has in fact been committed. Further, the very nature of tax fraud, the highly sophisticated cover-up frequently encountered in accounting records and in transactions between related tax-payers and their business entities requires of the special agent a skill that makes criminal fraud investigation a very special type of police work.

For these and other reasons, the administrative process embraces at least five levels of review before a criminal fraud case is presented to a grand jury. The review process starts after the special agent has concluded his investigation. If his report recommends prosecution, it is first reviewed by his group supervisor and then by the chief of the district Intelligence Division. In these instances, the report is examined for accuracy, completeness and the impartial presentation of the material facts as well as for the validity of the agent's conclusions. A third and fourth review are provided at the regional level, first in the office of the assistant regional commissioner (Intelligence) and then in the Enforcement Division of the regional counsel's office. Approval in the latter instance will result in the case being transferred to the Justice Department with a recommendation for prosecution. Here, a fifth review is made (some 10 per cent of cases are declined) before presentation to the grand jury, which, in effect, constitutes a sixth review.

In event the Enforcement Division believes prosecution is not warranted, the case is returned to the assistant regional commissioner with a memorandum. The assistant regional commissioner, in turn, remits the case to the district office for comment. After the appropriate parties at the district level have had their say, and if the assistant regional commissioner believes prosecution is warranted, the case is transferred to the Intelligence Division in Washington, where the decision is made whether or not to protest to the chief counsel. The final decision whether to recommend prosecution or return the case to the field is normally made on behalf of the chief counsel in the Enforcement Division in the national office.

The preceding administrative review may not be entirely a matter of examining documents. The taxpayer and his counsel are normally granted a conference at district, regional, and Department of Justice level if they so desire. While this may involve a problem of defense strategy from the taxpayer's viewpoint, it adds a new dimension to the administrative reviewing process as well as opportunities for settlement without the stigma of a criminal prosecution.

All of this reviewing is hardly prologue. The critical investigative work of the reviewed party, by the special agent, begins long before there is a need for review. His work is worth describing.

THE SPECIAL AGENT

As the special agent picked up the letter, he noted that it was on plain stationery; the envelope carried a local postmark and was addressed simply to "Internal Revenue." It was a "squeal letter," suggesting that the IRS check a named taxpayer's income tax.

Although some 100,000 Americans (jealous lovers, employees, wives, neighbors) volunteer information on other taxpayers annually, the Intelligence Division does not use paid informers or pursue a policy of appealing to the general public to inform, except with respect to violators of the wagering taxes. The Commissioner, however, is authorized by statute to pay rewards to informants and some 5 per cent of the information items received result in reward claims of which 20 per cent—less than 1,000 annually—are allowed.

The squeal letter, which produces some $20 million annually in taxes and penalties, is only one of the many sources of information available to the special agent that may lead to the disclosure of tax fraud. The most fruitful and most frequent source of leads are those uncovered by revenue agents during the course of audit examinations. Others may be provided by news stories pertaining to theft and other crimes.

Still other leads my be found in Treasury Currency Reports (TCR's) made by some banks to their Federal Reserve Bank, which disclose large cash deposits and withdrawals.

The handling of these various leads will normally call for a preliminary investigation to determine whether a full-scale investigation is warranted. Thus, if during the course of an audit examination a revenue agent finds indications of fraud, it will be referred to the Intelligence Division. After an initial screening, this lead may be assigned to a special agent for a preliminary investigation for its full investigation potential. Inquiry here may involve interviews with the taxpayer and third parties; it may involve an IRS file check on the taxpayer. Consideration will also be given to the taxpayer's residence (or place of the suspected crime) for proper venue, to whether the statute of limitations has or is about to expire, to the terms of the specific criminal statute, and to special factors, such as age or illness of the taxpayer, that would render conviction unlikely. The inquiry, in short, is to determine whether a potential criminal case exists.

Out of some 10,000 preliminary examinations conducted annually, approximately 2,000 full-scale criminal investigations result—the "jacketed" cases. Some of these will be conducted jointly with a revenue agent (or revenue officer). In these cases, although the revenue agent remains on the scene, his examination is subordinate to the criminal investigation work of the special agent. Until the criminal aspects of the case are concluded, the special agent is responsible for the direction taken by the investigation. When the Intelligence Division conducts an independent examination that results in a no-prosecution termination, the file with the special agent's report is transmitted to the Audit Division for examination on any apparent tax deficiencies and civil liabilities.

The work of a special agent in developing a criminal fraud case is often a tedious task, consisting of interviews and analyses of books of account and bank records, and, although his powers of investigation are broad and include the power to execute and serve search and arrest warrants, the special agent is constantly plagued by the need to prove beyond a reasonable doubt, with legally admissible evidence, that the taxpayer engaged in transactions that were indicative of the necessary willful intent required by the specific statute. Rarely will direct proof of such a state of mind be found; often what may appear to be willfulness will simply be neglect. While willfulness and intent may be inferred from such conduct as false book entries, keeping two sets of books, intentional destruction of books and records, hidden bank accounts, concealed assets, and use of an alias, frequently this type of proof is not available.

In some cases, all that is available is a pattern of lavish living—determinable only after prolonged inquiry—indicating that the taxpayer has some source of unreported income. In these and similar cases where adequate records are nonexistent, it may be necessary to establish a taxpayer's income through indirection. One available device for this is the net worth method. This method requires a determination of the difference between the net value of the taxpayer's assets at the beginning and end of the year, plus evidence of his nondeductible personal expenditures during the year. Any difference between the amount so determined and reported income may be treated as unreported taxable income. In these cases, much may depend on the credibility of the taxpayer's evidence as to nontaxable sources of income, such as claimed gifts, and on whether the government has made a reasonable effort to check out these sources as required. The outcomes of such cases have varied widely. For example, a taxpayer who asserted that his mother had left him $40,000 in an earthern crock in a basement in Iraq was found not guilty of fraud but still liable for a deficiency, because he failed to carry his burden of proof. In another case, the Tax Court, in a civil action, chose to believe a taxpayer who contended he had received $200,000 for marrying a wealthy widow nearly four times his age.

A device for proving income that may be used in conjunction with the net worth method is the cash flow method. This method requires an analysis of the taxpayer's cash expenditures in relation to his total acknowledged cash available for spending. A third method, the bank deposit method, consists of totaling the taxpayer's bank deposits, subtracting the gross income on the return and treating the difference as taxable income. This method has sometimes forced a taxpayer to reveal additional information and transactions, not disclosable during the course of an ordinary audit.

In other cases, records may be sufficient to utilize the specific item method, a method that has wide application and may include situations where there has been a manipulation of income and expense deductions between related corporations and individuals, the claim of fictitious dependents, or the omission of unrecorded cash sales from gross income. In these cases, the special agent focuses on the specific fraudulent transaction. Finally, a percentage method has been used successfully to reconstruct the tip income of waiters and taxicab drivers as well as the income of abortionists, gamblers, and numerous business enterprises, such as bakery shops, retail liquor stores, and pizza parlors.

All of this takes time. Normally, a special agent will be working on one to three cases at a time, but a production record of one good case a year is considered a satisfactory performance. Over-all, more than one-half of the some 2,000 full-scale investigations result in recommendations of prosecution, which, prior to 1968, were almost equally divided between income tax fraud and wagering tax cases. Eventual convictions—guilty and no-defense pleas—number some 600 on income tax cases and prior to 1968, 500 on wagering tax cases. Although actual trials are few in number (for 1968 there were eighty-nine income tax fraud convictions and thirty-one acquittals), the yield in tax and penalties for income tax fraud closings of all types amounted to some $110 million in 1968.

At the conclusion of an investigation, the special agent files a report, but his work does not stop there. He may be called upon to participate in the five-level review process described above, including conferences with the taxpayer and his attorney; he is required to assist the United States attorney in preparing for trial; and he may be required to testify before a grand jury and to appear as a witness during the course of the trial.

The special agent, therefore, must be prepared to handle a wide variety of tasks and must be able to keep pace with a constantly increasing sophistication in the concealment of assets, manipulation of transactions, and juggling of books and records. To meet these demands, the IRS imposes high entrance requirements and subjects new recruits to a rigorous training program designed to develop the full range of the varied and needed investigative skills.

Unless the applicant has other qualifying experience, entrance to the agency as a special agent requires a four-year college degree with twelve semester hours in accounting (or an LL.B. degree) and the passing of a civil service examination designed to measure investigative aptitudes—although a successful in-service recruitment program during 1967–68 resulted in meeting 65 per cent of IRS needs for this period on a noncompetitive basis. Upon selection and reporting for duty, the new agent is subject to a four-phase training program that includes seventeen weeks of classroom work in a basic income tax course and training in the Treasury Department's Law Enforcement School and the Special Agent's Basic School. Training is concluded with participation in a mock income tax trial. These courses are followed by on-the-job training under the tutelage of experienced agents. In addition, the special agent, during the course of his career, will attend advanced training programs designed to improve his skills and to enable him to keep abreast of developments in scientific investigation work.

The content of the special agent's formal training reflects

the tasks he will be called upon to perform. It will include training in income and excise tax law, criminal law, rules of evidence and criminal procedure, investigative techniques, use of firearms and electronic devices, interrogation of witnesses, report writing, and testifying.

The career advancement of the special agent is normally quite rapid. More than half of IRS special agents have entered the Internal Revenue Service during the past decade (the average age is 42); within two or three years almost all reach journeyman grade GS-11. A nationwide career program, launched in 1965 and designed to identify special agents for management positions, has helped many in their climb up the managerial ladder; some 13 per cent now occupy supervisory and management positions in grades GS-13 to GS-15. Special agents also may claim the benefit of the civil service rules pertaining to hazardous activity and retire at age 50 after twenty years of service.

ORGANIZED CRIME

In 1967, the President's Commission on Law Enforcement made the following statement:

> There is no accurate way of ascertaining organized crime's gross revenue from gambling in the United States. Estimates of the annual intake have varied from $7 to $50 billion. . . . While the Commission cannot judge the accuracy of the figures, even the most conservative estimates place substantial capital in the hands of organized crime leaders.

The magnitude of organized criminal activity funded primarily by illegal gambling (loan-sharking and narcotics are the second and third major sources) almost staggers the imagination. The source of its power lies in an estimated annual net profit of $7 billion, made possible by public apathy with respect to gambling laws. Basically a state and local government problem, organized crime did not confront the federal government as a national problem until shortly after World War II. The federal government's first action program came on the heels of congressional investigations led by Senator Kefauver in 1951, which provided the nation, through telecast public hearings, with the dimensions of the problem. These hearings and later studies revealed the modern racketeer as a sophisticated businessman type, guided by lawyers, accountants, and financial advisers, who functioned in large measure in organized groups. These hearings led to the establishment in the Department of Justice of the Organized Crime and Racketeering Section (OCRS), whose mission was to coordinate such enforcement activities in all federal agencies.

However, the OCRS remained a low-key activity until further congressional hearings by the McClellan Committee during the 1957–60 period brought out further evidence of the nature of organized crime's organizational structure (twenty-four Cosa Nostra "families" with a hard-core membership of some 5,000). These hearings led to a new move toward centralizing the federal government's crime fighting efforts in 1961, and by 1963 the OCRS was staffed with sixty attorneys, although it was still a coordinating agency without authority to direct enforcement.

Setbacks in this warfare occurred in 1965 because of what turned out to be illegal use of electronic surveillance devices and also because of 1968 Supreme Court decisions upholding taxpayers' rights to assert their privilege against self-incrimination in filing the returns required by the statutes applicable to the wagering taxes.

On the other hand, 1968 and 1969 saw renewed efforts at the federal level to combat organized crime. Legislation enacted in 1968, for example, provides for an extensive program of federal aid to local law enforcement, and fresh efforts to control interstate traffic in firearms (the latter laws, as described in Chapter VII, are administered by the IRS Alcohol, Tobacco, and Firearms Division). In 1969, the Nixon Administration began its campaign against organized crime with the establishment of a federal-state racket squad in New York City. OCRS field offices were opened in eight major cities, plans for twelve other such offices were announced, and requests were made for increased appropriations for these purposes. In addition, the Administration requested new legislation from Congress, including witness immunity laws, amendments to the wagering tax statutes, and laws making certain illicit gambling operations a federal crime.

Long before the establishment of the OCRS in the Department of Justice in 1954, the IRS Intelligence Division had begun its own private war against organized crime. As early as the late 1920's, the Intelligence Unit began paying special attention to the income tax returns (or lack of them) of known Prohibition era gangsters. This special attention was predicated on the proposition that, since these taxpayers were motivated in obtaining their income illegally, they were not likely to be possessed with the notion that they were obligated to share their gains with the government. Also, as the businessman type of racketeer began to emerge, and as evidence of the infiltration of major criminals into legitimate businesses began to mount, the Intelligence Division extended its "automatic audit" policy to these enterprises (98 of 113 of the nations's major crime figures have been found in 159 legitimate businesses).

In 1961 the Intelligence Division's special racketeer program resulted in the formation of an Operations Coordination Branch in the national office to coordinate organized crime cases. Coordinators in the regional offices worked in the field with OCRS attorneys during the course of investigations. At the functional level, the division maintained a file of names, provided in part by the OCRS (the Department of Justice list consists of about 3,100 persons considered to be leading racketeers), which were earmarked for special scrutiny annually. This list included, in addition to organized-crime figures, persons operating continuously in violation of local law. Further, the tax return of a known racketeer would be investigated in more depth than is usually the case, and administrative control would be maintained during the course of the investigation.

The conviction record (mostly for income tax and wagering tax violations) under this program was quite impressive. For the 1961–67 period, by utilizing 20 per cent of its manpower on these cases, the Intelligence Division conducted approximately 5,000 investigations, resulting in 2,198 convictions—60 per cent of all federal convictions against organized-crime figures during this period. Fines totaled $3 million and recommendations of tax $295 million.

Commencing in 1970, the Internal Revenue Service's independent efforts in the racketeer area were incorporated into Justice's new organized crime drive, and special agents and revenue agents are now assigned to Justice Department "strike forces," as they are established in the major urban centers in the country.

VI

International Activities

"For no country ever takes notice of the revenue laws of another"—thus spoke Lord Mansfield, one of England's most respected jurists almost two hundred years ago in the course of a judicial opinion. Surely this observation must be regarded as expressive of an archaic idea today, in a period when the need for working out the problems of international interdependence is regarded as so essential to the welfare of the people of all nation states. Unfortunately, such is not the case. This application of the doctrine of national sovereignty—an isolationism not tolerated generally today—seems to be rooted more strongly than ever in judicial doctrine and practices all over the world. Even though the Western judicial world has long subscribed—under the doctrine of comity—to the notion that private claims and debts may be enforced on an extraterritorial basis, the government's claim for taxes is still regarded as an attribute of its sovereignty, as a provision for its internal public order, and as being within the province of the legislature rather than the courts.

Consider what happened in 1963 when the Internal Revenue Service attempted to collect an income tax debt of some $640,000, which Mrs. Harden admitted she owed and for which a judgment was entered against her by agreement of the parties in a United States District Court. When Mrs. Harden moved to British Columbia, the United States followed her there and sued on the judgment. This, the Supreme Court of Canada held, was improper; the rule that denies the right of a foreign state to enforce its tax claims in another court, the Court said, is strongly rooted in public policy.

The limitations imposed on the IRS that stem from the inability to pursue normal judicial and administrative collection remedies constitute only one of the many dimensions of the problems attendant upon the enforcement of the U.S. revenue laws on a worldwide basis. The sovereignty notion lies at the source of many of these problems through the tax rules by which jurisdiction is asserted by the United States over its nationals and, in case of the income tax, over income from a U.S. source. Some knowledge of these provisions of the law dealing with jurisdiction is essential to an understanding of the problems of tax administration in the international area.

As one basic jurisdictional rule, U.S. citizens (and resident aliens) and domestic corporations (those formed in the United States) are subject to U.S. income tax on their worldwide income. However, if foreign income is generated in a foreign country that imposes an income tax, the foreign tax paid may be taken as a credit (deducted) from the tax on this income due the United States. Some additional rules: A U.S. citizen (other than a government employee) who is a bona fide resident of a foreign country (or who is present in foreign countries seventeen out of eighteen months) may exclude the first $20,000 of his earned income, as distinct from business and investment income. If he is a resident of Puerto Rico, all his Puerto Rican-source income is excluded from U.S. tax, since Puerto Rico has its own tax system.

The foregoing rules have generated a host of difficult problems of interpretation, but this is only the beginning of the complexities encountered in the international area. In addition to the earned income exclusion available to U.S. citizens resident abroad, Congress has seen fit to grant tax concessions to certain domestic corporations doing business in United

States possessions, in the Western Hemisphere, and in Hong Kong and Taiwan. These tax concessions, which are of long standing, were originally justified on the grounds that they were necessary to help United States interests meet foreign competition for these markets; currently, the corporate concessions are regarded as complementary to U.S. foreign policy, which is designed to aid less developed countries in their efforts to industrialize.

Many of the complexities in both the substantive rules and overseas administration can be attributed to congressional efforts to bring tax avoidance under some measure of control. The problems pertaining to individual taxpayers are minuscule compared to those pertaining to big business.

The starting point in the big business area is this: Subject to minor exceptions, a foreign corporation (or a nonresident alien individual) is taxable only on its U.S.-source income, and the revenue laws prescribe in some detail what income is to be so regarded. Prior to 1962, this jurisdictional rule was tailor-made for the following type of multicorporate operation.

X, a domestic United States parent corporation would establish Y as a Swiss (or Panamanian) wholly owned subsidiary at nominal tax costs in Switzerland. Y, in turn, could act for X in a wide variety of ways outside the United States, which could result in the accumulation of foreign income in Y without subjecting such income to U.S. tax. Y could act as an importer, an exporter, a sales agent, a service agent for licensing patents, or simply as a holding-company for stock in other country corporations in X's empire. Y's income could be used for loans to X or its other companies without being brought within reach of the U.S. tax collector. United States tax would be payable only when and to the extent X decided to have Y declare a dividend, in which case X would be entitled to credit for any income taxes paid by Y, or subsidiaries of Y, to foreign countries.

The preceding "tax-haven" abuse and a number of other abuses were brought under a measure of control in 1962.

However, the new rules—coupled with previous legislation designed to control the use of foreign personal holding companies, with the rules pertaining to foreign currency, with reporting of foreign investment, with foreign accounting, tax treaties, and other matters, such as limitations imposed in 1968 on direct investment abroad in order to limit gold drainage—have resulted in a body of law containing some of the most head-swimming rules ever devised by man. All of these must be taken into account in overseas tax administration. The task is not an easy one.

ORGANIZATION

Manila in December is most pleasant. The breeze comes in off the bay that opens into the China Sea, the tempo is unhurried, and the 'living is easy' in the jewel of the Orient. At least this was the case in 1936, as IRS's new "man in Manila" disembarked. However, it is doubtful that he was thinking of easy living; as the first overseas Internal Revenue Service representative, his thoughts were probably more on the ground he was breaking in tax administration—ground that still leaves U.S. tax administration unique among the world's tax systems.

In 1936, it had been apparent for some time to IRS officials that many Americans living overseas were not keeping up with their tax obligations, although the extent of noncompliance was a matter of guesswork at the time. In any event, congressional appropriations for at least some overseas enforcement had been secured, and Manila—the Philippines was then a United States possession with a good-sized American colony—seemed like a good base from which to service American taxpayers in the islands and other Far Eastern countries.

The opening of the Manila office was followed in 1938 and 1939 with new offices in Paris and London. All three offices were victims of World War II, and it was not until the smoke had cleared after the 1952 reorganization that IRS policy-makers were in a position to do something concrete about the tax administration gap in the overseas area. Up to this time, Americans living overseas simply prepared their returns as best they could—if they did this at all—and filed them with the collector where they had their legal residence or, if none, with the Baltimore district office.

A fresh start on overseas compliance was made in 1948, with the reopening of the Paris office and with a survey conducted by teams of revenue agents, who compiled data from Americans living in numerous cities in Canada, Europe, Latin America, and the Far East. This survey revealed a low level of compliance, due to a lack of taxpayer assistance (many thought the earned income exclusion applied to all income), as well as to a lack of systematic audit and collection programs. To meet these deficiencies, the Office of International Operations (OIO) was established in 1955, with division status, under the assistant commissioner (Compliance), with headquarters in Washington.

The OIO does not fit neatly into the usual decentralized structure of the Internal Revenue Service. It has a number of unique organizational features. In the first place, it is directly concerned only with U.S. citizens resident abroad and with non-resident aliens, foreign trusts and estates, and foreign corporations with U.S.-source incomes. In the second place, its four-divisional structure has a number of features that distinguish it from a domestic district office organization. Its Collection Division has a separate Puerto Rico Collection Branch, and its Foreign Operations Division, while charged with the intelligence function, has as its main function the coordination of the work of the nine foreign posts, located as follows:

Bonn, Germany	Ottawa, Canada
London, England	Paris, France
Manila, Philippines	Rome, Italy
Mexico City, Mexico	São Paulo, Brazil
Tokyo, Japan	

Each post is thinly staffed, is headed by a Revenue Service Representative, functions as a miniature district office, provides the full range of domestic district office services (taxpayer service, audit, collection, intelligence) and, in addition, provides certain services to domestic district offices. Finally, the Research, Tax Treaty, and Technical Services Division has essential management and field support missions, for which there are no district-level counterparts.

In short, the organization structure of the Office of International Operations is designed to permit the 550-man team to carry out its jurisdictional mission with respect to overseas-based taxpayers both in Washington and at the foreign posts. Jurisdiction over domestic-based taxpayers with foreign income is in the hands of the fifty-eight district offices, whose work is subject to the normal regional supervision.

OVERSEAS-BASED TAXPAYERS

In *United States* v. *First National City Bank*, Omar, a Uruguayan corporation, had been engaged in trading on the U.S. stock market from 1955 to 1961. When Omar's 1959 tax return triggered an audit resulting in proposed deficiencies, it transferred its funds out of the country. When the IRS discovered this, it made a jeopardy assessment of $19 million and obtained a court order, directing the defendant bank, a New York corporation, not to transfer any funds that Omar had on deposit in the bank's Montevideo branch. Could the U.S. tax collector reach the foreign taxpayer's foreign assets in this manner? Although the Court of Appeals said no, the United States Supreme Court, by a vote of seven to two, held that the procedure was proper. (To actually reach the money, however, if Omar refused to transfer the funds to the credit of the United States, the United States would have to secure a judgment against Omar and send an officer to Montivideo to make a demand on the branch.) The Court simply reasoned that the defendant bank was subject to suit, had control over its branches, and, if the action would be embarrassing to the U.S. Department of State, the courts were open to its plea.

The *First National City Bank* case, however, probably represents the outer limits of the ability of the IRS to reach a foreign taxpayer without assets located in the United States. If the bank had operated in Montivideo in foreign subsidiary form, there would have been no way to reach the taxpayer's assets. The locus of assets and ownership is thus critical.

Most disputes that arise are handled without incident in the filing and collection processes, which start with a return filed directly with the Office of International Operations in Washington. Returns filed elsewhere are forwarded. More than one million income tax, estate and gift tax, and information returns are processed annually by the Office Branch of the Collection Division (return processing at OIO has not as yet been integrated into automatic data processing). The branch also handles all funds, both taxes and withheld amounts, and performs the required delinquency checks in the overseas area. Its work with respect to the checking of returns on nonresident aliens and foreign corporations requires attention to a multitude of withholding rates, because of the differing provisions of twenty-two tax treaties, which vary the basic 30 per cent nontreaty withholding rate.

The Delinquent Accounts and Returns Branch of the Collection Division functions in a manner similar to the similar unit in a district office, assisted, when necessary, by the overseas-based revenue service representatives. The Puerto Rico Collection Branch, the official language of which is Spanish, functions in a manner similar to the Washington Collection Division with respect to returns originating in Puerto Rico and the Virgin Islands.

The work of the Audit Division, which handles about 20,000 audit examinations annually, is similar to that of a domestic district office division performing these functions, except that returns are not subject to a computer selection, and the Washington field and office audit groups may be required to seek aid from an overseas representative. In case of a proposed deficiency or processing of a refund claim, the usual statewide administrative and judicial review processes, described in Chapter III, are available to the taxpayer—district conference, appellate conference, and suit in the Tax Court, District Court, or Court of Claims.

Suppose that a foreign-based taxpayer has not filed a return as required or refuses to pay, or that IRS agents need books or records located abroad. What can the Collection Division in Washington do about it? Apart from turning the matter over to an overseas representative, who, as described below, may be even more handicapped, it has a number of collection tools at its disposal. At the investigative stage, not only is the IRS able to reach third-party books and records located in the United States, but, unless a foreign country's law so prohibits, it can also reach records of a U.S. business or bank located at the foreign branch.

If the collection process requires that a taxpayer's assets located in the United States be reached, the enforcement problems are the same as in the case of a domestic taxpayer.

In the case of an individual taxpayer in the process of removing himself or his property abroad, a number of procedures are available. In addition to a statutory jeopardy assessment and the closing of a departing taxpayer's tax year and immediate assessment, the U.S. collector may pursue a common-law remedy in a state court in form of a writ *ne exeat republica*, a court order to the taxpayer not to leave or remove his property from the country. Also, if the departing taxpayer is an alien, subject to certain exceptions, he is required to obtain a certificate of compliance (sailing permit) from his district director at the time of departure. This means that he will have to show that his taxes for prior years have been paid and that he has paid any taxes due for the current year up to the time of departure.

Finally, even if assets of a foreign-based taxpayer, especially a U.S. citizen, cannot be located or reached, the IRS may simply wait for the taxpayer to come home. The statute of limitations on collection is suspended when property is held or has been removed from the United States, and, in case of criminal fraud, the statute does not run while a taxpayer remains outside the United States.

But suppose an overseas-based taxpayer without reachable assets does not intend to return. As a general proposition, the Internal Revenue Service is then without foreign legal remedies, including even the power to examine the taxpayer's books and records and those of third parties located overseas. In a few instances, overseas collection efforts may run up against prohibitory disclosure laws. Swiss banking laws, for example, prohibit their banks from revealing the names of depositors, even to Swiss taxing authorities for Swiss nationals, and Swiss banks have developed an international reputation as a sanctuary for money from all over the world, having successfully resisted pressure from the highest of sources, including the powerful Nazi regime and the postwar allied military government.

Thus, if the taxpayer is an alien with no thought at all of leaving his own country, both investigation and collection may border on the impossible. However, if he is one of some 300,-000 overseas U.S. citizens, it may be quite a different matter. Here, the IRS has formulated a compliance policy that combines taxpayer assistance and education with persuasion and force, but which recognizes that the latter may be futile, as was the case with Mrs. Harden discussed above.

The Revenue Service Representative must execute this policy. He must not only be technically competent in collection, intelligence, auditing, and related areas, but he must be responsive to his status as a "tax administrator in striped trousers." He is attached to and quartered in the United States Embassy, responsible to the U.S. Ambassador as well as to his division director in Washington, and, in general, represents the United States in tax affairs in dealing with foreign government officials and businessmen. For these matters, he must have command of one or more foreign languages and a knowledge of foreign customs.

The duties of a Revenue Service Representative are numerous, and they extend over a wide geographic area. Each of the nine representatives have been assigned a definite geographic area of the world, so that, theoretically, they provide worldwide coverage for the IRS.

One of the representative's more burdensome duties is providing assistance to the 50,000 overseas U.S. citizens who request aid at tax return time. For this task, representatives are provided help in the form of twenty or more stateside IRS employees, who visit 120 cities in more than fifty countries during this period. The Internal Revenue Service also relies heavily on the propensity of overseas Americans to pay their income taxes on a voluntary basis. For example, two agents picked up $500,000 in four months during a compliance survey in 1954, revealing that most Americans need only to be informed or approached. For this reason, compliance programs have emphasized taxpayer education in the form of publications, available through U.S. embassies and consulates, and through special seminars and meetings.

One special overseas program is carried out in cooperation with the Army's Judge Advocate General's office; each year IRS teams conduct ten or more overseas tax schools for military advisers, who carry back to their units the ability to provide tax assistance to military personnel (who do not have the benefit of the $20,000 earned income exclusion but who are entitled to other more limited benefits). These schools meet the needs of some two-thirds of the assistance required by the overseas armed forces. As a more pragmatic matter, the IRS also has concluded agreements with the Department of Defense whereby the Department will accept levies on the salaries of both military and civilian overseas personnel. This has permitted the shifting of collecting from these taxpayers to domestic district offices, relieving the Office of International Operations of this sometimes difficult task.

As an example of a final task of a Revenue Service Representative, let us return to agent Jones of Chapter III, who is in the process of conducting an audit examination of Smith Company returns. Suppose Tom marks for further examination a claimed deduction for overseas branch office expenses, including salaries and rent. How does he know that such a branch even exists? On these, and other matters requiring information from overseas, Tom, as well as other U.S.-based IRS personnel, must rely upon the representative. If the information required involves a "peek at the books," the representative must often rely on his personality and charm or whatever other powers of persuasion he may have.

Domestic-based Taxpayers

Suppose revenue agent Tom Jones, during the course of his audit examination of Smith Company's books, uncovers this situation: Smith is selling its manufactured goods to its wholly owned domestic subsidiary Brown Company at cost. Brown, in turn, sells all it buys from Smith in Canada and Latin America at a large profit. If Brown qualifies as a Western Hemisphere trade corporation, as it could, it is entitled to a 14-point (approximately 30 per cent) corporate tax rate reduction. If this scheme is effective, Smith's manufacturing profits have been shifted to Brown, to be taxed at lower rates. Further, if Brown were a foreign subsidiary and resold the goods in the country where organized, no tax at all would be payable to the United States until Smith elected to have Brown declare a dividend.

Income-shifting in one form or another has been part of the "tax game" played by tax advisers and IRS representatives since the days of the first revenue laws. Success in exploiting this type of loophole has varied, but frequently the IRS has felt it necessary to ask for legislation from Congress to deal with transactions between related entities in the international area. In 1933, the Internal Revenue Service received broad legislative authority—now Section 482 of the Internal Revenue Code—under which it may reallocate items of income, deduction, credit, or allowances between related organizations. In the example above, the attempted shifting of income from Smith Company to Brown would normally run afoul of this provision. But this is not all. In 1962, as a result of IRS research under a directive from President John F. Kennedy, Congress responded with comprehensive legislation dealing with controlled foreign corporations (50 per cent or more owned by U.S. persons or corporations), which was designed to bring "tax-haven" abuses under some measure of control.

After the 1962 legislation had passed, and the smoke had cleared, it was apparent that the Internal Revenue Service was not only faced with a new dimension in tax administration but one with a technical content and volume with which a small centralized administrative unit in the national office was unable to cope, and that the response of tax administration to the unprecedented postwar overseas expansion of U.S. trade and investment (now some $55 billion in direct investment alone) would require decentralization in the district offices. This meant that the domestic revenue agent, for one thing, would have to be brought to a level of competency to deal with a multitude of new technical issues spawned by the 1962 legislation and by new detailed regulations issued as guidelines to a stepped-up enforcement program under Section 482.

To meet these problems, in addition to seminars and courses, a three-phase transitional international audit program was inaugurated, and in 1965 the Office of International Operations was restructured, and the Research, Tax Treaty, and Technical Services Division was established in the national office. This unit now provides both management and field support services in this critical area. It functions in two branches. The Research and Tax Treaty Branch, apart from its tax treaty functions, which are discussed below, conducts research in the international area, analyzes data provided on information returns in order to identify the nature and scope of the foreign activities of U.S. business interests, handles claims filed by taxpayers for relief available as a result of a Section 482 allocation, makes recommendations with respect to proposed changes in the law and regulations, and provides foreign tax law technical data to the field for determining the earnings and profits of controlled foreign corporations and other matters.

Of equal importance, especially to agents in the field, is the highly technical work of the Economic Advisory Branch, a unit which could just as well be denominated the Section 482 Branch. In exercising its power of allocation under Section 482, the IRS has often been confronted with the superior control and knowledge possessed by a large U.S. enterprise over its own pricing and other trade practices. To meet this challenge the IRS established the Economic Advisory Branch, a group of economists and agents whose primary task is to provide assistance to revenue agents and other personnel in meeting economic problems under proposed Section 482 allocations.

Tax Treaties

When Ingemar Johansson, the Swedish heavyweight, caught Floyd Patterson with a stiff left jab and followed with his famous right shot to Patterson's jaw, it was all over; Ingemar had won his fight and the world championship. He had prepared well for the bout and the results were what he had hoped for. He had also prepared for his bout with the United States tax collector, but not well enough; this time he lost (he also lost his championship in a return fight with Patterson).

In 1959, the year before the second fight, Ingemar became, ostensibly, a Swiss resident by opening a bank account and renting an apartment in Switzerland; he also secured a statement from the Swiss tax authorities that he was a Swiss resident. As a final step, a Swiss corporation was formed, which employed Ingemar under a contract, whereby he was to receive 70 per cent of the corporation's profits and a pension. The corporation would arrange his fights and pay expenses; its sole source of income and sole employee was Ingemar.

In this way, Johansson brought himself squarely within the literal terms of the United States–Swiss income tax treaty, which excepted from taxation the personal service income of an "individual resident of Switzerland," temporarily present in the United States not more than 183 days during the year and whose compensation was received as an "employee of, or under contract with," a Swiss corporation. The U.S.-Swedish treaty contained no comparable provision. On the other hand, the Collection Division of the IRS Office of International Operations wanted in excess of $1 million from Ingemar for his 1960 and 1961 fights, which were staged in the United States. The income was personal service income of an alien earned in the United States, said the Internal Revenue Service, and therefore was subject to United States tax.

The Fifth Circuit Court of Appeals agreed with the IRS. Under U.S. standards, the Court held that Johansson was neither a bona fide Swiss "resident," nor did the corporation have a legitimate business purpose. The corporation was merely a device to escape United States taxation. International trade, said the Court of Appeals, would not be "seriously encumbered by our refusal to grant special tax treatment to one only marginally, if at all, a Swiss resident and only technically, if at all, employed by a paper Swiss corporation."

The United States is a party to twenty-two bilateral income tax treaties, twelve estate tax treaties, and two gift tax treaties. These conventions, which take precedence over the revenue laws, carry imposing labels, indicating they are designed to prevent double taxation and tax evasion. However, from the standpoint of double taxation of U.S. taxpayers, they offer few over-all tax benefits, because the principal treaty device utilized to prevent double taxation is the grant of reciprocal credit for taxes, and U.S. taxpayers have had nontreaty or unilateral credit available under the general revenue laws for foreign taxes as a preventative of double taxation since 1918.

From the standpoint of the prevention of tax evasion, the machinery by which the parties to the treaty are able to enforce their respective tax laws on an extraterritorial basis cannot be regarded as truly effective. Most of the treaties provide only for an exchange of information and then only in specific cases upon demand; only four treaties provide for an automatic exchange of information. However, notwithstanding the limited utility of the information and collection provisions of the treaties, they undoubtedly have a psychological effect in limiting the use of a treaty country as a sanctuary and have proved to be of some aid in collection.

One matter is clear concerning tax administration: the tax treaties, which inject an additional dimension into a complex field, provide more than a few headaches and problems for the Internal Revenue Service. At the negotiation level, these problems are primarily research problems. Thus, although attorneys from the chief counsel's office assist the Department of the Treasury in the Department's ongoing negotiating work with respect to new treaties and amendments and protocols to existing treaties, the Research and Tax Treaty Branch of the Office of International Operations is responsible for the basic research function for compliance purposes.

Second, since the provisions of the various treaties override the provision of the U.S. revenue laws, the treaties also inject a measure of complexity throughout the compliance programs at both the district level and in the compliance divisions of the Office of International Operations. For example, each treaty modifies the usual 30 per cent statutory withholding rate on the investment income of nonresident aliens and foreign corporations. These modifications and others must be taken into account by OIO's Collection Division when processing thousands of tax and information returns.

Finally, there are the problems of interpretation. Once a

tax treaty becomes effective, each country appoints a "competent authority" as administrator of the treaty; in the case of the United States, this is the director of the Office of International Operations. This means that his office (through the Research and Tax Treaty Branch) must handle not only such routine matters as the exchange of witholding return information, but the sometimes protracted correspondence with foreign tax officials on questions of treaty interpretation.

The problem of arriving at a uniform interpretation of a treaty provision is not always an easy matter, and, on occasion, a bit of international pressure has been employed. For example, under Article 10 of the French treaty, compensation for professional services is exempt if the taxpayer does not maintain an office or base in the visiting country. When the French tax authorities interpreted this article as being limited to independent contractors, thereby excluding employed professionals such as teachers, the IRS felt forced to retaliate by reversing its broader interpretation for French teachers visiting this country. The French then relented and provided exemption in France for U.S. teachers and others. The IRS followed suit and reinstated its previous position.

FOREIGN TAX ASSISTANCE

During 1966, the international news services carried these items: in Peru a taxpayer was sentenced to prison for income tax evasion; in the Dominican Republic a revenue agent was convicted for accepting a bribe; in Uruguay a taxpayer's property was seized for nonpayment of taxes. Newsworthy? Yes indeed. Penalties for tax evasion, fraud, and nonpayment were common enough in the United States, but for these Latin American countries such occurrences were genuine "firsts."

The starting point for what the President of South Korea has labeled the "quiet revolution" in tax administration in less developed countries was a condition imposed by President

Kennedy at the signing of the Alliance for Progress charter at Punta del Este in 1961. The President cautioned that U.S. assistance under the charter, which included a pledge of all-out tax administration reform by the Latin American countries, would depend upon a demonstrated willingness to effect needed political, economic, and social reforms. In terms of tax administration, Secretary of the Treasury C. Douglas Dillon was explicit: Latin nations who requested it could have assistance from Internal Revenue Service technicians.

The ink was hardly dry on the 1961 Punta del Este charter when Chile knocked on the IRS door. The IRS response was immediate. Early in 1962, the first team of IRS technicians, on loan to the Department of State's Agency for International Development, arrived in Santiago ready to provide technical assistance in tax administration.

This early response from Chile triggered the formation of an assistance program. By the fall of 1962, the Foreign Tax Assistance Staff, headed by a director, was established in Washington in the office of the Commissioner of Internal Revenue, and program policies and procedures were promulgated. In brief, these contemplated: (1) the use of the best trained technicians available (mostly from within the IRS) for overseas assignments; (2) creation of a trained ready reserve for future assignment (most of the first class of trainees were assigned before completion of the course); (3) a management control system; and (4) a long-range training program to be conducted in the United States for key managers of foreign tax agencies (the INTAX program, described below, launched in 1966).

The average overseas tax team consists of 4 members, but they have ranged from 2 to 15; at present writing, some 69 individuals are overseas on 2-year terms (some are repeats) in 17 Latin American and 5 other countries (India, the Philippines, South Korea, South Vietnam, and Turkey). In addition, some two or three dozen individuals are sent overseas annually on short-term assignments to advise on particular problems of a more narrow range, such as audit and collection problems. Although most team members have been recruited from within the IRS, it has been necessary on occasion to resort to state tax agencies and private individuals because of lack of experienced IRS personnel, such as experts in property tax administration.

The work of the tax assistance teams is a "shirt-sleeves" effort (preassignment training includes language training where necessary) and, while the teams avoid involvement in individual cases, may cover the full range of tax administration: return-processing, auditing, collection, enforcement, training, taxpayer education, and planning.

Planning deserves special attention here, if for no other reason than, for many of the countries, it constitutes their first experience in working systematically in this area. Thus, after the original survey has identified the country's problem areas and weaknesses, the tax officials of the host country, in consultation with the tax assistance team, develop tax administration reform objectives and an annual work plan designed to meet the long-run objectives. Reform, however, is limited to reform in tax administration. Substantive changes in law and policy are within the province of the teams only in so far as they relate to administrative feasibility.

Every effort is made to provide balance in making improvements in tax administration; for example, an increased return-examination program would not be recommended without a corresponding capacity for collection. Special attention is paid to the critical functions of auditing and collecting by both the long-term teams and the short-term mobile teams. The latter normally consist of small teams of IRS audit and collection technicians, supplied from the long-term teams, who provide a concentrated 6-week course (in the language of the host country) on critical aspects of tax administration. Included in these classes are host country tax officials capable of carrying on training after the U.S. team leaves. For example, after one of these courses was given in Peru, Peruvian instructors who had attended the course trained a hundred additional revenue agents during the course of a year.

On an over-all basis, training is given as much, if not more, emphasis than any single facet of tax administration. Once an organized work program has been effected, the emphasis shifts to the establishment of effective training programs in the host country. (Chile, for example, the first recipient of aid in this area, now provides limited training for tax officials of other Latin American countries.) These programs are integrated in some measure with the U.S.-based phase of tax assistance, which is known as the International Tax Administration Training Series Program (INTAX).

INTAX is a series of regularly scheduled, 6-week courses on basic tax administration subjects (collection, auditing, training, personnel management) given to from fifteen to twenty foreign tax management officials or management trainees from eight to ten countries working in the same area (for example, auditing). The courses and seminars are given in the United States in the language of the participants and include observation visits to IRS and state offices. Of approximately 300 foreign tax officials visiting IRS headquarters each year, some 120 are INTAX students.

The Inter-American Center of Tax Administration is also expected to play an important role in the future in the area of foreign tax assistance. This organization of the heads of the tax departments of twenty-two American nations was formed at a 1967 Panama meeting and eventually will be permanently located there. It is intended to provide a forum and a means for exchange of information on tax administration, to conduct research in specialized areas, and, eventually, to coordinate the major Inter-American technical assistance effort.

The foreign tax assistance effort of the IRS costs the American taxpayer some $3 million annually. Is is worth it?

In terms of concrete results—discounting for inflation and increased economic activity—the answer is yes. Individual countries report substantial advances in enforcement. Audit assessments in Panama were up from 299,000 balboas in 1963 to 3.2 million in 1967; returns audited in the Dominican Republic increased from 667 in 1964 to 2,221 in 1966. The number and value of real property assessments in Guatemala in 1965 were double those in 1964. Returns received in Ecuador were up from 7,000 in 1963 to 87,000 in 1966. There is, in short, every indication that less developed countries receiving assistance under the IRS program have made substantial progress on the road toward a capability to go it alone—the ultimate objective of the effort.

VII

Alcohol, Tobacco, and Firearms

The case from the Atlanta Veterans Hospital was reported in the usual style of the medical investigator:

CF, a 47 year old white male . . . was admitted . . . because of swelling of the abdomen for a period of one week. He had a history of heavy alcoholic intake for many years, which had increased during the 3 or 4 months prior to admission. The swelling of the abdomen was accompanied by nausea and vomiting. Epigastric pain was likewise present. Previous history disclosed that he had an acute gastritis approximately 9 years prior to admission.

The physical examination revealed a poorly nourished, chronically ill white male. A definite lead line was present. . . . The impression was alcoholic gastritis with a possibility of portal cirrhosis and possible recurrence of pulmonary tuberculosis.

Upon admission . . . X-ray examination of the upper gastrointestinal tract revealed spasm of the lower esophagus, otherwise nothing remarkable. In spite of the history of the ingestion of illicit alcohol, the presense of a lead line, anemia, and basophilic stippling . . . the patient was not treated for lead intoxication. His course in the hospital was one of steady deterioration. . . . Upon his seventh hospital day, he was in extremis with severe bronchospasm and respiratory distress. Preparations were made to give him a course of calcium disodium versenate but he suddenly expired. The fact that the patient did not receive treatment for lead poisoning is unexplained, except that the resident physicians who cared for the patient were not aware of the serious danger of lead intoxication. . . .

The autopsy revealed black discoloration of the gingiva. . . . Toxicologic examination for lead revealed the following quantities of lead per 100 gram units of wet tissue: brain, 0.83 mg.; liver, 1.6 mg.; kidney, 0.78 mg.

The patient, one of five in the study, had been drinking moonshine whisky containing lead salts for a sufficient period of time to build up a lethal dose (less than the size of a pinhead). The lead salts, on the basis of parallel laboratory studies, had undoubtedly been contained in moonshine whisky distilled through automobile radiators or through equipment containing lead-soldered joints; the diagnosis of lead encephalopathy (poisoning) was not effected until after death.

The case of CF is hardly an isolated instance of the human tragedy and misery following in the wake of the manufacture and distribution of illicit moonshine whisky. Other studies in recent years reveal that this illegal industry has been responsible for one of the nation's most serious health problems, particularly in the Southeast, where the bulk of the poisonous spirits are manufactured. Thus, although the official Internal Revenue Service mission in this area is that of enforcing the revenue laws pertaining to the manufacture of alcoholic spirits, the IRS also plays a critical role in guarding the public health.

The enforcement of the federal revenue laws with respect to the illicit manufacture of alcohol is only one of the many functions of the IRS's unique Alcohol, Tobacco, and Firearms Division (AT&F), prior to 1969 the Alcohol and Tobacco Tax Division. While the work of the federal "revenooer"—AT&F's enforcement unit—has been frequently dramatized in the popular media (undercover work, the raiding and destruction of stills, hand-to-hand combat, and gunplay do make good copy), other segments of the AT&F have equally important roles in the division's over-all mission, which is not only the enforcement of the revenue laws pertaining to illegal spirits but also the enforcement of the details of, and the collection of, taxes on the manufacture of legal spirits and the regulation of the legal alcoholic beverage industry's trade practices, in addition to which AT&F enforces the occupational and excise taxes imposed on beer, wine, and tobacco products. It also enforces the occupational taxes imposed on importers, manufacturers, and dealers in firearms and functions as the federal regulatory agency of laws relating to firearms.

The Alcohol, Tobacco, and Firearms Division is thus, unlike its sister divisions under the assistant commissioner (Compliance), more than a tax collector engaged in providing the Treasury with some $6 billion in excise tax revenue on alcohol beverages and tobacco products annually. The roots of both its tax enforcement work and its regulatory work lie deep in the history and culture of the nation. An understanding of this historical and cultural background is essential to an understanding of the work of AT&F.

Although the origins of both the distilling and fermentation processes as productive of alcoholic beverages predates recorded history, there is evidence that both originated in the Middle East and that knowledge of the fermentation process goes back as far as 4200 B.C. Distilling, on the other hand, probably dates from the first or second century, and most likely originated with the Egyptians. Europe records a knowledge of the production of fermented beverages (beer and wine) by 800 A.D. and of distilled spirits by the twelfth century, when the first recorded descriptions by chemists and doctors indicate that the early European product *aqua vitae* (water of life) was regarded as a rare medicine. By the sixteenth century, however, the distilling of whisky for beverage purposes was an established industry. With the Industrial Revolution came a variety of technical advances in the production of a number of distillates (whisky, gin, rum), and by the middle of the nineteenth century, with the invention of the continuous-process Coffey still in Dublin in 1830, the basic technological fundamentals had been achieved.

Although the Indian tribes in America had fermented beverages of various types, the still was unknown in the New World until the arrival of the Europeans. A distilled product of grain was produced in the colony of New Netherland as early as 1640. Although gin and brandy were also produced, the most popular distilled beverage in colonial America was rum, which had been produced in the West Indies as early as 1650. Rum required the importation of molasses from the West Indies, and, with the advent of the Revolution and the decline of the "three-cornered" trade (Africa to the West Indies, with slaves; the West Indies to colonial America, with molasses; America to Europe, with tobacco), the new republic turned to whisky made of rye and corn. By the time of the Whisky Rebellion in 1794, "Monongahela rye" was an established product of western Pennsylvania. Rye was the money crop of the region. In a similar manner and at the same time, the early Scotch-Irish and German settlers of Kentucky were collectively and individually developing a distinctive American distillate: Kentucky bourbon. This whisky was made predominately of corn, a New World product (the proportion was later set at 51 per cent or more). The distillation of bourbon whisky has been credited first to a Baptist minister, the Reverend Elijah Craig, in 1789 at Georgetown, Kentucky (then in Bourbon County). The bourbon taste captivated not only the early western settlers but has grown to appeal to the majority of U.S. consumers. Kentucky remains to this date the center of the legal whisky industry in the United States, and corn remains the principal ingredient used in distilling.

Alcoholic beverages, especially spirits, have played more than a minor role in the development of American culture. Our political, economic, and social institutions have been subjected to a plethora of tugs and pulls over problems pertaining to the control and taxation of alcoholic beverages—problems that persist to this day. Although they are beyond the scope of this study, their presence is felt in the functioning of the IRS Alcohol, Tobacco, and Firearms Division.

While the use of distilled beverages is a part of our European heritage, the consumption of tobacco products is a result of the discovery of New World. By the time of the discoveries of Columbus in the late fifteenth century, the Indians of both North and South America had a developed tobacco culture, which followed the same production fundamentals adhered to today, including the spacing of plants, the pruning of side shoots, and curing. The introduction of the plant and the product into Europe in the sixteenth century made tobacco the primary export of a number of the early colonies and resulted in the rapid spread of the industry to all countries. Today tobacco is cultivated in twenty-two states in the United States. Historically, the industry has been a prime candidate for heavy taxation by both state and federal governments.

At the federal level, the Alcohol, Tobacco, and Firearms Division is charged with the issuing of permits for the manufacture of cigars and cigarettes and for the collection of excise taxes on cigars and cigarettes (you can make your own for your own use without tax), paid in accordance with a scale of rates based on size. Most cigarettes, regular and king-sized, are classed as small and are subject to tax at a rate of $4.00 per thousand. The tax is paid with a semimonthly return by the manufacturer after withdrawal from the factory. An importer pays to the customs collector on a customs return form. The manufacturer's excise taxes on cigars and cigarettes produce in excess of $2 billion in revenue annually for the federal government. Enforcement problems have been minimal. Arrests for tobacco tax violations are rare, and only occasionally has property been seized.

Firearms, like alcohol, have and continue to have an important role in an American society not too many decades removed from a period when the rifle was the principal means by which the wilderness was subdued. Although the twentieth century has seen the transformation of the nation from a rural community to one predominately urban, many older notions of the degree of freedom desirable in this area still obtain. However, in recent years there has been an increase in public awareness of the many problems of urban America—problems stemming from the assassination of public figures, from civil disorder and riots, and from the inferior political, social, and economic status of significant segments of the population. As a result, Congress provided additional firearms control legislation in 1968, which strengthened statutory measures enacted in the 1930's, and, as described later in this chapter, increased the regulatory work load of the Alcohol, Tobacco, and Firearms Division.

Tax Evasion

After the successful completion of the Indian Wars in the Southeast in 1869, the U.S. Seventh Cavalry Regiment was withdrawn from the Plains country for a much needed rest. Two years later, its commander, Lieutenant Colonel George A. Custer, found himself assigned to a two-company post at sleepy Elizabethtown, Kentucky, forty miles south of Louisville. Here, in the center of the blue-blood country, the Civil War hero entertained, hunted, and worked on his memoirs for a two-year period, while chafing for renewed action against the Indians. Action was to come in 1876 and to end disastrously at Little Big Horn. Meanwhile, detachments of Custer's own Seventh Cavalry were hunting moonshiners in Kentucky and elsewhere in the Southeast. While the record of these skirmishes is not clear, the warfare conducted here was even less decisive than that of which Little Big Horn was a part. Chief Sitting Bull and his Indians were eventually subdued; the moonshiners never have been.

If the history of the enforcement of the various taxes that government has seen fit to impose on alcoholic beverages has uncovered a singular feature it is this: tax evasion in this area is deeply rooted. Undoubtedly, a number of forces have contributed to this facet of the nation's culture. For one thing, the production and sale of non-tax-paid spirits in the United States has been long associated with a spirit of resistance to central government. Thus, the early Scotch-Irish settlers who populated the mountainous regions of the colonies brought with them a pattern of avoidance of an English excise tax imposed on distilled spirits dating from 1643, an avoidance effected through the production of illicit spirits on their farms. This pattern of avoidance was kept alive through the enactment by Parliament of the unpopular Molasses and Sugar acts in the years preceding the American Revolution. As already described in Chapter I, the unkindest cut of all to these independent people was the new republic's excise tax of 1791, which precipitated the Whisky Rebellion. While modern-day resistance to the taxation of alcoholic spirits through the production of illicit moonshine may be motivated more by greed than by notions of political freedom, there is still a remnant of the early spirit in the moonshine producer of the Southeastern United States.

A second factor that, historically, has contributed to tax evasion and has not been without its episodes of violence, is the propensity of the modern legislator to single out the alcoholic beverage industry for unusually burdensome levies. The 1791 Act lasted only until 1802, and, while it was revived during the War of 1812, from 1817 to the 1862 Civil War Act, the liquor industry was not burdened with federal taxes. As a result, it grew and prospered. By 1862 whisky retailed at prices ranging from 15 to 25 cents a gallon. However, the Act of 1863 imposed a tax of 20 cents a gallon; by 1865 the tax was $2.00 a gallon, and the stage was set for widespread evasion. This took two basic forms.

First, the production of illicit non-tax-paid whisky forced most legitimate distillers to suspend operations because of their inability to compete with the illicit producer. Some were forced into bankruptcy. The discovery of petroleum at this time and its use as a substitute for alcohol as a burning fluid also contributed to the legitimate distillers economic plight.

Second, a scheme of avoidance was developed that involved collusion between government agents, distillers, and politicians (so-called whisky rings). This collusion involved the payment of bribes, the removal of whisky from government warehouses without payment of tax, undermarking of the proof of whisky, and the reuse of tax stamps. Complicating matters was substantial public support for the illicit distiller, a support that more than once ended in civil disorder and the use of federal troops in a number of Eastern cities to suppress mobs interfering with the efforts of civil authorities to seize illicit distilleries. Although a reduction in the tax to 50 cents a gallon in 1868 (increased to $2.20 in 1917) provided a temporary solution, it was not until 1875 that the whisky rings were broken up as a result of congressional investigations.

A third factor bearing both directly and indirectly on tax evasion in this area has been the temperance movement. This worldwide social and political force had its origins in the early nineteenth century. It was then manifested by a variety of temperance societies as well as by local option laws enacted by some of the New England states. The movement reached its political high-water mark with the enactment in 1919 of the Prohibition (Eighteenth) Amendment to the Constitution. For fourteen years, until its repeal in 1933 by the Twenty-First Amendment, the Eighteenth Amendment declared that "the manufacture, sale or transportation of intoxicating liquors within, the importation thereof into, or the exportation thereof from the United States and all territory subject to the jurisdiction thereof for beverage purposes is hereby prohibited."

Characterized as America's most noble social experiment, the Prohibition Amendment had the immediate effect of ushering in the most broad-based tax evasion in the history of the nation; what had been the legal alcoholic beverage industry became the nation's largest illegal activity—the illicit production and sale of alcoholic beverages. This new industry was organized and controlled by such syndicate mobsters as Al Capone, Waxie Gordon, Dutch Schultz, and Eddie Fleischer. Living in an underworld of their own, they produced an estimated 800 million gallons in 1930 (some four times normal legal production). They allocated territory among themselves (sometimes by city blocks), enforced their rule by taking uncooperative gangsters on "rides," imported skilled builders of stills from Europe, used part of their immense profits to bribe officials, joined with licensed manufacturers of industrial alcohol in redistilling to produce a beverage product, counterfeited revenue stamps, and smuggled liquor into the United States through offshore "rum-running" operations in high-speed boats, which picked up their cargoes outside the 12-mile limit. They also discovered the small independent moonshine distiller, who was willing to provide them a source of supply. The nation has never fully recovered from this facet of life in the "roaring twenties."

Another aspect of the temperance movement, which persists to this day, is the support it lends to high excise taxes on alcoholic beverages, a support that is motivated not so much by the revenue the taxes produce or the control effected as by a desire to punish consumers for what members of the movement regard as an evil. Since 1951 the consumer has supported (in addition to the usual income tax) a federal tax of $10.50 a gallon on distilled spirits as well as state levies, a tax burden that, in the opinion of many, has led to continued widespread production of illicit spirits. These matters, of course, are critical in the consideration of the administration of this tax. Like the Prohibition Amendment itself, they are value judgments which have been made, and which are continuing to be made, by the American people.

ORGANIZATION

From the window in the loft of a warehouse in a New Orleans industrial district, Investigator Ted Johnson had a clear view of the platform directly across the street. Although it was past midnight there was sufficient light from the dock to read the plates on the truck. He did not need his sniper-scope; his binoculars were sufficient. What was going on was subject to a fair guess. A load of sugar was being readied for shipment to some distribution point in the moonshine belt. At regular intervals dock-wallopers emerged from the ware-house, trucking two-wheeled dollies loaded with bags. At the tailgate of the unmarked six-wheel truck, a checker with a clipboard was apparently counting the bags. Inside the van, two other men were loading.

Ted's mission was simply to keep the loading under sur-veillance and report by radio to two other agents stationed in a car, who would follow the truck in relays with other agents in the hope that it would provide a lead to the distri-bution setup of the sugar, the lifeline of the illicit moonshine industry.

Ted is only one of some 1,000 investigators in the enforce-ment unit of the Alcohol, Tobacco, and Firearms Division. He belongs to one of the three categories (the other two: special agents, and inspectors) of badge-wearing, gun-toting IRS agents with the power to make arrests and seize con-traband property. His work is apt to involve a wide range of activities, some of which involve more than a little risk. These include surveillance, raiding of stills, undercover work, preparation of material for court action, and participation in the Justice Department's drive against organized crime. In-vestigator Johnson is "average." He is 38 years old and mar-ried, and he entered the Internal Revenue Service after having passed the Treasury enforcement agent examination. Like other IRS employees, he has available a career development program, which, in his case, will include attendance at the Treasury Law Enforcement Officer's School, on-the-job training, and additional classroom study at the AT&F Investigator's School for both basic and advanced work in subjects related to his job.

AT&F, which had its origins in 1863 in common with other IRS enforcement units, has indeed come a long way since the days when Congress created the Office of Collector of Internal Revenue and authorized him to hire "not exceeding three revenue agents" to aid in ferreting out tax evaders. However, it was not until the advent of Prohibition in 1920 that the Bureau of Internal Revenue formed a distinctive unit for dealing with matters pertaining to alcoholic spirits. Prior to Prohibition, the Bureau's revenue agents and collectors had been charged with such enforcement matters as the investigation of illicit distilling and the making of arrests and seizing of property. In 1920, with an appropriation of $2 million dollars under the Volstead Act—the legislative measure supporting the Eighteenth Amendment and delegating enforcement to the Commissioner—the Bureau's newly formed Prohibition Unit swung into action against the developing illegal liquor industry controlled by mobsters and racketeers. A decade later, in 1930, Prohibition enforcement was transferred to the Justice Department, where it remained until the repeal of Prohibition late in 1933.

The year 1934 thus marks the origins of the modern Alcohol, Tobacco, and Firearms Division. With the reestablishment of the legal liquor industry, the IRS was charged with the enforcement of the excise taxes imposed on alcohol; this enforcement was delegated to a newly formed Alcohol Tax Unit, which, as a result of the 1952 reorganization, became the Alcohol and Tobacco Tax Division and was renamed the Alcohol, Tobacco, and Firearms Division in 1969.

As stated above, AT&F today is charged with the administration of excise taxes imposed on spirits, other products with an alcoholic content, cigars, and cigarettes, with regulation of the legal alcohol industry, and with enforcement of certain firearms legislation. The division is organized at two levels. The national office in Washington, headed by a director responsible to the assistant commissioner (Compliance), contains five branches: national office Laboratory Branch, Basic Permit and Trade Practices Branch, Enforcement Branch, Permissive Branch, and Tobacco Tax Branch. The field organization is structured in a manner similar to the Appellate Division. An assistant regional commissioner (Alcohol, Tobacco, and Firearms) at each regional headquarters heads a three-branch unit: Laboratory, Permissive, and Enforcement. Permissive (legal-industry) activities and enforcement (illegal-industry) activities are carried out through branch and area offices located in each region. The thirty-six branch offices in some instances house both a chief inspector, who is responsible for permissive activities, and a chief special investigator, who directs the work of the special investigators in carrying out enforcement work. Area offices for both these basic units are headed by area supervisors, who are responsible to a chief inspector, or chief special investigator, as the case may be.

The AT&F Laboratory Branch provides essentially a support function for both the permissive and enforcement missions. The national office laboratory provides management support in the fields of chemistry and physics, conducts research to improve and develop analytical techniques, and coordinates both national office and regional laboratory programs. Both national and regional offices engage in extensive sample analysis work (some 40,000 samples a year) for both the AT&F and Treasury's Bureau of Narcotics. In addition, personnel from the regional laboratories testify as expert witnesses in court actions and provide advice and guidance to branch offices on laboratory matters.

As described in Chapter 4, an associate chief counsel (Litigation) heads a five-division litigation unit in the chief counsel's office. One of these divisions, the Alcohol, Tobacco, and Firearms Legal Division, which has a counterpart in the field in each regional counsel's office, is responsible for the performance of all the legal services in connection with the administration and enforcement of the laws governing AT&F's permissive and enforcement functions. As a result, this division of the chief counsel's office is unique with respect to legal services rendered in that they include the whole range of services otherwise divided among the various divisions in the chief counsel's office. These activities include the drafting and review of regulations and legislation, the preparation and review of rulings, the representation of the assistant regional commissioner and the Commissioner in administration permit hearings, the processing of refund claims, and advising with respect to assessments and litigation.

The AT&F Legal Division, it should be noted, does not conduct litigation in the federal courts. As in the case of other taxes outside the jurisdiction of the Tax Court of the United States, litigation involving violations of all types and action on claims in the federal courts is conducted by attorneys from the Department of Justice.

INDUSTRY REGULATION

Placed at strategic spots in many of the nation's regulated distilleries are signs such as this:

IS A DRINK WORTH YOUR JOB?

Such signs reflect more than an employer's parental interest in his employees' sobriety and more than an interest in the prevention of pilferage; most relevant is the interest the employer has in being free from being forced to explain shortages to the AT&F on-the-premises inspectors engaged in carrying out the permissive mission of the division (there are some four hundred such AT&F agents).

Probably no private industry in the United States is as closely regulated as the legal alcohol beverage industry. Let A. Theriault, Seagram's government relations superintendent, tell the story in his own words:

Our Plant at Baltimore is one of the largest distilled spirits plants in the country. Currently, there are seven government officers assigned to it. Like other distillers, we operate pursuant to a basic permit issued by the Basic Permit and Trade Practices section of the Alcohol and Tobacco Tax Division. A detailed registration must be filed for each permit and upon approval thereof, the government assigns each Plant a registry number. . . . We must post a continuing bond with the Government, the penal sum of such is determined by the type of operations conducted.

All distilled spirits on which tax has not been paid must be stored in bonded warehouses. Such warehouses are under the joint control of the Government and the warehouse proprietor. However, the entrance door to each warehouse is under government lock, and access can be had to these warehouses only at such time that a Government Officer is present. As a daily routine, such Officer unlocks these doors in the morning and locks them up at the close of the day's activities. Practically all movements of distilled spirits in bond from one distilled spirits plant to another are made via sealed conveyance; that is, the Government Officer at the consignor plant affixes seals to the truck or freight car, and upon arrival of the shipment, the Government Officer at the consignee plant checks to see that such seals are intact. In the event a seal is found to have been broken, a detailed report along with affidavits must be submitted in explanation of the circumstances.

Government regulations call for the maintenance of a closed distilling system. This means that from the time that distilled spirits come into being in a still until such time as they are deposited in a receiving tank under government lock, no access can be had to such spirits except through a sampling device which records the number and quantity of such samples taken. This requirement for a closed distilling system calls for the affixation of government seals to all flanges and other detachable connections in pipe-lines. . . .

As a general rule, before any handling or processing of distilling materials or distilled spirits may be undertaken on our part, some form of prior approval must be secured from the Government. For instance, our distilling procedures, any changes in equipment, applications to transfer distilled spirits in bond, blending formulas, labels for bottles must be approved by the Government before any action is initiated with respect thereto.

The Government's requirements respecting records of all transactions and reports to be filed are quite extensive. For instance, daily reports of the kind and amounts of grain received at our distillery for mashing as well as the amount of fermenting material set in each fermenter must be submitted to the Government Office in Charge. Similar daily reports must be submitted respecting distilled spirits entered into, manipulated or removed from the warehouse as well as distilled spirits rectified, bottled, or packaged in the rectifying and bottling premises. Comprehensive monthly and annual reports reflecting all operations are transmitted by us to the Alcohol and Tobacco Tax Division at the Regional level.

The annual production of alcohol products varies with the inventory needs of the industry. The greater amount of total production, however, is designed for industrial use after denaturing (adding of substances to render it unfit for consumption). For example, in 1966, some 215 million gallons of all types of beverage spirits (whisky, brandy, gin, vodka, and alcohol) were withdrawn from bonded warehouses (at which time tax is paid) for marketing, while 576 million gallons of alcohol were withdrawn tax-free for denaturing and industrial use.

The tax-free withdrawal privilege of alcohol intended for industrial use reflects in some measure the punitive aspect of the high excise tax rate imposed on beverage spirits. The problem was first encountered in 1865 when the rate on all spirits was increased to $2 a gallon. A temporary solution was found in 1868 with the reduction of the rate to 50 cents a gallon, and in 1906 the present legislative policy was established, which permits the tax-free withdrawal, after denaturing, in order to eliminate this burden on the thousands of products in commerce that use alcohol in production. Industrial alcohol is produced largely from petroleum products rather than grain.

During the 1870's, Congress established the present policy of allowing the tax-free withdrawal of undenatured spirits for government and scientific purposes, which includes use by hospitals, blood banks, clinics operated for charity, and colleges, universities, and laboratories engaged in research. Undenatured alcohol used in medicines and food products is normally taxed at the rate of $1 per gallon.

The close regulation of the beverage spirit industry is not limited to the production processes; it extends all along the marketing trail down to and including the retail dealer. A convenient starting point for this portion of the story is the period after the Civil War when the various producers began to develop trade brands through the use of distinctive Kentucky family names. Trade practices, however, were largely unregulated at this time, and the nationwide marketing of quality products under brand names was not possible until the first decade of the twentieth century, when Congress provided the needed legislative controls. The 1906 Pure Food and Drug Act and additional legislation in 1909 legally defined the various types of whisky (rye, bourbon, etc.) and required that labels disclose both the production processes and the product source of the beverage. Prohibition and the limiting of beverage production during World War II slowed the development of brand-name marketing, but after the war depleted inventories were replaced, and brand-name products now dominate in the marketing of beverage spirits.

The actual regulation of marketing commences with the storage process. Normally, whisky intended for consumption is stored in barrels in a bonded warehouse owned by the proprietor but in control of an AT&F agent who holds the keys.

Whisky may be stored for aging up to twenty years without payment of tax. Tax is paid only upon withdrawal. While most beverage spirits are withdrawn for bottling elsewhere, they may also be bottled while in storage (bottled in bond), in which case tax is deferred until actual withdrawal.

All of the preceding regulatory measures are designed primarily to protect the federal revenue. Since 1940, the AT&F Division has also been charged with the enforcement of the Federal Alcohol Administration Act. This is the primary mission of the Basic Permit and Trade Practices Branch. The legislation is designed to regulate competition and protect the consumer. It greatly extends the earlier statutes pertaining to identification and labeling. It includes a licensing system that requires beverage distillers, importers, and wholesalers to secure permits. These permits (some 20,000 annually of all types) are issued only if the applicant meets certain statutory criteria and complies with all applicable federal laws and regulations. These include the prohibition of certain trade practices binding producers and wholesalers to retailers (exclusive outlets, commercial bribery, consignment selling) and restrictions on selling in bulk and on labeling and advertising. Regulations under the Act establish standards of identity for all beverage products (vodka, straight bourbon, Scotch, Canadian whisky, cognac, brandy, etc.), and prescribed bottle sizes. Label control is maintained by requiring a certificate of label approval, and advertising is subject to surveillance in order to determine whether the statutory provisions have been met.

THE MOONSHINE INDUSTRY

It was a planned guerilla operation with air reconnaissance. It had been preceded by a massive propaganda campaign. The time was late October, 1965. In the crisp predawn darkness, the men moved into five staging areas. They were armed with rifles, handguns, explosives, and walkie-talkies. They knew their targets, the terrain, the cover, and the line of march. Some of them had been over the ground in the preceding weeks in "walk-throughs." Their line of communications was well protected. But even though the planning seemed complete, there was more than a little apprehension.

As dawn broke the men moved out of the staging areas. Thirty-eight minutes later, a charge of explosive went off. They had made their first hit. At the end of the day they had scored 56 hits; at the end of the third, 135; by the tenth day the total reached 340, and six weeks later, 600. At their rear an equally carefully planned operation had also been executed with success: some 165 of the enemy had been rounded up.

A planned DMZ raid by the Green Berets? An assault on a Viet Cong stronghold in the Iron Triangle? Nope. And the action in the rear—was that a roundup of infiltrators in Saigon? Nope. It was the second stage of Operations Dry Up. The targets were backwoods moonshine stills in northern Georgia. The enemies were the operators of the stills, and the "troops" were a picked team of AT&F agents, state revenue agents, and local police. The air cover consisted of small spotter planes and helicopters, whose pilots could detect the thin, telltale wisps of smoke from a still. (Electronic sniffers, capable of detecting mash odor, were also available.) The propaganda campaign that preceded the operation consisted of a series of articles in the *Atlanta Journal,* focused on the $70 million annual loss of federal and state tax revenue from Georgia stills. The rear-guard action was a roundup of "nip joint" operators and peddlers of "white lightning" in Atlanta.

The first phase of the special tactical, large-scale, combined-forces raiding operations known as Operations Dry Up had been staged in South Carolina in 1963; the third phase was launched in Alabama in 1968. Have the three operations been successful? Undoubtedly. Still seizures dropped 1,500 in Georgia in 1967. Does this mean that the illicit moonshine operator has been driven out of business? Hardly. Ever since

President George Washington's march on western Pennsylvania to put down the Whisky Rebellion in 1794, the federal tax collector has carried on intermittent guerrilla warfare with the moonshine operator—warfare that has resulted in making the AT&F the most hazardous of all federal police agencies, not excluding the FBI, the Secret Service, and the Narcotics Bureau. Currently, the moonshine industry is suffering an annual loss of some 17,000 stills of varying sizes (down from a high of 25,000 in 1956), of which AT&F's share is some 6,500. The decline in these figures in recent years is due to a shortage of personnel as well as to a change in tactics aimed at increasing the number of arrests, which run about 5,000 annually. Although the over-all problem no longer approaches that of the Prohibition era in size, and although, in some instances, the lone-wolf independent operator may have his back against the wall, informed estimates indicate that some 43 million gallons of illicit moonshine —much of it containing poisonous lead salts—is consumed annually by the American public—or one of every eight bottles of beverage spirits consumed.

The paradox of enforcement faced by the AT&F, as well as by state and local agencies, is that, as new techniques are developed to ferret out stills and violators and as the risks to the operator increase, the market price of moonshine increases (although only rarely to the point where it is cheaper to turn to legal liquor), and so do the temptations of high profits. A $4.00 quart of moonshine will yield a $3.75 profit; a $6.00 quart of legal liquor is burdened with $3.50 in taxes. The moonshine industry can no longer be characterized solely by the lone-wolf backwoods hillbilly marketing his product locally in jugs and Mason jars. Today it is a syndicate-controlled industry. Although some 90 per cent of its product is produced in the eleven Southeastern states, two-thirds of its consumers are found in the urban centers in the Midwest and along the Eastern seaboard. It is thus an organized industry, which, in many of its forms, parallels the legal industry in respect to managers and workers, production and distribution specialists, and ready financing. A destroyed still is simply one of the costs of doing business.

There are, of course, significant differences between the legal industry and the illegal moonshine business, and these differences give rise to the many problems created by the functioning of a large-scale industry almost entirely outside the ground rules established by society. These problems go beyond the annual loss of some $600 million in taxes to the federal and state governments—a loss that must be made good by the rest of society. Compare, for example, the detailed supervision required for the production of legal beverage spirits to the lack of supervision that exists in the production of moonshine whisky. Then consider the conditions under which moonshine whisky is produced. The contents of the mash may consist of two parts sugar and one part corn meal, with yeast added to speed the fermentation process. But this is only part of the mash story. Vats have been found hidden in garbage dumps. Commercial fertilizer, lye, and manure have been added to speed fermentation, and animal and snake carcasses, bees, and flies are not uncommon ingredients.

After fermentation, four days more or less depending on the weather (good corn whisky takes at least ten days), the mash is ready for the cooker—sometimes simply a stir kettle —and heating. From here, the vapor is led to the condenser, whose coils, immersed in water, liquefy the vapor and produce the clear liquor variously denominated as moon, corn, white lightning, rotgut, or perhaps, more properly, simply as sugar whisky. But consider the condenser: probably an old automobile radiator or a jerry-rigged affair with soldered tubes. In either event, the final product undoubtedly contains a quantity of poisonous lead salts.

After distilling, the cutting begins, either at the still (perhaps with water from a pool or swamp) or during the distribution process (sometimes in convoyed trucks). Aging is that period of time it takes to get the moonshine to the consumer. The consumer may wind up with a 60 proof product (30 per cent alcohol) that produces a hot burning sensation— a kick like an army mule—not from the proof (most legal whisky ranges from 80 to 90 proof) but from the impurities.

The attack on the moonshine industry has centered on its production centers in the Southeastern states, where perhaps 85 per cent of the moonshine is distilled. But no one knows exactly how many stills operate at any given time, how much they produce, or how much reaches the market. Pockets of illicit production have been found in a number of Northern cities, including Detroit, Philadelphia, Brooklyn, Newark, and Boston.

FIREARMS CONTROL

John Herbert Dillinger was gunned down by three FBI agents in the alley outside Chicago's Biograph Theater on July 22, 1934. This marked the start of a fresh effort by the federal government to control some of the most blatant criminal activity ever witnessed in the nation. During the preceding ten months, Dillinger and his gang had left a trail of ten murders, seven men wounded, four bank robberies, and three jailbreaks (which involved the plunder of police arsenals). Dillinger himself was only a symbol of the then existing lawlessness, which was represented by such incidents as the Kansas City Massacre, the cold-blooded killing of four police officers and their prisoner in a rescue effort, a highway killing of two FBI agents, and innumerable kidnapings, including the abduction and death of the Lindbergh baby.

Out of all this developed an insistent public demand for federal efforts to curb the widespread criminal violence. At the same time that the Dillinger gang was cutting its wide swath through the Midwest, Congress was considering a series of bills designed to strengthen the federal government's fight against crime. One of these measures became the National Firearms Act of 1934, designed to prevent criminals from obtaining gangster-type weapons such as submachine guns, short-barrel shotguns and rifles, and silencing devices. The main thrust of this legislation, which is based upon the federal taxing power and administered by the AT&F, consists of the imposition of annual occupational taxes ranging from $10 on dealers in special-type guns to $500 (now $1,000) on importers and manufacturers of the gangster-type weapons indicated above. In addition, these weapons must be registered and can only be transferred in accordance with the terms of the statute. Prior to the enactment of modifying legislation in 1968, there were some 100,000 firearms registered under the National Firearms Act, mostly to law enforcement agencies; this was less than one-tenth of one per cent of the estimated 100–200 million firearms of all types presently owned in the country. The National Firearms Act also contains provisions designed to curb the use of firearms by criminal elements. For instance, it makes it a crime for anyone to transport these weapons in interstate commerce while under an indictment, a measure which has been but infrequently utilized.

In 1939, under its then growing power to regulate interstate commerce, Congress took a second step toward strengthening all the nation's enforcement agencies—federal, state, and local—with the enactment of the Federal Firearms Act. Although not a revenue measure, the administration of this law was assigned to the Bureau of Internal Revenue's Alcohol and Tobacco Tax Division, since the division was then engaged in enforcing the 1934 tax legislation. The Federal Firearms Act, unlike the National Firearms Act, embraced all firearms and was essentially a dealer licensing measure. It required that licensed dealers maintain purchase and sale records of all firearms. In general, it prohibited the transportation or receipt of firearms in interstate commerce by felons, by persons under indictment, and by unlicensed dealers and purchasers required to have a license to purchase under state law.

Both the foregoing acts, however, left some significant deficiencies in the control of the firearms traffic. One particularly glaring defect was the ease with which firearms could be secured by mail and over-the-counter purchase by nonresidents. A second was the difficulty found to exist with respect to the control of imported firearms. Although all states have legislation controlling firearms in some measure, these vary considerably in strictness, and, even in the case of the eight or so states with strict permit and registration laws, these laws could be easily circumvented by mail-order purchases.

Notwithstanding the apparent need for additional federal controls, it was not until the mid-1960's that Congress became sufficiently aroused to provide the needed legislation, a matter that provoked the opposition of a number of interest groups (40 million gun owners are a lot of votes). However, the assassinations of President John F. Kennedy, his brother, Senator Robert Kennedy, and civil rights leader Dr. Martin Luther King, coupled with widespread civil disorder and riots in many urban areas, finally commanded sufficient attention to move Congress to provide additional legislation. It did this in 1968 in two measures: the Omnibus Crime Control and Safe Streets Act and the Gun Control Act. The first replaced the Federal Firearms Act and the second amended the National Firearms Act and portions of the Omnibus Act.

The 1968 legislation, recognizing that law enforcement is essentially a local problem, is designed to encourage the establishment of effective programs at the state level. At the federal level, the legislation is concerned with the elimination of the more glaring defects in the 1934 and 1939 acts. In brief, the features of the new laws at the federal level, are:

Prohibition of interstate mail-order sales (to other than another licensee) of handguns, rifles, shotguns, and their amunition;

Prohibition of over-the-counter sales to nonresidents unless the purchaser satisfies the requirements of the laws of both states;

The provision that a person carrying a firearm while committing a federal crime of violence may be subject to life imprisonment;

Restrictions on the importing of firearms;

Expansion in the scope of the weapons restricted under the National Firearms Act (gangster-type weapons); and

Increases in occupational taxes.

Where registration is required (gangster-type and destructive weapons), disclosure of information is restricted in order to avoid conflict with the constitutional right of a prisoner to claim his privilege against self-incrimination. It is worth noting that the Administration vigorously sought but that Congress refused to provide for general federal registration and licensing of most firearms and to provide for taking a national inventory of the estimated 100–200 million firearms owned by the nation's citizens.

The 1968 legislation greatly expanded the activities and responsibilities of the enforcement unit of the Alcohol, Tobacco, and Firearms Division. Even before its enactment, however, there had been an increase in such activity. In recent years, the enforcement unit has devoted more time to the Attorney General's organized crime drive, including the opening up of a number of organized crime cases. It has also conducted several large city firearms surveys and made extensive inspections of firearms dealers. For fiscal 1968, apart from the manpower expended in the moonshine belt (the Southeast Region), 40 per cent of AT&F's time was expended on firearms investigations. Arrests for firearms violations also have increased, although they constitute but a small fraction—450 of some 5,400 for 1968—of all division arrests, most of which are for alcohol violations.

VIII

Relations with Other Government Agencies

"No man is an *Iland* intire of it selfe." Neither is the Internal Revenue Service as respects its relations with other government units. In fact, without interdepartment cooperation it is difficult to see how modern governmental agencies could function effectively. Consider, for example, what would be the results in the following cases without the cooperation of other federal agencies.

X Corporation, a contractor working on a Department of Defense contract, was short of cash and refused to turn over withheld employment taxes. *X* was confident that the district Collection Division would not seize its property (its inventory was sufficient to cover its liability), because it regarded its work as vital to the national defense. Through regional counsel and the chief counsel's General Litigation Division in Washington, contact was made with the Department of Defense, which informed the IRS that, although offsetting of the amount owed *X* under the contract was not possible, because the contract had been assigned to a bank as security, the contract was not considered vital. Faced with this information, *X* paid up.

In another case, *Y* Corporation, during the course of preparing a registration statement for approval of the Securities Exchange Commission, executed a lease on certain property, which gave it a substantial tax advantage. When regional

161

counsel took the position that the lease would not be recognized because it lacked substance, the taxpayer contended that the Securities Exchange Commission required that it be drawn in this manner as a prerequisite to registration and public listing of *Y*'s stock. A check through the Washington office with the chairman of the Securities Exchange Commission revealed that there was no foundation for *Y*'s position. *Y* conceded, and litigation was avoided.

In still another case, *Z* Company, operating a television station, made an ostensible tax-free transfer of its assets and its broadcasting permit through a temporary trustee for the benefit of the ultimate recipient. The district Audit Division contended that the use of the trustee was a sham and that the Federal Communications Commission would not approve the trustee as a permit-holder. A check with the commission through the IRS assistant commissioner (Technical) in Washington revealed that such was the case. Result: another possible conflict was avoided.

Internal Revenue Service cooperation with other agencies is not a one-way street. Although interdepartmental cooperation can hardly be placed on a *quid pro quo* basis, as described below the IRS gives as much, if not more, than it receives, and its organizational structure, especially at the national level, assigns specific information and advice-giving responsibilities to the various divisions and branches on matters within the areas of their operations.

STATE TAX AND LAW ENFORCEMENT

Between 1950 and 1955, Wisconsin's Tax Department was able to report the collection of an additional $3 million of income taxes, penalties, and interest; at the end of one year, Minnesota's Commissioner of Taxation reported additional income tax collections of $860,000, and North Carolina almost $1 million in additional taxes on some 6,000 assessments.

This data reflects only a few of the early results from joint

IRS-state audit programs, which were formalized with a limited number of states in the 1950's. Today, the Internal Revenue Service has entered into formal tax information exchange agreements with forty-four states (all except Alabama, Connecticut, Louisiana, Nevada, Rhode Island, and Texas) and the District of Columbia, which are designed to provide both state tax agencies and the IRS with data for compliance purposes.

The informal exchange of information between federal and state tax authorities dates from the early years of the republic; however, it was not until the enactment of the 1909 excise tax on corporate income that Congress provided specific legislation authorizing state tax officials the right to inspect federal corporate tax returns, and not until 1935 that the right of inspection was extended to individual income tax returns. Further, it was not until 1950 that efforts were made by the Bureau of Internal Revenue to put the exchange of information on a formal basis. After a 1949 conference of state and federal tax officials, formal income tax audit agreements calling for an exchange of abstracts of income tax audits were entered into between the Internal Revenue Service and Wisconsin, North Carolina, Kentucky, Montana, and Colorado.

While these early arrangements proved to be largely one-sided affairs with the major benefits moving to the states, a renewed interest in the programs was generated in 1957 with the signing of a new and broader type agreement with Minnesota. This agreement provided the prototype for the type in current use.

The slowness in the development of the federal-state tax administration cooperation program has undoubtedly been due to a number of causes. One major reason has been the lack of compatability of federal and state tax structures and the multitude (some 13,000) of state and local taxing authorities. For example, while the backbone of the federal tax structure during the past decades has been the income tax, and some three-fourths of the states utilize an income tax on individuals or corporations, only a few state income tax structures conform to the federal structure. A further reason has been the lag in the technical development of state tax administration compared to the degree of sophistication that has been achieved by the Internal Revenue Service. Many, if not most, states have been plagued with small audit staffs, multiple tax agencies at the state level (to say nothing of hundreds of local taxing authorities), and inadequate appropriations for training and development. As a result, they just have not been able to keep up with the needs of a modern tax administration organization. However, there are indications that substantial progress is being made in closing many of the tax administration gaps at the state and local government level. Hopefully, the new and broader type of IRS-state cooperative agreement will speed this progress.

Program guidance and coordination is provided at the national level by the IRS Research Division. The current type of agreement is designed to ensure that the specific program (1) will be broad-based, in that it will provide the means for cooperation with respect to all taxes other than the alcohol and tobacco taxes, (2) will be tailored to the individual state, and (3) will provide for a balance between benefits and costs. For example, the Virginia agreement signed in 1963 by Commissioner of Internal Revenue Mortimer Caplin and Governor Albertis S. Harrison, provides for the establishment of exchange programs by certain state officers (state tax commissioner, state highway commissioner, employment commissioner, and corporation commission) and the IRS district director at Richmond.

The Virginia agreement makes express provision for four categories of taxes: income taxes, the federal highway use tax, unemployment taxes, and estate and gift taxes. The provisions pertaining to federal and Virginia income taxes call for exchange programs between the IRS district director and the Virginia tax commissioner with respect to audit adjustments resulting in deficiencies, overassessments, and lists of persons delinquent in filing returns. The tax commissioner will provide the district director with lists of persons who receive state tax refunds in excess of an amount mutually agreed upon (such amounts would normally constitute taxable income for federal income tax purposes), and efforts will be made to explore the use of computers in making comparisons of tax returns.

The Virginia agreement, in common with other agreements, prohibits the exchange of income tax audit information where criminal prosecution is pending or under consideration. In such cases, audit information will be provided only after the criminal aspects of a case have been finally disposed of. This provision reflects federal (and state) legislation designed to keep income tax returns confidential. For example, overriding any agreement are provisions of the Internal Revenue Code that limit inspection by state and local tax officials of federal income tax returns to tax administration purposes, and then only upon written request of the governor; further, any state official who makes an unauthorized disclosure is subject to a $1,000 fine or 1-year imprisonment, or both.

The provision in the 1963 Virginia agreement pertaining to the use of computers has been advanced to the point where the Internal Revenue Service now has agreements with twenty-seven states and the District of Columbia under which the IRS provides (on a user charge basis as authorized by federal law) magnetic tapes of selected data from its individual master return file. This program, which has not supplanted the exchange of audit abstracts on a manual basis, was inaugurated in 1966 after an IRS survey of state agencies revealed that all but one of the states with income tax laws utilized computers for return-processing. Thus, the harnessing of the computer to federal-state cooperative programs promises to add a new dimension to tax administration in the United States, which may be particularly meaningful for compliance at all levels of government.

The principal use of the tax return data by both the states

and the IRS has been to determine whether comparable returns have been filed; however, a full evaluation of the benefits of the program (the indirect benefits are obviously substantial) in terms of dollars has not been made, although a study of audit exchange data for 1964 of eighteen states and the District of Columbia revealed additional collections, directly attributable to the information exchanged, of $25 million by the latter and $7 million by the IRS. (Apart from the budding computer program, the Internal Revenue Service has been provided some 250,000 audit abstracts annually.)

Finally, additional IRS-state relationships of a continuing nature arise in the law enforcement area. Thus, the Alcohol, Tobacco, and Firearms Division, as described in Chapter VII, frequently conducts its campaigns against the moonshiner in conjunction with state and local law enforcement agencies, and the IRS inspection units have cooperated with local authorities when these units have uncovered facts (for example, the solicitation of money from taxpayers under the guise of having to pay off revenue agents) that constitute violations of state but not federal law.

DEPARTMENT OF THE TREASURY

During the course of Congress's deliberations on the Internal Revenue Act of 1964, its tax-writing Ways and Means Committee was informed that the Treasury proposed repeal of the 4 per cent dividend-received credit would result in a tax increase for a substantial number of taxpayers, notwithstanding the over-all proposed reduction in rates. Not unmindful that taxpayers with sizable amounts of dividend income are apt to be influential citizens, Ways and Means wanted more detailed verification of the Treasury contentions that such was not the case. They had this verification the next morning. Turning to their "back-up" colleagues in the Internal Revenue Service, the Treasury tax policy-makers arranged for a computer comparison of the proposed changes with the then newly operational IRS individual income tax model (a random sample of 100,000 returns on tape which can be blown up to yield a result of the universe of taxpayers). The result: a convincing demonstration of the soundness of the Treasury position and eventual repeal of the 4 per cent credit.

Not all of the many points of contact of the IRS with its parent organization, the Treasury Department, can be presented with the drama involved in the roles that each plays in the tax legislative process. Yet these points of contact are many and varied, notwithstanding that the Service is basically an autonomous operating bureau within the Department, with a well-defined mission limited to the administration and enforcement of the internal revenue laws enacted by Congress. Few IRS units are without interdepartmental relationships and obligations, a number of which have been noted in preceding chapters. The Commissioner, as a member of the staff of the Secretary of the Treasury, participates in periodic staff meetings and makes a printed report annually to the Secretary; the chief counsel, the Commissioner's legal officer, is also assistant general counsel in Treasury's office of general counsel; the Investigative Techniques Branch in the Intelligence Division provides instruction for, and collaborates in the direction of, the Treasury's operation of the Federal Law Enforcement Center; the Investigations Branch of the Internal Security Division conducts personnel background investigations for certain other Treasury bureaus; the Alcohol, Tobacco, and Firearms Division's laboratories analyze samples for the Bureau of Narcotics, now in the Justice Department; and the IRS Data Center in Detroit prepares the Treasury Department's payrolls.

However, few of the coordinating activities of the Internal Revenue Service can match the role it plays in support of the Treasury Department's legislative program. For an understanding of this role, some knowledge is necessary of the organizational structure of the office of the assistant secretary of the Treasury for Tax Policy and of the tax legislative process.

As previously indicated, while Congress has seen fit to charge the Secretary of the Treasury with the general administration of the revenue laws, it has also established the office of Commissioner of Internal Revenue; the effect of this is to separate—at least formally—the administration of the revenue laws from the formulation of the administrative tax policy, that is, from the formulation of what the Secretary of the Treasury believes the revenue laws ought to be. This latter mission is within the jurisdiction of the assistant secretary for Tax Policy, whose office performs a staff or service function without a field organization and is divided into two main units: the Office of Tax Analysis, and the Office of Tax Legislative Counsel (not to be confused with the legislative counsel of the House of Representatives). The Office of Tax Analysis, a group of economists headed by a director, is primarily concerned with the analysis of proposed tax legislation as it affects the national economy, the assembly of statistical data, and the projection of over-all economic trends. Its collaborative IRS counterparts in the making of studies are found in the Research and Statistics divisions of the assistant commissioner (Planning and Research).

The Tax Legislative Counsel heads up a group of lawyers who provide legal advice and analysis with respect to the Treasury's tax legislative programs, assist in the development of the regulations, and participate with congressional staff members in the analysis and presentation to congressional committees of tax proposals and in drafting legislation in accordance with the decisions of such committees. Its collaborative unit in the Internal Revenue Service is the chief counsel's forty-lawyer Legislation and Regulations Division, which provides drafting aid in preparing the basic documents utilized by the assistant secretary for Tax Policy in his effort to sell the Treasury's tax program to Congress and in presenting IRS's own proposals for legislation (to be described in Chapter IX) as part of the over-all Department of the Treasury program.

All revenue bills must be introduced in the House and

referred to the Ways and Means Committee, which normally conducts a public hearing on an Administration-sponsored bill before it reports the bill for floor consideration. After House passage, the bill is sent to the Senate, and the process repeated through the Senate Finance Committee, which reports its version back to the Senate. After passage, differences between the two bills are worked out in a conference committee composed of members of both House and Senate committees. From the conference committee comes the final bill. The process is, of course, truncated, and the original Treasury proposals may hardly be recognizable by the time a revenue bill reaches the President's desk; the process is political.

Although the IRS plays a role only secondary or supporting to the assistant secretary for Tax Policy in the over-all Treasury Department's tax programs, IRS officials, during the course of legislative consideration of revenue legislation, may be called upon to explain or to provide supporting data on a variety of issues.

DEPARTMENT OF JUSTICE

In Chapter III we saw that, if revenue agent Tom Jones discovered what he contended was an underpayment in his audit examination of the Smith Company's books, Smith Company would be faced with a choice of judicial remedies if it wished to contest the asserted deficiency in the courts. Without payment of the deficiency, Smith Company could petition the Tax Court of the United States for a review, or, as an alternative, could pay the asserted deficiency, file a claim for refund, and upon disallowance of the claim sue the United States for a refund in a federal District Court or the Court of Claims. In a Tax Court review, the defendant Commissioner would be represented by a field attorney from the chief counsel's regional office. In the case of a refund suit, the United States would be represented by an attorney from the Department of Justice. Further, in case of an appeal from either the Tax Court or a District Court to a Court of Appeals—and in all other cases, including criminal prosecutions, suits to collect amounts due the United States, and Supreme Court matters—the government is represented by the Department of Justice.

This divided jurisdiction (between the IRS chief counsel and the Department of Justice) in the handling of tax litigation is primarily a product of the establishment of the Tax Court in 1924 (then the Board of Tax Appeals) as an administrative court in order to provide taxpayers an independent administrative review of deficiencies asserted by the Commissioner for income, estate, and gift taxes. For the purpose of this review, it was felt that the Commissioner should be represented by his own staff, leaving general representation of the government in the legislative and constitutional courts in the hands of the Attorney General as head of the Department of Justice. However, the growth of the income tax to the point where it constitutes the principal source of federal revenue, coupled with the development of the Tax Court into a judicial entity in a very real sense, has necessitated a corresponding refinement in interdepartmental coordination between the Internal Revenue Service and the Justice Department in the formulation and execution of litigation policy. Some understanding of this relationship can perhaps be gained from a description of the organizational structure of the Department of Justice as it relates to tax litigation and from the five-divisional litigation structure of the chief counsel's office.

The exclusive jurisdiction of the Department of Justice over tax litigation other than in the Tax Court had its modern origins in legislation enacted in 1932, implemented by executive order in 1933, and the establishment of Justice's Tax Division in 1934. Thus, the Tax Division, headed by an assistant attorney general, and Justice's Office of Solicitor General constitute the key organizational units utilized in carrying out Justice's tax litigation mission, with attorneys from the

Tax Division responsible for the actual trial of cases other than those before the Supreme Court.

The role of the solicitor general in tax litigation is basically twofold: (1) the determination of whether an appeal should be taken from a decision adverse to the government in the Tax Court, District Court, or Court of Claims, and (2) the supervision of tax litigation in the Supreme Court. In the exercise of his appeal determination function the solicitor general normally relies on recommendations made by the IRS chief counsel's office, the Justice Department's Tax Division, or the United States attorney, as the case may be.

It is clear that, if anything approaching national uniformity is to be achieved in tax litigation policy-making, the work of the chief counsel's office—especially as regards its exclusive jurisdiction over the conduct of litigation in the Tax Court—must be fully coordinated with that of the Justice Department. To this end, the chief counsel's litigation work is organized under an associate chief counsel (Litigation) into five divisions: Tax Court; Refund Litigation; General Litigation; Enforcement; and Alcohol, Tobacco, and Firearms.

All of these divisions other than Refund Litigation have their regional counterparts, but the major coordinating work with Justice's Tax Division is centralized in Washington. Thus, the Tax Court Division in Washington, in addition to review and coordination of regional office Tax Court matters, prepares recommendations to the Department of Justice for the Commissioner's appeals and for settlements in civil actions. The Refund Litigation Division shares with the Tax Court Division the responsibility for maintaining control over consistency in legal position on a national basis and to this end works with Justice's Tax Division in disposing of refund suits.

The General (formerly Collection) Litigation Division functions in a manner similar to Refund Litigation with respect to the collection of claims due the United States; the Enforcement Division with respect to criminal tax cases; and the Alcohol, Tobacco, and Firearms Division with respect to alcohol, tobacco, and firearms taxes.

The relations of the Internal Revenue Service with the Department of Justice are not limited to litigation matters. The IRS has a long history of coordinated efforts with Justice in criminal investigation work of many types, including the enforcement of the older federal Prohibition and kidnaping laws. Today, however, as described in Chapters V and VII, the principal coordination in this area consists of the important aid provided by the IRS Intelligence Division and Alcohol, Tobacco, and Firearms Division in the Justice Department's drive on organized crime.

OTHER FEDERAL AGENCIES

Although the full range of IRS relationships with all government agencies can hardly be explored here, it is worth recalling that almost all IRS overseas activities are dependent upon a functional relationship with the State Department. This is especially true with respect to various Office of International Operations compliance and education programs designed to ensure that United States citizens living overseas are aware of their continued obligation to the U.S. revenue. The embassy-based Revenue Service Representative—tax administrator in "striped trousers"—and the teams sent out in the tax season to provide tax return aid all reach the overseas taxpayer through embassies and consulates maintained by the Department of State. Also, initial contact in a foreign government's request for tax administration assistance, as well as the funds for the program, come from State's Agency for International Development.

Since the State Department does not have a monopoly on overseas activities, the Internal Revenue Service has frequently found itself dealing with other government agencies in such activities as the conducting of overseas training schools for Department of Defense tax advisers, technical assistance provided to United States possessions and to Micronesia (a United Nations trust territory) at the request of the Department of Interior, and participation in a task force, along with Interior and Treasury representatives, to study the special facets arising out of the relationships between the United States tax structure and the tax structures of the possessions.

The IRS also maintains continuous and important relationships with the Social Security Administration, which administers the various federal welfare programs, with the Civil Service Commission in connection with recruitment, employee classification, and other personnel matters, with the Bureau of the Budget in connection with the preparation of the IRS budget, with the General Service Administration with respect to needed space and equipment, with the Bureau of Customs in the joint operation of eight field laboratories, with the Department of Agriculture and the Small Business Administration in conducting tax education programs for farmers and businessmen, and with the General Accounting Office in connection with the auditing activities of the Comptroller General of the United States. In short, there are few operating agencies in the federal government that do not, at one time or another, come in contact with the federal tax collector—the Internal Revenue Service.

IX

Relations with Congress

At the conclusion of the hearings before the House of Representatives Subcommittee on Appropriations for the 1970 budget, Chairman Tom Steed of Oklahoma cited a number of instances in which the Internal Revenue Service had been of assistance to him with respect to a number of tax matters of importance to the governor of his state, to the state legislature, to an industry of major importance, to communities within the state, and to a few individuals who needed guidance or help from the agency. "In some of these cases," he was moved to say, "time was of the essence and in some it required some very serious policy decisions and I am happy to testify . . . that in each instance I received the utmost assistance, and the Service acquitted itself in a very exemplary manner."

While the foregoing testimonial hardly reveals the nature of the services rendered to Congressman Steed, it does indicate that IRS management officials and employees are frequently called upon to provide technical aid and information to members of Congress. The performance of such services may be more than a matter of doing what is routinely expected of professionals. Unlike many federal regulatory agencies (National Labor Relations Board, Interstate Commerce Commission, Food and Drug Administration, Federal Trade Commission, Federal Aviation Administration, Securities Exchange Commission), the Internal Revenue Service does not have a private constituency—the group regulated—that it can call upon for political support. In this respect, it lacks the political power often needed to do battle in the sometimes whacky, sometimes mysterious political world of congressional-executive department relationships.

On the other hand, there is a mutual awareness on the part of both the IRS and Congress that they need each other; in the present scheme of things there must be some large agency to administer the federal tax system, and to do this efficiently and fairly this agency requires support from Congress. This support may be given grudgingly, in a manner to make the lives of IRS managers uncomfortable to say the least. Today, however, even if harmony does not always reign, there are no indications of any widespread dissatisfaction on Capitol Hill with the manner in which the Internal Revenue Service is doing its job of administering the tax laws enacted by Congress. Notwithstanding occasional disclosures of internal corruption and abuse of the power granted the agency in enforcement, there is no evidence of a congressional revolt, no indication of a trend toward reducing or limiting the powers granted the IRS or of a major reorganizational shake-up. Today Congress appears to consider that the problems encountered by the Internal Revenue Service can be solved by the agency itself.

JOINT COMMITTEE ON INTERNAL REVENUE TAXATION

The foregoing does not mean that the IRS and Congress do not clash or that Congress has relaxed or defaulted in the exercise of its surveillance function. Congress not only has subjected IRS behavior and practices to sometimes critical review before special investigating committees (to say nothing of swipes in the *Congressional Record* by individual congressmen), but its standing and permanent tax-writing committees (the House Ways and Means Committee and Senate Finance Committee) and appropriation committees also perform periodic reviews. Since 1926, Congress has institutionalized certain of its relationships with the IRS and the Treasury through the establishment of a Joint Committee (House and Senate) on Internal Revenue Taxation.

The fifteen-member Joint Committee (five from the House Ways and Means Committee, five from the Senate Finance Committee, three from the majority party, and two from the minority party) functions through a small staff of economists, lawyers, and accountants. The committee has a dual mission: (1) review of taxpayer refund claims of $100,000 or more, and (2) the preparation of tax studies and recommendations to the tax-writing committees of Congress.

Through the staff of the Joint Committee Congress participates directly, though in a limited area, in tax administration by approving or rejecting large refund claims (the taxpayer, of course, can sue on a rejected claim). These claims, which number some 500 a year and which account for a good portion of the IRS's annual interest costs of $136 million, are handled under special guidelines at the district level and are subject to special review treatment at both the regional and national levels.

With respect to the committee's research role—its relations with the Internal Revenue Service are mostly indirect. While the Joint Committee staff has participated with the Treasury and the IRS in making some tax studies, it, rather than the Internal Revenue Service, has sometimes been resorted to by members of Congress as a source of technical information and aid; when this is done, it is arguable that the political position of the IRS is correspondingly weakened. Although the Joint Committee has no formal role in the tax legislative process, it has been utilized by Congress for studies that have sometimes taken positions contrary to positions maintained by the Department of the Treasury and the IRS. It has also served as a means of reviewing administrative action taken by the agency.

IRS-sponsored Legislation

In a 1955 case, the Tax Court of the United States concluded that the taxpayer, Sanitary Farms Dairy, had shown a sufficient business relationship (through an advertising campaign) between the costs of an African safari by the dairy's president-owner, a hunting enthusiast, and his wife to qualify as a deductible business expense of marketing dairy products. Nor was this an isolated example of the manner in which taxpayers had been combining business and personal pleasure at the expense of the revenue. The scope of the problem was revealed by Secretary of the Treasury C. Douglas Dillon at the hearings on the Revenue Act of 1962. Mr. Dillon testified that an audit of 38,000 returns revealed claimed deductions totaling $5.7 million for club dues, $2 million for theater tickets and similar amusements, over $1 million for hunting lodges and fishing camps, $2.6 million for yachts, and $11.5 million for business gifts.

Here then was an abuse, uncovered during the course of its audit examinations, that the IRS felt required remedial legislation. This Congress provided with the enactment of Section 274 of the Code, which, in three pages of fine print, imposes substantial limitations on the availability of a deduction for travel and entertainment expense.

This IRS-sponsored legislation was not achieved without a struggle. Arrayed against it were some of the most powerful interest groups working at all levels of the tax legislative process. Consider what was involved besides high-living business officials: restaurants, hotels, vacation spas, chambers of commerce. If the legislative proposal had not been properly dramatized and timed as an important part of a new Administration's tax program, enactment may well have been questionable, at least in the form in which it eventually became law. This much at least is evident from the fate of the

IRS-sponsored legislation in the same revenue act that was designed to require withholding of tax by payers of dividend and interest income. Service studies had revealed substantial underreporting of such income, and withholding on wages had been in effect for two decades. What could be more just than similar treatment for taxpayers receiving dividend and interest income? However, the IRS underestimated the strength of the large corporations, banks, and savings and loan associations, who launched a shareholder-depositor grass roots, letter writing campaign that overwhelmed Congress. The result was that this Administration-sponsored measure was defeated and the IRS had to be satisfied with additional information reporting requirements on this type of investment income.

In short, what often appear to be rather innocent technical proposals designed to improve tax administration or to correct demonstrated abuses will turn into major issues of tax policy and force the Internal Revenue Service to do battle on the political front. It is ironic that the organization best qualified to evaluate equity and fairness in action lacks meaningful political power of its own, but in all such cases the IRS must rely upon the power of the Treasury and the support of the President. If Presidential support is lacking or a proposal has any adverse effect on important interest groups, too much success cannot be anticipated. However, if the proposals are in the nature of "relief"—in that they do not shift a tax burden or the opposition is weak—IRS-sponsored legislation may have relatively easy going.

The Internal Revenue Service may also find itself involved in the tax political process as a result of congressional legislation designed to reverse IRS interpretations of existing law. During the 1950's and 1960's state and local governments made increasing use of their power to issue tax-free bonds to finance industrial development programs under which private industry would acquire property and establish plants. Because the proceeds of the bonds enured to the benefit of private persons, the IRS concluded that this was an abuse of Section 103 of the Code, which exempts interest on state and local bonds from federal income taxation. Consequently, in March, 1968, the agency proposed amendments to the regulations that would have withdrawn the interest exclusion for certain industrial development bonds. With this proposal, the IRS was up against what is probably the most powerful interest group in Washington—the states—and it was probably only because the change was proposed at a time of widespread public dissatisfaction with tax preferences that congressional reaction did not take the form of complete rejection. In any event, the reaction of Congress was almost instantaneous; by May 1, 1968, Section 103 had been amended, and, although the amendment endorsed the basic position of the proposed regulations, it littered the general rule with such a large number of exceptions that it is difficult to conclude that the state and local governments would be hampered in any substantial manner in the use of tax-free bonds in their industrial development programs.

Political skirmishes originating in the foregoing manner have been many. However, while they have sometimes raised the ire of individual congressmen, they do not normally leave lasting scars. Both sides appear to regard these political conflicts as a necessary part of the taxing process.

BUDGET AND APPROPRIATIONS

Fiscal years 1968 and 1969 will live long in the memory of IRS managers. Consider what Commissioner Randolph W. Thrower had to say in May, 1969, when testifying on the 1970 IRS budget before the House Subcommittee on Appropriations:

In the last two fiscal years the Service's operations, especially its Compliance programs, have been cut back below the levels approved by Congress in the annual appropriations acts. About

18 months ago—after we had hired most of the new revenue agents and revenue officers authorized for fiscal year 1968, we encountered the expenditure restrictions. This caused certain dislocations in that year that have been compounded by the continuation of hiring restrictions in fiscal year 1969.

As you will recall, one requirement of section 201 of the Revenue and Expenditure Control Act placed a limitation on full-time permanent employment in the Government until the level of June 30, 1966 is reached. This required that one of every four vacancies after June 30, 1969 be left unfilled. As a result of needs recognized elsewhere in the government, the Service was eventually limited to filling 70 percent of its vacancies.

In short, the IRS had been trapped in the higher politics of the infighting between President Johnson and Congress. When the President asked Congress for a 10 per cent surtax on income in 1967 as a means to combat inflation and to meet the mounting costs of the Vietnam war, Congress responded after months of delay, but made the tax conditional upon reduced executive department spending and hiring mentioned in Commissioner Thrower's testimony. The net effect of these restrictions on the revenue has been quite startling; $21 million savings in Internal Revenue Service operating costs will result in an estimated $700 million loss in tax revenue for the fiscal years 1968–70 and an incalculable loss from lessened voluntary compliance (a drop of 1 per cent in voluntary compliance costs an estimated $1.7 billion in tax revenue).

This across-the-board technique of cutting back on appropriations—which Congressman Tom Steed termed a monstrosity—is not a common tactic of Congress. The Revenue and Expenditure Control Act of 1968 must be regarded as an aberration. Normally, congressional controls over executive department spending are exerted in the formulation of a department's budget, which must be justified before the appropriation committees. The IRS budget process starts early, and much effort is expended by the various units long before the Commissioner and his staff appear before the subcommittee handling the Treasury Department appropriations—which occurs a few months before the start of the government's fiscal year (July 1–June 30).

Primary responsibility for IRS budget is assigned to the assistant commissioner (Administration), and the work of assembling the needed data is carried out by the Budget Branch of the Fiscal Management Division. This unit must also work with the Bureau of the Budget (in the Executive Office of the President), which has over-all authority for the preparation of the annual budget presented by the President to Congress.

The IRS budget is structured functionally, without regard to the national office-field organizational structure, into three major divisions: salaries and expenses (3 per cent), revenue accounting and processing (25 per cent), and compliance (72 per cent). The Appropriations Committee hearing begins with a general statement by the Commissioner pertaining to the major items in the budget. For answers to questions by committee members and detailed supporting data, the Commissioner frequently relies upon his attending staff members (assistant commissioners, chief counsel, and in some instances national office division directors). Questions pertain to the effect of new and proposed legislation, new programs, and their needs and costs. Committee members also ask for explanations of administrative problems encountered during the preceding year, especially those that have received considerable public exposure. However, even the most embarrassing of these issues—such as complaints of too much supervision of employees and taxpayer harassment—are handled in a low-keyed manner, and the general atmosphere is one of a team working together in the common good.

It is rarely suggested that the IRS is uneconomical in conducting its operations. Committee members frequently avow that they will continue the battle for improving IRS salaries, which comprise more than 80 per cent of the agency's operating costs, to meet the high attrition rates in some employee categories and to turn the IRS into a truly blue ribbon organization. Perhaps one reason for this lack of more detailed attention to costs is the wealth of statistical cost data provided in the budget. Another may be the ability of the Internal Revenue Service to demonstrate that it is indeed unique among the world's tax collecting agencies on the basis of the unit cost of revenue collected. The unit cost of internal revenue collections reached a high of $5.30 per $100 of collected revenue in 1871. Since the advent of the broad-based income tax of World War II, unit costs have ranged from 30 to 50 cents per $100 (slightly more than 40 cents for fiscal year 1970, on the basis of an $800 million budget and estimated collections of $200 billion).

A multitude of forces—growth of the economy, inflation, tax rates, type of taxes—affect unit costs, making this standard a questionable yardstick of administrative efficiency. On the other hand, the unit cost of the collection of some $200 billion annually by the United States tax collector, most of it voluntary with a minimum of coercion, is viewed by most observers as no mean accomplishment. Foreign tax administrators who visit the United States often find this accomplishment bordering on the incredible, especially since some 70 per cent of it is derived from what is regarded as the world's most difficult tax to administer, a progressive income tax. In short, many of these observers regard the Internal Revenue Service as a model of efficiency.

CONFRONTATIONS

When Sheldon S. Cohen took over as Commissioner of the Internal Revenue Service in January, 1965, he found that he had inherited a problem that was, in effect a backlash of congressional reaction to what might be termed—charitably—an overzealous effort by the Department of Justice's organized crime unit to secure convictions of racketeers, an effort which, as described in Chapters V and VII, has included a major role for the IRS Intelligence Division and the Alcohol, Tobacco, and Firearms Division. The overzealousness consisted of the widespread use by both federal and state investigating agents of electronic surveillance devices, including wiretaps (which will be discussed in Chapter XI). Congressional reaction took the form of a series of investigations by a Senate committee on the invasion of privacy, which covered the practices of many federal agencies as well as practices utilized in private industrial espionage.

Six months after he took office, Commissioner Cohen was confronted by Senator Edward V. Long of Missouri, Chairman of the Senate Subcommittee on Administrative Practice and Procedure:

SENATOR LONG: Mr. Commissioner, before you start your statement, you will recall that the subcommittee has requested various documents from you, from your Department. . . . It is my information and my recollection that you have secured from many of your agents—whether all of them or not—affidavits dealing with wire tapping and with snooping here. . . . Now, do you have those documents in the possession of your Department?

MR. COHEN: Yes, sir.

SENATOR LONG: We have asked you that the committee be furnished with those documents or copies of them. Are you prepared to comply with that request this morning?

MR. COHEN: Not at this time, sir.

SENATOR LONG: Do you indicate by that you either will or will not furnish them to us?

MR. COHEN: As I explained to the chairman and his counsel on a number of occasions, there are many instances in running the Revenue Service or any other executive department, where a superior must call on his subordinates for full and frank information, daily reports, critical analyses of proposals. In order to have full and frank discussion within the department and in order to elicit information on which to operate a department, one must have complete confidence in members of the staff expressing themselves in the fullest and to the extent that such documents are allowed outside of the department one cannot rely on the future of full and frank discussion, because everyone will be looking over his shoulder to say, if I say it this way, how will it look in public, if I say it that way, how will it look in public? We feel it is in the interest of good government all the way up and down the line that this type of information not be discussed in public. However, as I have indicated to the chairman and to the counsel and your staff, I am willing to discuss all of these affairs fully and frankly, and I have made available to your staff and to you each of the individuals that you have requested involved here, so that you might fully and frankly discuss any of these matters with them. . . . If the chairman has read the copy of the statement that I delivered to your staff last night, you will discover that I have no intention of covering up anything. I have full intention of bringing to the light of day any of our acts that are beyond the pale. I am as vitally concerned as the chairman is with the fact that the IRS shall operate within the law. I am, as I have mentioned to you, a member of the American Civil Liberties Union myself and I would have no countenance with any actions that might be beyond what both of us agree is the legal limit.

SENATOR LONG: I have read your statement, too, and you mention three or four instances of wire tapping there. I happen to know there are many more than that. We will have evidence as we go along. The thing I want to know is—will you make those affidavits available to the committee or will you not? That is my present statement.

MR. COHEN: My present inclination is not to make them available to the committee, sir.

During the course of these same hearings, Commissioner Cohen also refused to disclose the names of IRS agent involved in a certain wire tapping attempt, as well as the diaries kept by special agents on grounds that they contained names of informants and others, which he was forbidden by law to disclose, since they were not yet a matter of public record.

Other IRS personnel, for like reasons, refused to disclose to the committee similar data upon orders of their superiors.

Confrontations of IRS managers and members of Congress have not been uncommon throughout the history of the organization. Perhaps the most notorious of such encounters in modern times were those involved in the investigations and disclosures of the King-Kean committees in the early 1950's, which, as described in Chapter II, served as a catalyst for a complete reorganization of the IRS in 1952. The reorganization was hardly four years old when, in 1957, the House Ways and Means Committee launched a critical review of what had been accomplished by the 1952 reorganization. This evaluation was carried out by a subcommittee headed by Congressman Wilbur D. Mills (now chairman of Ways and Means), which enlisted the aid of an advisory group of practicing lawyers and accountants.

The generally favorable report of the advisory group demonstrates how sound an organizational structure was formulated in 1952 and testifies as well to the recovery of the IRS image in the short span of four years. While there was some considerable probing in depth (for example, on the functioning of the internal auditors, on their effect on employee morale and efficiency, and on the work of the regional commissioner's offices), the basic impression was that of a congressional committee seeking information and understanding. The committee members made repeated offers of aid with respect to a number of knotty problems, many of which persist to this day, such as the adequacy of salaries and taxpayer utilization of settlement procedures within the agency.

Although confrontations between IRS managers and Congress reflect congressional concern with such problems as possible abuse of power and insufficient enforcement in particular areas (for example, tax-exempt organizations in recent years), there is no indication that these members of Congress are dissatisfied with the IRS in the over-all execution of its mission.

X

Relations with the Public

A high rate of citizen literacy is not enough, the Internal Revenue Service has discovered, to ensure effective voluntary compliance with the federal revenue laws. Often the literal terms of the Internal Revenue Code require more than a little explanation. Take the case reported by the district director at Buffalo a few years back. A taxpayer had deducted a bad debt from his income as he was entitled to do; however, he had taken a deduction for the same debt three years in a row, reasoning that it was still bad at the end of each year. It took some explaining to convince him that he could only deduct it once. (If he had ever recovered the debt, still more explanation would probably have been required to convince him that he would have to report the recovery as income because of the tax benefit from the previous deductions.)

This illustration demonstrates only one facet of the many-dimensioned public information task of the IRS, faced as it is with communicating effectively with more than 110 million individual and 5 million business taxpayers each year. The Internal Revenue Service is second only to the Post Office Department in the number of contacts it makes with the public. The field of taxation has been characterized by one judge as "probably the single greatest area of contact between individuals and the force of the state."

Spearheading the IRS public communication effort is the Public Information Division in the office of the assistant commissioner (Administration) in Washington. The division is formally charged with the development of information programs, the evaluation of public response, and the recommending of corrective measures where indicated. This work is directed from the national office and carried out in the field by the assistant regional commissioners (Administration) at the regional level and through corresponding units at the district and branch office levels.

However, public information personnel (in private industry more often called public relations) have more to do than hand out press releases, consult correspondents and writers, and, in general, advance and preserve the image of the Internal Revenue Service. When pockets of corruption have been exposed or when other events demand that the IRS position be reported accurately, the public information director frequently finds himself involved in public relations "firefighting" missions. For example, when the Long Committee of the Senate opened hearings on the invasion of privacy in Kansas City in 1965, it discovered (to the vexation of its chairman Senator Edward V. Long) that IRS's director of information had preceded the committee to Kansas City and opened a line of communications with the local press.

The formal dispensing of information through the Public Information Division is only a small part of the total information-dispensing task of the Public Information Division. All IRS officials participate in one way or another. A former Commissioner has indicated that perhaps three-fourths of his time was devoted to other than administrative matters. The test of effective public relations lies in what the Internal Revenue Service does rather than in what it says; this means that truly effective public relations is dependent upon how the revenue agent, the special agent, the revenue officer, the taxpayer service representative, and all the other front-line workers do their jobs. Experience shows that a public relations problem may arise in assisting a taxpayer with his return, in communicating with the taxpayer by computer after processing the return, in auditing, and in collecting. IRS managers are well aware of this and utilize not only the standard public relations methods and techniques developed over the years in public relations work but also a wide variety of unique IRS information and assistance programs, designed to deal with the taxpaying public.

These programs, it is worth noting, have in no measure been prompted by the Freedom of Information Act of 1967, whose purpose is to make knowledge of many of the internal procedures of the various federal agencies available to the public; the Internal Revenue Service, however, has provided public reading rooms in response to this law at its national office and at its seven regional offices.

INFORMATION AND ASSISTANCE

The basic theme at tax return time—the first three and one-half months of each year—is

READ THE INSTRUCTIONS

During the 1968 season, this message was emblazoned on posters carried by 50,000 United States mail trucks. The posters depicted an income tax return, folded in the shape of a schoolboy glider and carrying the additional legend:

ACCURATE RETURNS DON'T COME BACK

This poster campaign is but one example of the massive effort made by the Internal Revenue Service to forestall the millions of errors made by taxpayers on their income tax returns each year. The IRS information program is not only a year-round effort. It is also aimed at individuals in a pre-taxpayer status. For example, the Training Division in Washington, with the aid of district coordinators, provides course materials for a "Teaching Taxes" program for the nation's high school students. Some 4 million students annually in 25,000 schools taking business and social studies are exposed to the fundamentals of the federal tax system, with emphasis on the preparation of form 1040, the individual income tax form.

This form, the Internal Revenue Service's "primary direct line of communication" with the general public is, in fact, the focus of attention of much if not most of the IRS information-dispensing effort. The return forms themselves are subject to almost constant review and change by the Technical Publications and Services Division in Washington and, incredible as it may seem, always with the aim of making it easier for the taxpayer to make his own assessment. For example, the agency has experimented with the use of color and has just recently revised the basic individual form 1040 by combining short form 1040-A (which, in the past, could be elected by taxpayers with income under $5,000) with long form 1040. Studies revealed that a number of taxpayers had overpaid, simply because they had elected the short form. The new form 1040—with larger spaces for entries—will be based on a "building block" principle; page 1 will call for the same question as the old short form, plus a few lines designed to ensure that the lower income taxpayers (31 million, or 40 per cent of all individual taxpayers) are aware of all their rights in making a choice in reporting, and to provide tie-in lines to the more complex schedules (the building blocks) on the following pages, which are needed by taxpayers in the higher brackets.

A second new form, form 1040X, which was issued for the first time in 1968, has been designed to ease the burden of amending a filed return; it permits the making of the changes without duplicating the nonessential data on the original return.

However, in final analysis, and regardless of IRS solicitude, the task of filling out an income tax return is an annual nightmare for many taxpayers. The world's most complex income tax law, subject to annual changes made by Congress, guarantees this. To lighten the burden, when the IRS mails out the tax return blanks in December to all taxpayers listed in the master file, it provides a number of immediate aids. The return kit contains an instruction booklet which articulates to some extent the items which must be included in income, the available deductions and credits, and, in some cases, the manner in which they are to be computed.

It would be a rare income taxpayer, and one almost wholly out of contact with the rest of the world, who could overlook his obligation to file. Early in January each year the information dissemination program shifts into overdrive. National, regional, and district office mimeograph machines work overtime on press releases (district offices release some 5,000 items annually); articles on income tax appear in newspapers and magazines; cooperative distribution programs with banks and financial institutions are carried out; by radio and television (some 4,000 local programs in 1968) the taxpayer is informed of his obligation and given tips on how to discharge it. The businessman and professional are not immune. They may not be allowed to enjoy their chicken and cold peas at Chamber of Commerce or Rotary luncheons without being reminded by a speech or film clip that income tax time is approaching.

The message relayed in the outpouring during the filing period is basically the same: Get it right. To this end, error registers are maintained weekly, and district offices select the appropriate manner to publicize the predominant errors in their territory. And the errors are plentiful. In addition to mathematical errors made by some 4 million taxpayers in 1967, processing at the service centers caught 2.3 million omitted or erroneous Social Security numbers, 903,000 uses of wrong tables or columns, 466,000 returns without withholding tax forms, and 309,000 without signatures.

After the filing period, with 50 million taxpayers looking for their refund checks, the message changes. Now it is: Patience. Articles and releases emphasize the number of errors, the mechanics of processing, and the difficulty of programing computers to communicate effectively and promptly with taxpayer inquiries. Also utilized during this period is a 2-minute television program in color, available to local stations, which provides information on the reason for refund delay, the audit process (which for 2.5 million taxpayers follows the filing of a return), and household servant employment taxes (a low-compliance area).

The information activity during the filing and post-filing period, however, is only a portion of the over-all taxpayer assistance effort. At the most basic level in this area is the year-round assistance program for taxpayers seeking help from the Internal Revenue Service over the phone or by personal visits to IRS offices. This program, under the direction of the Collection Division at all three administrative levels, has been formalized as a separate management activity with the development of a special front-line employee category, the taxpayer service representative (formerly tax assister). While aid is available at all IRS locations, this special group of 900 full-time employees (supplemented at filing time by 450 temporary assistants), located at 500 IRS field offices and providing itinerant services at 150 other locations, has been trained to provide personal aid to some 27 million taxpayers annually (17 million by phone and 10 million by personal visit). Critical in the training of this group, who are in the GS-5 to GS-7 civil service grade range, has been the need to keep them up to date on tax developments. This is accomplished through a special internal information publication, TAXNEWS, which focuses on new and proposed legislative changes and enables personnel servicing taxpayer inquiries to keep up with new developments as they occur. The inquiry program is also utilized as a means of keeping an account of the major taxpayer problems. The top twenty-five inquiries are reviewed by management periodically and a number of changes have been made in the tax form instruction booklet as a result of these reviews.

Recognizing that the instructions accompanying the tax return forms do not provide much help for many problems encountered by taxpayers in reporting their income, the IRS has conducted over the years an extensive publications program, (with an annual printing bill of about $15.5 million) administered by the Technical Publications and Services Division. At the head of the list of some eighty booklets and pamphlets is the best-selling *Your Federal Income Tax*. This 160-page, 60-cent booklet, with annual sales of 1 million copies, covers the income tax in nontechnical terms. The *Tax Guide for Small Business*, equal in length and price, has an annual sale of 250,000 copies. Pamphlets from 2 to 64 pages in length are distributed free, and often provide ready answers for both taxpayers and IRS representatives handling taxpayer inquiries. A few of these are *Tax Guide for United States Citizens Abroad*, *The Farmer's Tax Guide*, and *A Guide to Federal Estate and Gift Taxation*.

Private Rulings

Suppose that the owners of *X* Corporation and *Y* Corporation decide to merge corporations. If the assets of the companies or the shares of stock of the owners have increased in value over the years, as normally would be the case, both the corporate taxpayers and the individual owners may face the horrifying fact that the various exchanges of assets and securities involved in the merger could generate capital gains tax for all concerned. However, Congress has recognized that certain transactions, including corporate mergers and formations, constitute merely formal changes in ownership and has therefore provided that, if a merger is carried out in a prescribed manner, gain or loss on the exchanges involved will be postponed to a time when the taxpayer makes a final disposition of the property, assets, or shares. As a result, somewhere in the mountain of paper work providing the legal foundation for the merger of X and Y will be a critical clause that subjects the agreement to a favorable ruling from the IRS. Without a favorable ruling from the Internal Revenue Service for tax-free treatment, the deal is off.

The IRS system of providing U.S. taxpayers with private (unpublished) rulings for prospective transactions is unique among the world's tax systems. It had its origins in 1938 legislation authorizing the IRS to enter into formal closing agreements with a taxpayer under which both parties are legally bound to the interpretation agreed upon for the particular transaction. However, it was early discovered that the closing agreement procedure was much too cumbersome to meet taxpayer needs for promptness. Starting in 1940, the IRS began informing taxpayers by letter, when inquiry was made, of the position it would take if a closing agreement were entered into. By 1953, this procedure had developed into the present-day two-part, private-letter-ruling program: (1) the office of the assistant commissioner (Technical) in Washington, upon written request from taxpayers (30,000 to 40,000 annually) will in certain cases provide a letter ruling on the proposed transaction outlined in the taxpayer's request; (2) a district director will issue a "determination letter" (mostly on pension trust funds and tax-exempt-organization status) in response to a taxpayer inquiry based on certain completed and certain prospective transactions.

The letter-ruling program, which the Internal Revenue Service regards as a definitive public service to the individual letter recipient only, must be distinguished from other interpretative programs, including regulations, revenue rulings, and revenue procedures. As described in Chapter IV, regulations (as general guides to the law) and revenue rulings and procedures published in the *Internal Revenue Bulletin* (as more specific applications of the law) are intended as planning guides for all taxpayers and IRS personnel. Letter rulings and determination letters, which normally lack substantive rationale, are basically solutions to the problems of particular taxpayers.

Letter rulings and determination letters must also be distinguished (1) from the technical advice available from the national office as a field support function at the request of a district director during the course of an audit examination, (2) from the acquiescence program of the IRS, whereby it publishes its agreement or disagreement—and little more— with the decisions it loses in the Tax Court of the United States, and (3) from a number of releases, such as Information Letters, News Releases, and Technical Information Releases, which are issued as guides or cautions and are informative rather than interpretative in nature.

The importance of the private-letter-ruling program in the administration of the highly technical areas of the revenue laws can hardly be overstressed. Although the program does not affect the general body of taxpayers, it is critical to the high-taxpaying business community, especially the larger corporations, who provide the bulk of the $30–$35 billion collected annually from the corporate income tax. The program serves a deep-felt taxpayer need for certainty (one practitioner has referred to a letter ruling as a policy of insurance) in the sense that Allen Dulles referred to the desire for advance information as "rooted in the instinct for survival"—and it does so with reasonable dispatch (most letter rulings are processed within ninety days) and on a uniform basis. The importance to the taxpayer of the letter-ruling program is best illustrated by the large volume of critical literature written by tax practitioners on the subject. Law reviews, accounting journals, and tax institute proceedings devote no small amount of space to tax practioners' critiques and their advice to each other on ruling-request strategy.

From an administrative point of view, the ruling program provides the Internal Revenue Service with a number of advantages. Letter rulings are the major source for the published-rulings program and promote national uniformity in interpretation. Also, audit examinations are simplified, and litigation is decreased. Finally, the large volume of requests enables the IRS to keep up with the type of transactions being considered by taxpayers, especially in the business community.

However, the private letter-ruling part of the program is not easy to administer, since such rulings frequently require the application of highly technical rules to complex fact patterns. This burden falls on the assistant commissioner (Technical) at the national office and his 450 to 500 lawyers, accountants, engineers, and actuaries, most of whom are classified as "tax law specialists" for civil service purposes. Their annual case work load of all types ranges from 40,000 to 50,000, including 30,000 to 40,000 requests for letter rulings. Most letter rulings are issued at the branch level without review, but published rulings are subject to review by the Interpretative Division in the chief counsel's office.

The bulk of the determination letters issued by the audit divisions in the district director's offices (more than 104,000 in 1968) pertain to pension, profit-sharing, and similar plans, to self-employed plans, and to determinations of the tax-exempt status of charitable and other organizations.

A number of final questions remain: How reliable are letter rulings and or determination letters? Can they be revoked? If so, can they be revoked retroactively? In brief, the Commissioner of Internal Revenue has the power to revoke (except with respect to excise taxes not passed on by the taxpayer) and to revoke retroactively if a ruling is contrary to law. However, revocation is rare, and, if a mistake has been made, Congress has authorized the Commissioner to exercise his discretion as to whether revocation will be retroactive. The taxpayer can rely on IRS rulings and letters to the same extent as he can on regulations and published rulings. Only in a rare case will a revocation be made retroactive to a taxpayer's detriment. In short, private rulings and letter rulings involve a minimum risk to the taxpayer. Proof of their reliability will be found in the fact that the program has in large measure

supplanted the closing-agreement device for prospective transactions, which is legally binding on both the taxpayer and
the IRS.

THE TAX PRACTITIONER

The tax practitioner's view of the Internal Revenue Service
has perhaps been best articulated by the American Bar Association's Committee on Professional Ethics in its *Opinion
314*:

> The Internal Revenue Service is neither a true tribunal, nor
> even a quasi-judicial institution. It has no machinery or pro-
> cedure for adversary proceedings before impartial judges or
> arbiters, involving the weighing of conflicting testimony of wit-
> nesses examined and cross-examined by opposing counsel and
> the consideration of arguments of counsel for both sides of a
> dispute. While its procedure provides for "fresh looks" through
> departmental reviews and informal and formal conference pro-
> cedures, few will contend that the Service provides any truly
> dispassionate and unbiased consideration to the taxpayer. Al-
> though willing to listen to taxpayers and their representatives,
> and obviously intending to be fair, the Service is not designed
> and does not purport to be unprejudiced and unbiased in the
> judicial sense.

The estimated 200,000 lawyers and accountants who comprise the amorphous "tax bar" regard the IRS as an adversary
who must be bested in the various conflicts that arise between the represented taxpayer and his government. Although
this role of an advocate is hardly surprising as regards the
lawyer, it is a relatively new notion for the accountant. Traditionally, the accountant has viewed his primary role as that
of a certifier of financial statements, which often requires him
to act independently of, or adversely to, his client's interests
in the discharge of his obligation to his client's creditors,
which, in any broad view, would include the government.
However, the largest accounting group, the 68,000-member

American Institute of Certified Public Accountants (CPA's), is currently struggling with a proposed statement pertaining to erroneous tax returns that affirms, with respect to tax practice that "it is appropriate for the CPA to serve as an advocate for his client."

Further proof of the dominance of the advocacy role assumed by both lawyers and accountants may be gleaned from their writings in law and accounting journals, where the "warm zeal" normally exercised in advocacy is frequently carried into print in critical analyses of IRS positions and policies. One leading practitioner has recently suggested that the Internal Revenue Service should pursue a policy of "non-aggression" by resolving ambiguities in favor of the taxpayer, should make no attempt itself to close loopholes, and should take no account of "trifles" if they affect taxpayers adversely.

The fact that tax practitioners regard their primary role as that of an advocate does not mean that they have not and do not contribute substantially to the administration of the federal revenue laws. Not only is the adversary system itself productive of much that is good by providing stability, flexibility, and a measure of certainty, but the organized practitioner groups have often labored arduously for reforms that would promote tax administration. They frequently close ranks in support of the IRS when the agency is subject to outside attack. The reaction of the chairman of the 12,000-member Tax Section of the American Bar Association to a *Reader's Digest* attack in 1967 was that it was clear from his own experiences "that the Service is operating generally in a fair and reasonable manner and that no general alarm is warranted." The IRS has received support from other organized groups—the 87-member Division of Federal Taxation of the American Institute of Certified Public Accountants, the Tax Executives Institute, the American Society of Public Accountants, the National Association of Tax Administrators, and the American Law Institute.

This is not to say that the Internal Revenue Service and

these professional groups have never clashed. The legislative programs of the American Bar Association Tax Section and the Division of Federal Taxation of the American Institute of Certified Accountants are extensive and frequently embrace proposals that run counter to IRS and Treasury positions. For example, the IRS and the organized professions, including the medical profession, carried on a running battle for almost two decades over the question of whether professionals should be able to qualify for corporation status so that the members of a group, who ordinarily operate as a partnership, may be employed by the corporation and thereby enjoy the numerous tax benefits available to employees provided by the revenue laws. To achieve these tax benefits for themselves, the legal, accounting, medical, and other professional groups lobbied long for appropriate federal and state legislation. At the federal level they achieved a measure of success in 1962 when Congress granted certain tax deferral pension benefits to self-employed persons. At the state level, local bar associations spearheaded programs of state law reform that would permit professionals to operate as professional associations and thereby qualify as corporations for federal tax purposes. The IRS countered this state action by amending its regulations to the point where, as a practical matter, a group of professionals could not qualify as a corporation for tax purposes. This, in turn, has been followed during the past several years by a series of refund suits, all won by the taxpayers, which held that the regulations were invalid and that the particular taxpayer group did qualify as a corporation. During the summer of 1969, the IRS gave in and announced that it would no longer contest this issue.

Needless to say, during the course of this battle, IRS policy was subjected to no small amount of harsh comment by tax lawyers and tax accountants. However, these conflicts do not mean that both the agency and tax practitioners do not find it desirable to work in tandem for the development and improvement of tax administration. The Internal Revenue Service has

called upon tax practitioners, its "special public," for aid with
a variety of problems and keeps lines of communication open
in a number of ways. IRS officials are frequently invited to
speak at meetings of organized professional groups. Their
articles are found in the journals of such organizations. Both
speeches and articles attempt to explain IRS policies and problems and the manner in which tax practitioners can aid in
their solution. In recent years, members and committees of the
Tax Section of the American Bar Association have received,
in the words of the chairman of the Tax Section, "assignments"
and requests for aid on such matters as suggested revenue
rulings, the identification of automatic data processing problems, a proposed power of attorney form for client representation, review of tax forms, the revaluation of the policy with
respect to letter ruling, and district conference procedure.

Of even more importance as a means of communicating
effectively with the tax bar is the IRS advisory group system.
At the national level, a Commissioner's Advisory Group of
attorneys, accountants, business executives, economists, and
educators is appointed annually. Its members meet with top
IRS officials four times a year to provide constructive criticism of IRS policies, procedures, and programs. At the
regional and district levels, similar advisory groups meet regularly with regional and district staff members and other IRS
officials for the purpose of thrashing out problems that arise
out of the day-to-day practice of tax law. Discussions at these
meetings in recent years have embraced such problems as the
by-passing of district conferences by practitioners, the consideration of new cases that arise at appellate conferences after
a protest is filed, procedure for reopening cases, and tactics of
revenue agents designed to secure agreement after audit.

Does the IRS benefit from the advice and aid offered by its
tax practitioners? Concrete examples of the utility of these
cooperative efforts are much too numerous to tabulate. A few
examples, however, should serve to indicate their range and
usefulness. Of over-all and primary utility in recent years was

the study by the Committee on Administrative Practice (of the American Bar Association's Tax Section) on the limitations imposed by the Revenue and Expenditure Control Act of 1968 on IRS hiring. After approval by the Association's Board of Governors, a unanimous resolution proposing that the IRS be exempted from such across-the-board limitations was dispatched to appropriate government officials, and discussions were held. At this writing, legislation embodying the essence of the resolution has passed the House of Representatives.

A further example of cooperation between the Internal Revenue Service and its practitioners is to be found in the aftermath of 1962 legislation designed to provide a measure of control over the use of foreign corporations in avoiding income taxes. These rules, some of the most complex rules imaginable, required that the accounting system of a foreign affiliate be correlated with accounting principles used in the United States. Knowledge of foreign accounting systems is not widepread in the United States. In drafting the regulations under the new law, the IRS found the aid it needed in a committee of accountants from the major firms working in the international area.

A final example is worth noting. Although only two officials in the Internal Revenue Service are subject to Presidential appointment—the Commissioner and the chief counsel—both these top offices are invariably filled by lawyers or accountants with a substantial background in tax practice. The present incumbents of these offices have had years of experience in tax practice and as officers in the Tax Section of the American Bar Association. This appointment-making policy ensures that working relationships between the Internal Revenue Service and tax practitioners will remain at the highest cooperative level.

XI

Controversies and Conflicts

According to Saint Matthew, a former tax collector himself, Jesus was criticized by the Pharisees for eating with "tax collectors and sinners." It is perhaps understandable that a Hebrew tax collector in the employ of the occupying Romans would not be likely to rise to a place of high esteem in the eyes of the members of his own community; it is not so easy to understand why a modern tax administration in an advanced twentieth-century democratic society must struggle constantly to maintain a reputation for fair treatment of the taxpaying public. This is clearly the case with the Internal Revenue Service. The preceding chapter revealed in some measure the nature and dimensions of the agency's public relations undertaking; here we will focus on some of the specific controversies and conflicts that have been engendered by its administration of the revenue laws enacted by Congress.

This chapter will treat with conflicts that have substantial public impact and contemporary relevance. It will not deal with controversies that have plagued the IRS in the past—or with such matters as internal corruption, organizational structure, and oversupervision of front-line employees. Nor will it treat those conflicts of internal organization and functioning that constitute the way of life of all large public and private entities, or such conflicts as may be involved in adjusting to the replacement of keypunch machines by direct data entry scanners, or in handling "sensitive cases" in which, in auditing the return of a highly placed political figure, the revenue agent files a special internal report to alert his superiors that such an audit is being conducted.

Finally, although the Internal Revenue Service is not infrequently charged with unfairness because of inequities in the rules enacted by Congress, this chapter will not concern itself with tax policy issues except in so far as they affect the administration of existing laws.

Many controversies and conflicts in the administration of the revenue laws by the IRS have their origins in taxpayer complaints. These complaints may be manifested in a number of ways. Most frequently, a taxpayer's complaint takes the form of a letter to his congressman. While most complaints manifested in this manner do not result in controversy, if these letters reflect a common, recurring theme and are written by influential taxpayers, there may be basis for a conflict—especially if they become the subject of a formal congressional investigation. Controversies may also be generated by the press, when reporters and newsmen who pursue a special interest in governmental agencies fan taxpayer complaints into controversies by forcing public recognition of the issues. Other controversies may be the result of a special interest maintained by particular congressmen in specific facets of tax administration, or conflicts may be generated as a by-product of congressional investigations in other areas. Such conflicts often serve as tests of decent tax administration and may perhaps best be regarded as political phenomena of a democratic society— phenomena not infrequently charged with emotional content and political dogma

Tax Administration Gaps

During the course of the 1970 budget hearings, Commissioner of Internal Revenue Randolph W. Thrower and his deputy, William H. Smith, were asked by Congressman Tom

Steed whether their requests for 1970 would restore the IRS to where it was prior to the imposition of the hiring restrictions imposed by the 1968 Revenue and Expenditure Control Act. The dialogue went like this:

MR. STEED: If your budget is approved as it now stands, and if the hiring restriction is removed, where will you be at the end of 1970 in numbers of average positions more than you now have? What will that increase it to? Will that restore the 3,000 plus average positions you lost this year and add any more? Do we put it this way? You go from a total average position at the end of the year to a total for the end of the following year.

MR. THROWER: We go from the total appropriated for this year of 69,356 to 69,775.

MR. STEED: So essentially the total number of average positions, the increase for 1970 is mainly to recover what you would have had had you not had this restriction in 1969.

MR. SMITH: I think perhaps a way to express it would be like this, Mr. Chairman: The recovery will be virtually complete with respect to revenue accounting and processing and would also allow the additional positions which would be required in that area for growth in the upcoming fiscal year. On the other hand, because of our inability to recruit and assimilate the numbers required in our audit and other enforcement operations in the compliance appropriation, the total provided for compliance will fall short of what the loss has been over the preceding years. In short, as of 1970, this budget will not restore compliance to a level that would make up the losses. In the aggregate the losses will be made up.

Apart from illustrating some of the difficulties currently facing the Service in recovering from the hiring restrictions imposed by Congress in 1968 and 1969 (assuming they are not to be continued), the preceding dialogue contains an implication that Congress wants no more than a certain level of enforcement of the revenue laws. Since this level is rarely, if ever, made articulate, for the most part it must be discovered by IRS managers indirectly, largely on a hunch-and-feel basis, and the annual requests for appropriations for compliance programs constitute only the end product. For example, under its long-range planning in 1961, the IRS contemplated an increase in the over-all audit work load from 4.5 to 10 per cent in 1971. By 1963 it had achieved a level of 5.6 per cent for individual returns, but by 1969 it was estimating that only 2.7 per cent of individual returns could be audited for fiscal 1970. While improved selection methods during this period had the effect of lessening the need for coverage, a sharp increase in the number of more complex individual returns would seem to have had the opposite effect. In brief, the IRS is currently auditing less than one-third of the tax returns it had planned to do a decade ago. Why? The answer would appear to be that sometime during the past ten years IRS managers discovered that Congress did not want 10 per cent of the taxpaying public being subject to audit examinations.

Some of the more telling indicators of this congressional policy are to be found in the reaction of Congress to a number of attempts made by the Internal Revenue Service to close specific tax administration gaps. It will be recalled (Chapter IX) that, when the IRS requested statutory authority to require withholding on dividend and interest income, Congress rejected the request after extensive lobbying against the proposal by financial institutions and corporations. In a similar vein the agency was forced to backtrack on proposed regulations to enforce legislation limiting deductions for travel and entertainment expense when pressure was exerted by a large bloc of congressmen.

However, the general policy that limits total enforcement sometimes rises to haunt Congress when the IRS pursues programs designed to maximize actual appropriations. Late in the 1940's, the first of the IRS taxpayer compliance measurement programs was launched—audit sampling programs designed to determine whether the level of compliance was increasing or decreasing and to develop discriminant-function formulas for use in computer selection of returns for audit examination. (Small corporations were included in the audit sample for the first time in 1969.) But taxpayers soon forget the laudable purpose of such a program, and so do congressmen who receive letters from taxpayers included in the sample. Many taxpayers complain quite bitterly about the intenseness of the examinations carried out in the name of the program. They complain of agents who make repeated demands for substantiation of expenditures extending down to the minutiae of the costs of paper clips and rubber bands. One taxpayer complained that the examination was so thorough that he felt as though the agent was moving in with him. Although these complaints have not as yet provided a basis for a revolt against the program, the Internal Revenue Service has found it necessary time and again to explain the purpose of the taxpayer compliance measurement program, and it is a fair guess that taxpayer reaction in this area fortifies a belief held by many congressmen that enough enforcement is enough.

On the other hand, the existing degree of enforcement is not enough for Senator John J. Williams of Delaware. When spring comes to Washington, so does the Senator to the floor of the Senate to present a report on the inventory of delinquent taxpayers. For fifteen years Senator Williams has scored the IRS on a district by district basis ("Brooklyn, New York: This is another office that needs attention. . . . St. Paul, Minnesota, has a good record. . . . Reno, Nevada: This office has a bad report"), deploring, in general, the rise in total delinquencies over the years and employer trust-account turnover delinquencies in particular.

Senator Williams's watchdogging in this area (the year-end inventory of delinquent employers has ranged in recent years from a high of 400,000 in 1955 to a low of 212,000 in 1965) does not seem to have created much consternation in Congress or in the IRS, and for the past two fiscal years the agency has had a ready answer: The 1968 Revenue and Expenditure Control Act, according to Deputy Commissioner Smith, resulted in 755 fewer man-years in fiscal 1968 for collection work than the number of man-years approved by the House Appropriations Committee.

Broadly speaking, the IRS collection policy on delinquent accounts is designed to maximize the ultimate yield. This necessarily means that the agency is frequently forced to allow additional time for the tax debtor to pay past obligations. The execution of this policy is not without some risk that the IRS will be charged with granting special concessions. A 1967 *Reader's Digest* article suggested that the Internal Revenue Service was pursuing a double standard when it settled a $40,000 unpaid tax debt of a union official who had contributed to the Democratic Party "for a token $17,000 plus an agreement that he would pay more if his income rose." However, the article did not mention that the full amount had already been paid off in two additional installments by October, 1966.

Documentation of this type cannot be regarded as evidence of political corruption, and there is no indication that Congress regards the IRS as having subverted its collection policies and practices to political pressure. One tax administration gap, has provided more than a little embarrassment for the agency, especially during the past decade. This is the problem of the allocation of auditing manpower to the examination of the returns of the growing number (some 20,000 annually) of tax-exempt organizations.

An understanding of the conflicts in the tax-exempt organization area requires some knowledge of the revenue laws granting tax exemption. The Internal Revenue Code exempts from taxation nineteen types of nonprofit organizations that would otherwise be subject to taxation as corporations on their net income. Certain of these entities, including so-called charitable organizations, qualify for charitable contribution deductions.

The conflicts in this area during the past decade have been generated in large measure by a House Subcommittee on

Small Business headed by Congressman Wright Patman of Texas. Starting in 1962, this committee conducted extensive investigations into the activities of tax-exempt organizations in general and privately controlled charitable foundations in particular. At the conclusion of the first round of hearings in 1964, there was evidence that the IRS had not been allocating sufficient manpower to auditing in this area. Overshadowing this gap in administration, were alleged abuses of private foundations for which the Internal Revenue Service frequently received an unfavorable press, but many of which were quite unrelated to tax administration, such as the growing power of charitable foundations in the economic sector.

On the other hand, the Patman investigations did have two major effects. The first was a study by the Department of the Treasury that resulted in a detailed report in 1965 on private foundations (20,000–25,000 out of a total of some 1.5 million tax-exempt organizations of all types). This report included recommendations for legislation to control six areas of abuse: self-dealing between the founder and his foundation, delay in benefits reaching charitable objectives, involvement in business, family use of foundations to control corporations and property, financial transactions unrelated to charitable functions, and narrowness of foundation management. Four years later, most of these recommendations found their way into the Tax Reform Act of 1969.

The second major effect of the Patman committee investigations has been a revitalized effort on the part of the IRS to increase its surveillance in this area. Thus, as part of its 1965 report, the Treasury related that the Internal Revenue Service had increased its annual audit coverage of tax-exempt organization returns from 2,000 in the 1950's to 10,000 in 1964. This was accompanied by an increase in the amount of information about foundation behavior, some of which was acquired through revised information returns. At the same time the agency had improved its internal controls and established a tax-exempt organization master file. Efforts in the litigation area had also been increased (not without some set-backs), as had IRS efforts to improve voluntary compliance.

In 1967, a fresh development rocked the boat. Widespread publicity in the press and in additional hearings conducted by the Patman committee disclosed that a Barrington, Illinois, organization, Americans Building Constitutionally (ABC), had been formed to instruct businessmen and professionals (for fees up to $10,500) how to operate their businesses (and their homes in some instances) as tax-free foundations. Many congressmen apparently feared that the foundations formed pursuant to an ABC plan were getting away with something —that a foundation founder could report only a small salary income as an employee of his own foundation and leave large balances free from tax. By 1968, Commissioner Cohen was able to report that most audited ABC-generated foundations had given in to the IRS contention that they were not genuine charities and that others were under investigation or in litigation.

By 1969, additional steps had been taken to augment the national control of tax-exempt organizations, maintained through a 100-man branch unit in the office of the assistant commissioner (Technical); here certain types of requests for rulings for exempt status are forwarded from district offices that would otherwise issue determination letters on such requests. The new steps consisted of the establishment of an Exempt Organization Branch in the national office Audit Division, the formation of an internal coordinating committee of top IRS officers, and the appointment of a special outside committee for advice in developing administrative specialists in the area. Finally, in mid-1969, the IRS announced that all tax-exempt organization information returns were to be filed with a single service center (Philadelphia) for processing by a specially trained staff.

Occasionally, the IRS has found itself in hot water when it has proceeded against a charitable organization whose contributors are entitled to deductions. This was the case when the agency moved against the powerful San Francisco-based 20-chapter, 38,000-member Sierra Club, an organization devoted to the conservation of the nation's natural resources. The case had its origins in the legislative activities of the club, because the revenue law allows deductions for contributions to a charitable organization only if "no substantial part of the activities . . . is carrying on propaganda, or otherwise attempting to influence legislation."

As early as 1931, the IRS had ruled that the Sierra Club qualified for exempt status; contributions to it qualified for deductions, and its name was listed as a qualifying organization in IRS Publication 78, a constantly revised document available to contributors. However, on June 13, 1966, the Internal Revenue Service issued a press release designed as a warning to Sierra Club contributors, indicating that the club had been notified and that the IRS was "no longer prepared to extend advance assurance of deductibility of contributions to the Club." (Four days previous to this release, the club had taken full-page ads in Washington and New York papers, urging readers to protest a proposed bill in Congress that would authorize the building of hydroelectric dams on the Colorado river and assuring contributors that contributions would be deductible.) This advance warning, for which the IRS was criticized, was contrary to its usual procedure of disallowing deductions only after the qualified status of an organization had been actually revoked and an announcement made. The procedure taken was justified by what the IRS regarded as the blatantly disqualifying legislative activity evidenced by the newspaper ads, coupled with the club's assurances that contributions were deductible.

Six months later, after an in-depth audit of the Sierra Club, the IRS revoked the club's status as a charitable organization, but leaving it a tax-exempt social welfare organization. This would leave it free to engage in legislative activity, but contributions would not be deductible. In the meanwhile, the Internal Revenue Service faced a sometimes hostile press, which forced it to explain to Congress and the public that the legislative-activity limitation was not an administrative innovation but a legislative mandate going back to 1934 and that the soundness of an organization's legislative program or the public welfare nature of its objectives were quite irrelevant.

Some final conflicts generated by tax administration gaps are worth special mention. These are the conflicts that arise out of the relationship that exists between Congress's own General Accounting Office and the IRS. In the exercise of its surveillance function, the General Accounting Office may single out a particular area or income item for study. For example, the Comptroller General of the General Accounting Office, on the basis of data revealed in the 1970 appropriation hearings, complained to Congress of his inability to secure information from the Internal Revenue Service, apparently contending that the IRS should have allocated enforcement resources differently with respect to underreporting of state tax refunds. The IRS replied that the law not only forbids the General Accounting Office access to tax returns but that the allocation of enforcement resources is an IRS function, not subject to General Accounting Office review. As of this writing, the conflict remains unresolved.

OVERENFORCEMENT

Early in 1968, Vincent L. Connery, president of the 25,000-member National Association of Internal Revenue Employees, the IRS employees' union, testified before the Senate Subcommittee on Administrative Practice and Procedure. Part of what he had to say was this:

Aside from outside pressures, however, it is our considered judgment that certain IRS management policies and procedures tend to generate and foster a climate in which offensive practices may well take root and flourish. We have in mind specifically management's emphasis on quotas and production goals. The pressure begins in Washington, is transmitted to the Districts through the Regional pipelines, and is vented on the working Agent and Revenue Officer. Under such a system, quality of performance is a casualty, and in too many cases the taxpayer may be a victim of an over-zealous Agent or Officer frantically trying to meet his quantitative goals or quotas imposed on him from higher up in the IRS management structure. When talking to IRS employees, and even management officials, we frequently find them using the term "statistical rat-race" to describe the set-up.

In point of fact, your continued vigilance is the key to the prevention of fresh tyranny or impropriety by Federal investigative organizations—at least until very sophisticated legislation is put on the books, and maybe not even then. The reasons for this are (1) the incredible advance in the technology of surveillance, coupled with a lag in judicial development of law; and (2) the constant temptation of investigators to take short cuts to get results, to make a case.

Charges that the Revenue Service maintains a quota system for measuring the productive efforts of its front-line professionals—revenue agents, revenue officers, and special agents —have been leveled against IRS managers periodically, ever since modern tax administration eliminated the practice of farming out the collection of tax revenue on a percentage basis. Periodically, events occur that bring this problem into the public spotlight. During the past decade there have been at least two such events: the investigations of the Long committee on the invasion of privacy, and a 1967–69 series of three articles in the *Reader's Digest*, which generated additional press comment, wherein the IRS was charged with (among other thing) the maintenance of a production quota system for agents.

Since it is generally accepted that an individual production quota system in tax administration is an unmitigated evil that can lead to enforcement abuses, IRS managers have frequently been faced with the need to explain their policies and practices in this area. Since the early 1960's at least, they have categorically denied the existence of an individual quota system, contending that the performance of their agents is based on an over-all evaluation of their work. However, IRS managers can hardly deny their own statistical reporting to Congress and the public; they do acknowledge that production records —and perhaps, by implication, quotas—are maintained on a nationwide, regional, and district basis, and that on each audit examination a control record is maintained that includes the amount of any deficiency or overassessment. This system they regard as consistent with, if not required by, the accounting they must make to Congress. To put it another way: basically, Congress (and the public) expect a certain level of measurable production from Internal Revenue Service in general and from each IRS employee in particular.

What is frequently overlooked in the many comments on this conflict is the deep-seated competitive spirit in American society, a spirit that can be traced back to the founding fathers and beyond. Former Commissioner Sheldon S. Cohen referred to this competitive spirit in this way:

> Our revenue agents and our other employees are human beings, and even if we don't impose a quota on them and we do not— we carefully do not—sometimes they get the competitive notion that if Joe down the hall has closed ten cases this month, and I only closed eight, I'd better get on the ball and try to meet Joe's capacity.

On the other hand, even if the intenseness of the competitive factor serves as an explanation, it hardly constitutes a solution to the conflicts that may arise in the wake of a system that is one step removed from an individual quota system. Here, the vital question is not whether a quota system may lead to such undesirable results as taxpayer harassment and deterioration of professional development of IRS employees, but whether the policies maintained are sufficient protection to individual taxpayers and at the same time consistent with the maintenance of the present tax system's reliance upon voluntary compliance. In the final analysis, the balancing of these competing interests must be made by Congress and the public, rather than by the Internal Revenue Service. Only to the extent that the IRS fails to provide Congress with the information Congress needs for its lawmaking function, or to the extent the IRS performs its administrative tasks outside the guidelines established by Congress can the agency be regarded as at fault. And these guidelines do include statistical reporting.

In making value judgments in this area, Congress has undoubtedly relied in substantial measure on the rights available to a taxpayer under the Constitution and the judicial machinery available to enforce them. Thus, although it has granted substantial enforcement powers to Internal Revenue Service agents, it does not follow that Congress has been unmindful of American society's deep-seated fear of the abuse of governmental power, a fear going back to the struggle of the early colonists with the British Crown, which was manifested in the first ten amendments to the Constitution (the Bill of Rights). These constitutional guarantees notwithstanding —and some considerable judicial expansion of them during the past two decades—some students of the tax administrative process view the statutory powers granted IRS agents as too broad. Their proposals for reform range widely and include the extension of the privilege against self-incrimination with respect to taxpayers' books and records; the establishment of jurisdictional prerequisites or more limiting procedural devices for a summons, a subpoena, and the conduct of investigations; and the establishment of an office of ombudsman, a prestigious citizen with powers to investigate and act on citizen complaints against the Internal Revenue Service.

To date there is no indication that Congress believes there is a present need for such legislation and no indication that the present devices—the congressional standing and investigating committees, and the pressure that can be exerted by individual congressmen, professional organizations, and the popular media—are regarded as inadequate to control administrative abuse and to protect the security of the individual —and at the same time to leave a sufficient measure of flexibility to protect society's interest in uniform tax administration.

The conflicts pertaining to overenforcement by the Internal Revenue Service have centered on revenue agents, revenue officers, and special agents. In one of its sixteen case studies (which the IRS branded as mostly misleading half-truths) the *Reader's Digest* contended that an unidentified revenue agent had threatened a traffic officer with a tax investigation when the latter refused to stop writing a ticket for speeding. (The IRS replied that it had been unable to identify the agent, but the officer's return had been selected for office audit by normal procedures, and the audit had resulted in no change.) Other revenue agents from time to time have been accused of threatening individual taxpayers with fraud examinations and corporations with imposition of the penalty tax on unreasonable accumulations of income as a means of securing agreement to a deficiency after a normal audit. (The IRS reply: these agents should be reported, and disciplinary action will be taken if warranted.)

Revenue officers have been subject to an equal if not larger number of complaints of intimidation and harassment in the exercise of their extensive statutory collection powers, which include the right of seizure of property and garnishment of wages. Perhaps the most extensive list in recent years was compiled in two articles by the *Reader's Digest*. In one case, it was charged that the Internal Revenue Service had threatened to seize the car of a waitress for a $275 claimed tax deficiency, which had been assessed when the taxpayer and her husband failed to substantiate claimed deductions for dependents. The IRS answered this charge before the House Appropriations Committee with a long story of the taxpayer's failure to show up for repeated appointments; it stated that a collected deficiency was later refunded when all the facts were available. A second case concerned seizure of a bank account without notice. The IRS contended that notice had been given, but admitted that the seizure was in error.

These cases and others like them cannot be retried here; they were, however, exposed to House committee scrutiny. Congressman Silvio Conte felt that the Internal Revenue Service had offered good explanations for all sixteen cases, except the one in which an agent (apparently a special agent) was accused of opening a letter linking the taxpayer to another woman and showing the letter to the taxpayer's wife in an effort to get her to inform against her husband (the agent, a 12-year employee with an otherwise good record, was subjected to an official reprimand). Congressman Otto Passman was even more satisfied. He stated that during his twenty-one years in Congress he had been confronted with many disgruntled taxpayers. He had referred all these cases back to the IRS and had "never known of an instance where a taxpayer has actually been mistreated."

Special agents, because of the nature of their work and the length and depth of a fraud investigation, come in for an unusually large number of complaints. Perhaps a third of the sixteen listed cases in the August, 1967, *Reader's Digest* article involved fraud investigations. The article also drew upon the Long committee hearings, which had disclosed that during the early 1960's IRS special agents had utilized electronic devices in investigating organized crime cases.

It seems clear that any dispassionate analysis of public records pertaining to the conduct of special agents during the past decade would require that separate consideration be given to organized crime cases and to what appears to have been no small amount of vacillating policy-making on the part of both Congress and the Department of Justice, which has provided the leadership for the drive on organized crime since the 1950's. As a starting point for an analysis of these cases, consider the statement made before the Long committee in 1968 by Vincent L. Connery, president of the National Association of Internal Revenue Employees:

> We are well aware of the fact that your Committee has reviewed a number of cases in which IRS employees, while acting as agents of the IRS and the U.S. Government, were accused of disregarding the rights of taxpayers and their representatives. Considering the total number of taxpayer contacts made by IRS employees during the course of a year, such cases, fortunately, represent a very small minority. Equally significant, however, is the fact that the controversial techniques used were ordered, authorized, tolerated, sanctioned, or condoned by responsible IRS management officials. To be perfectly frank, I must say the scuttlebutt in IRS circles is that many of these incidents occurred as a result of pressures from the Justice Department.

A number of events prior to this testimony need to be related in order to put these pre-1965 investigations into perspective. In July, 1965, President Lyndon B. Johnson issued an order to all federal enforcement agencies prohibiting the use of electronic devices except in internal security matters, an order which the Commissioner carried through in the IRS. In 1966 the Supreme Court, affirming a prior position taken in 1963 in the Lopez case (see Chapter IV) sanctioned the use of recording devices where the consent of one party to a conversation is obtained. On July 6, 1967, the Attorney General issued guidelines for federal agents in their use of recording devices; a week later the Commissioner issued a news release and a report to the Long committee on the findings of a special inquiry board, covering the 1958–66 period. The report revealed 910 instances (including 723 uses of pen registers, which record dialed phone numbers only) of the use of electronic devices, both legal and questionable, by all three IRS investigative units. All cases involved investigations of criminal or illegal activities with no overlapping of ordinary audit examinations.

This was not the end by any means. In 1968, in reaction to large-scale public disorders and limited progress in the drive against organized crime, Congress passed the Omnibus Crime Control and Safe Streets Act, which authorizes electronic surveillance in certain instances under judicial safeguards. Evidence secured under such procedures is admissible, but only if such procedures are followed strictly. In addition, penal sanctions are provided for the unauthorized use of electronic devices, but not for public enforcement officers. Finally, the new Administration in 1969 included an increased budget for crime fighting for the new Attorney General, who has indicated that use will be made of the new wire tapping legislation. Where does this leave the Internal Revenue Service now? Commissioner Thrower has provided this answer: The Attorney General will make the determination when wire tapping is to be used in organized crime cases. Thus the pendulum swings on vital issues in a democratic society.

If the preceding recital permits the electronic surveillance conflict to be laid to rest for the time being, it hardly provides an answer to charges of other types of mistreatment of taxpayers which have been attributed to special agents. The first *Reader's Digest* article, for example, recited a number of instances where the author contended that certain taxpayers had been subjected to abuse. The third article, January, 1969 ("The Tragic Case of John J. Hafer") was a case study of a long and involved investigation of a taxpayer operating a dozen or more businesses, for which he had not kept separate records. Furthermore, he had mixed both business and personal transactions. Although the taxpayer was subsequently fully exonerated from both tax liability and criminal charges of assaulting a federal officer (a matter hardly conclusive on the subject of harassment), his returns had been selected for audit because of a large disparity between annual gross receipts of some $250,000 and less than $1,500 of taxable income. He had also claimed his privilege against self-incrimination, refusing to open his books for one of the tax years involved when the special agent appeared on the scene.

The facts of the Hafer case as presented by the *Reader's Digest* and the Commissioner's explanation of the case in the hearings on the 1970 budget illustrate the impossibility of evaluating such a controversy, but these recitals, as well as the testimony of the taxpayer and the special agent during the Long committee hearings, do indicate some apparent misunderstanding regarding the task facing the special agent who is seeking to determine whether a crime has in fact been committed. When a taxpayer asserts his privileges, it is standard procedure for the agent to make third party inquiries—banks, suppliers, customers—as the only practical means available to verify the taxpayer's own reporting. This is indeed a delicate matter, and it is perhaps easy for the taxpayer under investigation to arrive at the conclusion, during the course of what may be a long and involved process, that he has been singled out for special mistreatment.

The courts at times have been highly critical of the conduct and motives of special agents. The Ninth Circuit Court of Appeals in a 1967 case involving a two-and-one-half-year networth investigation of a taxpayer-attorney was highly incensed over the agent's report, which indicated to the Court that the agent was engaged in a "witchhunt" because of the taxpayer's leftist "thinking on the subject of Cuba, Laos, China." More recently a District Court, in suppressing certain evidence introduced by the government, characterized the transfer of an audit examination to a new revenue agent and a special agent —who identified himself but failed to explain his function— and the subsequent securing of additional information as a "deliberate scheme to deceive" the taxpayer and keep him from realizing he was under a criminal investigation.

Although the judicial process, as well as the extensive review of a special agent's recommendation of prosecution, may provide some measure of taxpayer protection from abuse in fraud investigations, the Internal Revenue Service does not rely on these protective devices only, by any means. It does believe, however, that its policies and practices with respect to control of all its front-line agents provide the most effective means of arriving at a decent balance between the individual interest in security and the social need for uniformity in tax burden to the extent possible under existing laws. It contends that a vigorous pursuance of its inspection mission, coupled with selective recruitment programs and followed by continuous inservice training has led it toward the development of a corps of front-line professionals who will, and do, temper their actions in their dealing with the American taxpayer. This task, like the need for continuous congressional and public overview, is never-ending. Pressure on the Internal Revenue Service from the outside need not cause a loss of integrity; democratic institutions require this pressure so they may change for the better.

UNIFORMITY AND CERTAINTY

Although Congress has been creating administrative agencies since 1789, and at an ever increasing pace as American society has grown more complex, many lawyers apparently still have difficulty accommodating themselves to the public need for the agencies and their processes. Kenneth Davis has suggested: "If attitudes of lawyers toward the administrative process were charted on a graph, with enthusiastic approval on the left side and complete condemnation on the right, the bunching near the center would be pronounced, but the peak would probably be well to the right of center." While a comparable graph of tax practitioner attitudes toward the Internal Revenue Service probably would find a bunching to the left of center, there is no doubt that there is more than a remnant of the traditional lawyer hostility toward administrative agencies still present even in this group of specialists. As indicated in the preceding chapter, the tax practitioner has assumed the role of critic toward tax administration; however, not all of this criticism is provided in a spirit of constructive aid. Frequently the bitterness is but thinly disguised, as when the IRS is charged with misconduct, such as the usurping of legislative powers and the making of overrefined interpretations.

Much of the controversy in this area may be analyzed in terms of the sometimes conflicting desiderata of uniformity and certainty in tax administration, objectives that both the IRS and the tax practitioner agree upon, but which often generate conflict when the agency has exercised its rule-making power. For example, in 1940 the Supreme Court held in the case of *Helvering* v. *Clifford* that, where a grantor transferred property to a five-year trust for his family, naming himself trustee with broad administrative powers, the grantor, rather than the trust, was taxable on the trust income during the 5-year period; the Court reasoned that the combination of a short term (he would get the trust property back after five years), the retention of extensive administrative powers, and the family beneficiaries left the grantor with substantial ownership of the trust property, despite the fact that legal title was in the trust. After this decision, short-term trusts, then as now a favorite device for reducing taxes on family income, were brought into review in over one hundred cases at the Court of Appeals level alone; the tripodal foundation of the Clifford decision made it extremely difficult to develop a satisfactory body of case law. In 1946, in an effort to provide a measure of certainty, the IRS issued its complex Clifford Regulations, which articulated in considerable detail the terms under which the grantor of a trust would be regarded as the owner of the trust property and would therefore be taxable on its income. These regulations (which in 1954 formed the basis for new statutory rules) attributed trust income under prescribed circumstances to the grantor in any one of three alternative situations. This, charged one prominent practitioner, constituted an invalid exercise of congressional power, setting off an extended debate in the law journals.

This charge of administrative lawmaking has been frequent and has taken many forms. The Internal Revenue Service has been accused at times of ruling on particular issues after requests for corrective legislation on the subject have been rejected by Congress. One congressman has charged the IRS in sweeping terms with taking "a comparatively simple bill" and writing "a myriad of regulations around it." He sees in this "one way in which the executive branch has gradually eroded the law-making power of Congress." Another practitioner would have Congress write the revenue laws so that regulations and rule-making by the IRS would be unnecessary.

On the other hand, Congress itself has delegated rule-making power to the Internal Revenue Service, and, while many practitioners remain distrustful of the agency in its exercise of this power, most of them, at least recognize the need for an IRS rule-making power. They appreciate the fact that neither Congress nor the courts can respond with needed interpretative solutions quickly, and that IRS experts are the ones most qualified to provide the needed technical rules for a complex and dynamic economy. Some too would agree with the late Randolph Paul that, with extended administrative rule-making power, "Congress would be free to devote much more of its precious time and energy to fundamental problems of tax policy."

However, if most tax practitioners accept the need for IRS rule-making power, many have been highly critical of the agency for abusing its power in refusing to rule in certain instances, for failure to make private letter rulings public, and for delays in ruling and in providing the guidelines needed to enable taxpayers to plan their business affairs with reasonable assurances of the tax consequences. Delays in ruling are likely to be particularly burdensome when Congress has enacted new complex legislation with a broad impact, and when the IRS is contemplating—or in the process of making—a change in enforcement policy. One practitioner has suggested that Congress should provide a time limit on the production of regulations. Another complained that enforcement by the IRS Office of International Operations (OIO) of Section 482 of the Code (permitting reallocation of income and deduction items between related entities) in the foreign area was being conducted without adequate regulations and that "both the OIO agents in the field and we in accounting need guidelines desperately."

These conflicts involving delay can hardly be analyzed out of the context of particular statutory rules. Where the legislation is complex or has a broad impact, delay may be inevitable. As former Commissioner Mortimer Caplin observed:

> Everyone is interested in the issuance of regulations as rapidly as possible. At the same time everyone wants good regulations, and often he wants to be heard before final action is taken. This usually involves informal meetings with professional or business groups, publication of proposed regulations, submission of written comments, formal hearings, analysis and investigation of testimony and written materials. On some occasions, there might even be intervening Congressional hearings on the proposed regulations. Then final regulations must await Treasury Department approval.

Interpretative rule-making is bound to invite criticism when the guidelines for it are limited, as they are, to basic notions of fairness and speculation as to whether a court would view particular interpretations as going beyond a fair view of the applicable statute. The bulk of tax practitioner criticism in the tax administrative process probably centers on positions taken by the IRS on issues that are adverse to taxpayers with whom practitioners harbor an innate empathy. Only rarely is the Internal Revenue Service criticized for not going far enough and in such cases the criticism will ordinarily come from the academic world or from Congress. In either event, these conflicts only infrequently become public; normally they remain buried in law or accounting journals.

An exception is worth noting. In 1961, General Electric, Westinghouse, and twenty-seven other companies (and forty-five corporate officers) pleaded guilty or no contest to anti-trust price-fixing charges, which resulted in the payment of some $400 million in treble damages to their customers. In 1965, as these payments were being made, the IRS ruled for the first time publicly that such payments constituted deductible business expense and did not fall within the court-made rule that denies deductions for such payments as fines and penalties (three years earlier the IRS had taken a contrary position internally). The agency subsequently argued that it felt reasonably certain that the Supreme Court would not regard such payments to private persons as penal in nature. Therefore, evenhanded administration, said Commissioner Caplin, required their allowance.

This ruling, made one year after a conference with the taxpayers and after considerable internal study and discussion, resulted in a tax benefit of some $200 million; to a number of congressmen it was a "giveaway" and called for an investigation. The ensuing hearing (the ruling was reversed by statute in 1969) resulted in considerable probing for evidence of political influence. Also of importance was the testimony of two university tax law professors on the role of the Internal Revenue Service in ruling on these borderline cases. Professor L. Hart Wright suggested that the Commissioner was faced with a choice of either assuming his usual role of an advocate who should litigate an important matter even if he believes the odds are against him or of taking the position of a judge—the one chosen—and ruling against deductibility only if he believed the odds favored the government.

It is this usual posture of an advocate that has frequently subjected the IRS to criticism with respect to its litigation policy, especially when it has persisted in maintaining a position on an issue in the face of a number of adverse decisions in the appellate courts. Although the IRS does follow a broad general policy, as stated by one former chief counsel, "to conform our position after two adverse circuit court decisions," this policy will not be followed as an inflexible rule if, as still another chief counsel observed, it interferes with the agency's "public responsibility for the equitable and reasonable interpretation and development of the law." As we have seen in Chapter X, the making of litigation policy is a complex matter, which requires that such policy not only conform to ruling policy but that it be formulated in cooperation with the Justice Department's Tax Section and that consideration be given to the two-way effect of particular court decisions. In short, the IRS argues that, in the making of litigation policy, certainty must be tempered with flexibility in the interests of uniformity. In any event, broadsides aimed at IRS litigation policy cannot be taken seriously under the present federal judicial structure, which permits eleven different Courts of Appeal to arrive at different legal positions on the same issue. Short of reform in the judicial appellate structure (which has been proposed), IRS litigation policy may be legitimately subjected to criticism only in the context of specific cases where the competing considerations of national uniformity and certainty are taken fully into consideration.

Specific cases may indeed be another matter. Most tax practitioners could probably cite instances that they regard as unfair because the taxpayers have been the victims of long and costly litigation. One practitioner has gone so far as to suggest that "where the IRS appeals from an adverse decision of the courts and loses on appeal, the taxpayer should have compensatory relief." Another has suggested:

> There should be a joint Congressional Committee to review court cases decided in favor of taxpayers, to determine, in each case, whether the Government was *reasonably* justified in putting the taxpayer to the expense (visible and invisible) of defending his position. Where injustice is found, someone should

be called upon to explain, and steps taken to avoid similar actions in the future.

Apart from litigation policy, taxpayers and tax practitioners have also complained of a wide variety of compliance costs. Some of these complaints have been attributed to the position assumed by the IRS as an advocate, which, it has been contended, prevents "evenhanded treatment" and results in narrow "legalistic, hairsplitting" approaches that force taxpayers to fight hard for their rights. These general complaints are sometimes articulated in detail. The ink was hardly dry on the 1968 Gun Control Act regulations when congressmen began to receive complaints that the Internal Revenue Service was not only requiring that ammunition purchased include the purchaser's name but also a detailed description of the ammunition. The answer to these charges of technicality and resultant compliance burden (many by small-town merchants) is that the law as enacted by Congress requires that this information be kept by the seller.

In fact, many if not most charges of compliance burdens may be more fairly attributed to Congress than to the IRS and in some instances may have their source in taxpayer abuses. This, it is arguable, was basically the case with respect to the furor caused by the highly technical proposed regulations governing the statutory rules enacted in 1962 setting limits on, and requiring substantiation of, deductions for travel and entertainment expenses. The statutory rules, it will be recalled, were a product of demonstrated abuses of claimed deductions for costs of maintaining yachts and hunting and fishing camps, costs of club dues, business gifts, and the like. One tax practitioner has referred to this causal relationship as the "Beget Rule," observing that "one technical rule to correct a so-called abuse begets another technical rule to ensure that the first rule is not abused."

The preceding recital hardly exhausts the many conflicts

that arise out of the Internal Revenue Service's effort to carry out its mission in a uniform manner and at the same time provide needed certainty for taxpayers in the conduct of their business and family affairs. These conflicts may appear at times to expose minor irritants only, but their critical nature in tax administration cannot be stressed too strongly. Their exposure provides an important means by which adjustments can be made to accommodate both uniformity and certainty in tax administration in a democratic order; and there is no evidence that both the tasks of exposure and of adjustment are not being carried out adequately.

XII

The Future of the
Internal Revenue Service:
Career Opportunities

The history of the Internal Revenue Service mirrors the history of the nation and the events and philosophies that have molded its political, economic, and social institutions. This undoubtedly will continue to be the case in the future. Today's events, including the almost revolutionary resistance to traditional values by a large segment of the young, will undoubtedly affect the Internal Revenue Service of tomorrow. While the nature of the changes resulting from today's unrest can hardly be predicted, the apparent frustrations of many of our youth would seem to lend even more meaning to Carlyle's words: "Blessed is he who has found his work; let him ask no other blessedness."

While unpredictable events may well provide the major impetus for change in the IRS in the years ahead, there are discernible trends today that throw some light on the future of the agency and on what may lie in store for the career-minded who seek their "blessedness" in tax administration. These trends are the major concerns of this final chapter.

Career opportunities in taxation, of course, are not limited to tax administration. Many of the nation's 450,000 accountants and 300,000 lawyers engage in tax work. For most lawyers and for many accountants, the federal income tax is a major factor in many of the transactions that cross their desks daily. The formation, operation, and termination of all forms of business enterprise require a consideration of the tax consequences. The family trust, the family business, even the termination of the marital relationship by divorce or death, all bring into play same of the most complex rules of the revenue laws. The proper drafting of leases, contracts, and wills requires knowledge of the applicable income tax rules. The securities owner contemplating a shift in his investments must consider the costs in terms of the capital gains tax; likewise the buyer and seller of a business must bargain in terms of tax costs. In short, no lawyer or accountant can remain ignorant of federal income taxation and still serve his clients and the public effectively.

Fortunately, the career-minded may pursue the same formal training for meaningful service in both tax administration and private tax practice; movement between these public and private sectors is possible. For the most part, this training will be through a business school or a law school, with the greater number finding entry into the Internal Revenue Service through a business school accounting program. However, unlike the IRS entrant of the past, the business and law school graduate of the future will undoubtedly have more extended opportunities for pre-entry intern and clinical training, as well as greater exposure to more meaningful courses in high school, college, and law school, designed to acquaint him with career alternatives.

As described in Chapter IV, the present-day recruitment program of the IRS is directed nationally by the Personnel Division in Washington, although actual recruitment and hiring is decentralized. Each regional office, service center, and district office has a personnel officer, and authority to hire has been delegated. Most career recruits are hired by the district offices, whose personnel participate in the regional coordinated college recruitment programs. The district offices (and their local offices), along with college placement offices, thus constitute the principal source of information for employment opportunities. However, a number of national office units—such as the chief counsel, assistant commissioner (Technical), and the Office of International Operations—do their own recruiting. Information concerning employment in these units may be secured either locally or directly from the applicable national office unit or from the national office Personnel Division.

At present, apart from grade GS-3 and GS-4 clerical positions, the majority of career recruits are hired at grades GS-5, GS-7, GS-9, and GS-11. In-grade increases in salary and promotions come rapidly. In 1962 Congress adopted a policy of keeping federal salaries comparable with those in private industry and, in general, has been responsive to inflationary pressures in legislating salary increases.

ELECTRONIC DATA PROCESSING AND BEYOND

> There are over 60,000 computers revolutionizing data processing in the U.S. today. In an average year's operation, they'll spew out a stack of paper thousands of miles high. At a cost of billions of dollars. For the paper, for the handling and for the time.

Thus runs the advertisement of a computer manufacturer, pointing up the advantages of a microfilm printer, which, if hitched to a computer, will print a computer's output ten times faster than impact printing. It will print "onto microfilm at speeds up to 120,000 characters a second, 115,000 pages per eight-hour day. Our desk-top inquiry stations then can retrieve and display selected information at the push of a button."

This advertisement not only symbolizes the effect of the communications revolution on the Internal Revenue Service but seems to predict that this agency, along with the rest of the world, is only in the threshold of a second Industrial

Revolution. The principal impact of computer technology on the IRS today has been in return-processing and revenue-accounting, with an almost complete shifting of the processing of returns from district collection divisions—where only remnants remain—to regional service centers.

For the most part, this transformation was accomplished through a phase-in process that resulted in a minimum of human frustrations and dislocations. Even more important, perhaps, it opened the door to new career opportunities both in the national office and in the field. For example, college graduates with majors in economics, mathematics, statistics, or business administration (recruited by national office's Personnel Division) are now able to participate in the development of financial and economic programs, based on computer output, that were hardly possible a decade or so ago—programs that give a new dimension and meaning to such positions as statistician, mathematical statistician, and economist. The new computer technology has also opened up a whole new career area in data processing itself. Thus, for computer work at the service centers and the national office, the IRS has conducted extensive recruiting for trainees for the positions of digital computer assistant, digital computer systems operator, programer, systems analyst, and scheduling and control officer—positions that lead, through data processing management training programs, to middle and top management positions.

Today one-third of the IRS work force is engaged in data processing—at the regional centers, the National Computer Center, the service centers, and at the national office in Washington. This work force is engaged primarily in these functions: return-processing (including routine correspondence with taxpayers), revenue-accounting, refund-processing, providing hardware for statistical studies, making initial selection of returns for audit, and providing data in support of the Collection Division's delinquent accounts and returns programs. Data processing tomorrow may be quite different.

As we have seen in Chapter III, tax return–processing it-self has recently witnessed a major technological change that saw keypunch operations eliminated by the Direct Data Entry System (DDES), as well as experimental use of tax returns filed by taxpayers on tape compatible with the agency's com-puters. The preparation of tax return forms on computer tape by outside firms is a growing industry, and more extensive use of returns on compatible tape can be anticipated in the dec-ades ahead. A long look ahead may even see relief for the taxpayer who prepares his own return. Thus, the individual wage earner of the future may find that he will be able to discharge his return-filing obligation by filling out an IRS-designed questionnaire for machine computation of his liabil-ity, and end result will be the printout of a refund check or a bill for the balance.

It is at least clear that the future will see improvement in direct communications between taxpayers and the regional computer center system, which will result in prompter process-ing of returns and refunds as well as an expansion of the federal tax deposit system by businesses, which will speed up the availability of tax money to the government and eliminate the flow of millions of checks and remittances through the service centers.

Of overriding importance for the decades ahead will be the increased utilization of the computer in compliance programs and in management control and planning systems. The Inter-nal Revenue Service appears to be only on the threshold of significant changes in these areas.

COMPLIANCE

Today two-thirds of the IRS work force—the heart of the agency—are in the compliance divisions under the assistant commissioner (Compliance). This is likely to hold true for the immediate future, but changes are clearly in the offing for revenue agents, revenue officers, special agents, lawyers, and others in the compliance categories.

Important as any change on the horizon is the possibility of increased service to taxpayers (and IRS personnel) through expansion of the service-center-based Integrated Data Retrieval System (IDRS), now under development. Utilized primarily by the Collection Division today in the Southwest Region, the system is designed to retrieve information from the thousands of documents (notices, payments, adjustments) affecting taxpayers' annual accounts—information that otherwise must be retrieved manually. The system consists of television-type screens at the regional service center and typewriter keyboards tied to a computer. The computer is fed tape with information on the various documents. The keyboard is used to request the information, which is displayed on the screen. Display-inquiry stations are also located at district offices and major area offices in the region.

From this system, it is but a short, though perhaps expensive, step to the establishment of remote terminals or consoles in district and local offices and the retrieval of the desired information on a nationwide basis. Thus, a taxpayer making inquiry of a local taxpayer service representative, a revenue officer seeking the status of an account, or a revenue agent wanting a facsimile of a tax return or other document would have almost instant response from a regional or national computer.

The auditing function of the Internal Revenue Service, which is carried out by 13,000 revenue agents, 3,000 tax auditors, and their clerical and management support, is regarded by IRS managers as the keystone of the compliance effort. Auditing also provides the single largest area of entry into the IRS. As of fiscal 1970, tax auditors and 20 per cent of the revenue agents were recruited at grade GS-5. Of the remaining revenue agents, 50 per cent were recruited at grade GS-7, 15 per cent at GS-9, and 15 per cent at GS-11. Revenue agents normally reach GS-11 journeyman status within two and one-half years. Of the 1969 revenue agent force, 55 per cent earned from $11,230 to $15,800 annually, and the top 25 per cent from $15,800 to $32,800. The balance were recruits.

The work of a revenue agent in the top grades requires knowledge of a highly technical body of tax law, skill in a unique auditing technique, and the exercise of judgment normally demanded of a professional. The revenue agent, in fact, has been moving ever more perceptibly toward professional status. Tomorrow will undoubtedly see an acceleration in this trend. The pre-entry training of tomorrow's revenue agent, in response to forces both inside and outside the business school, may well include a more thorough grounding in tax law and revenue auditing. It most likely will include some substantial exposure to computer technology. His in-service training will include more in-depth training in specialized areas and in computer auditing techniques, and many of his courses will be taken at training centers located on the campuses of major universities. On the basis of present trends, he will find opportunities for specialization in such areas as natural resources, foreign income, deferred compensation and pension plans, corporate reorganizations, and tax-exempt organizations. With specialization will come greater stratification in grade and salary.

The revenue agent a decade or so from now will find marked changes in the auditing processes. He will find computer selection of returns for audit for potential change more reliable, with the result that the present 40 per cent of no-change audits will decrease steadily during the years to come. He will also find greater compatibility between IRS and business computer systems, a greater willingness on the part of the agency to gear its operations to business operations, with the result that the use of the IRS auditape system (Chapter III) will become commonplace, and the higher-grade agents will be able to audit "through the computer" as easily as they do today "around the computer" with conventional records and accounts. The examining agent of tomorrow may also find that the service center computer will discover errors on returns that today's agent must dig for manually, and that it will provide leads to other errors, which will materially shorten the examination process, especially in team audits of large cases.

Finally, in the decades ahead, the revenue agent seeking information and technical advice during the course of an audit examination may find a more prompt response, as suggested above, from more elaborate data retrieval systems, and, at the conclusion of his audit, he may conceivably be able to enlist the aid of the computer in a printout of his revenue agent's report.

For a number of careerists in the IRS, duty as a district or appellate conferee may be an important experience. Here, too, trends are discernible. During the past decade, the more complex income tax returns, with adjusted gross income in excess of $10,000, have more than doubled to an estimated 20 million for 1970, while the over-all total has risen only slightly. These returns, with their more complex issues, have been responsible in large measure for the downward trend in return coverage, while auditing manpower has remained substantially the same. The effect of these trends is that the IRS has had to make a special effort to settle more of the simpler cases at the district level by encouraging taxpayer representatives not to by-pass the district conference and by expanding the authority of the district conferee. There are no indications at present of any reverse trends in these and related developments. The future may well see a more meaningful role for the district conferee in the form of increased training and authority, perhaps even a separation from the district Audit Division and acquisition of an independent status similar to that now enjoyed by the Appellate Division conferee.

Most revenue officers for the Collection Division are recruited at grade GS-5, one notch below the usual entry level for revenue agent. However, the work of the revenue officer, the modern counterpart of the old-line collector, has been subjected to substantial revaluation in recent years. IRS managers have come to realize that the knowledge and skills required of the revenue officer have vastly increased as a result of new legislation, technological advances, and increasing taxpayer resistance. This realization has resulted in a substantial number of revenue officer upgradings (in fiscal 1970, almost 10 per cent were raised to grades GS-11 and GS-12), and it may be only a question of time before the revenue officer recruit will enter the IRS at the GS-7 level.

The computer already has had a substantial impact on the work of the revenue officer. Multifiling of returns has been substantially eliminated. The bulk of taxpayer errors are being resolved by direct communication between the computer and the taxpayer. Refund claims are subject to computer search and to deductions of amounts due the government by the claimant. And the revenue officer and other collection personnel have a developing information retrieval system that may be utilized in the collection process and promises to eliminate much duplication in the reinvestigation of uncollected accounts and in the identification of taxpayers and taxpayer accounts.

However, notwithstanding improved account controls, there is no indication that the electronic computer will eliminate delinquent returns and accounts. One of the critical problems facing the Internal Revenue Service today and in the years immediately ahead is maintaining effective control over delinquent accounts and returns. The fiscal 1970 year-end inventory of 800,000 delinquent accounts and 550,000 investigations of delinquent returns, plus the inauguration of a new return compliance program designed to identify taxpayers who have never filed returns, promises to provide an acceleration of the present collection effort. Thus, in addition to personal contacts with taxpayers, the revenue officer of tomorrow will pore over state records—including those available under expanded federal-state audit programs—interview businessmen, and otherwise attempt to run down nonfilers.

Trainees for special agent (Intelligence Division), investigator (Alcohol, Tobacco, and Firearms Division), and inspector (Internal Security Division), all of whom are concerned with unique types of criminal investigation work, must first pass the special civil service examination given to all Treasury Department enforcement agents. Most active recruiting is for special agents, who constitute the largest group. The normal entry grade for all three categories is GS-7, with premium pay provided in lieu of overtime for some assignments, such as those connected with an organized crime drive.

In the future, the varied work and risks of these investigating agents will be subject to a number of significant trends. For one thing, more special agents (and revenue agents) will be assigned to strike forces in the Justice Department's drive on organized crime in cases that will be affected by the future legal testing of the use of the growing arsenal of electronic surveillance devices. For another thing, if current studies in the nonorganized crime area prove fruitful, the special agent can anticipate the development of a data base for use in investigation that will identify noncompliance areas—and perhaps even cases—on the basis of qualitative factors.

Finally, the Alcohol, Tobacco and Firearms Division investigator can anticipate the continuation of the Southeastern Operations Dry-Up program described in Chapter VII, with substantial elimination of large-scale illicit liquor operations, but not (if history teaches anything at all) the elimination of the traditional small still producer. The Alcohol, Tobacco, and Firearms Division will also utilize an increased work force in enforcing the new firearms legislation enacted in 1968.

The Internal Revenue Service provides law school graduates interested in taxation with a number of unique opportunities. The entry grade salaries, GS-9 and GS-11, provide beginning compensation comparable to those in most large-city law offices, and compensation in the form of experience may be even greater. Normally, after a trial period, an attorney in one of the chief counsel's litigation divisions will be acquiring trial experience in taxation not available elsewhere except perhaps in the Tax Section of the Department of Justice. Law school graduates interested in research and in the policy-making process may find their niche in the Interpretative Division, in the Legislation and Regulations Division, or in the ruling branches of the assistant commissioner (Technical), or as an estate tax attorney in the field audit activity.

Tomorrow, the IRS attorney in the field will be aided in his work with improved data retrieval techniques, and attorneys in the national office can anticipate an increased use of computers in both basic and applied research, especially in tax policy studies. Both the national office staff and field attorneys may well look to substantial changes in their work if legislative proposals to overhaul trial and appellate procedures in the tax field are made into law by Congress.

MANAGEMENT

A decade ago a student of management observed at a seminar on management and the computer that it was tempting to predict that the ultimate impact of the computer on top management might well be the professionalization of management. This indeed would be a most radical development if it means, as Professor Chadarck Haberstroh puts it, "a divorce of managerial functions from organizational status and an acceptance of mobility between organizations as a normal step at any stage of a career."

While adherents of the senior civil service concept have long envisioned just such a managerial corps for the federal government, this has yet to materialize, except on a limited basis. Today, one will find occupying the top rungs of the various Internal Revenue Service career ladders "organization men," who have devoted much of their career time to the IRS and have been "rewarded with a degree of control over the organization's affairs." And the IRS executive development program described in Chapter IV is designed to ensure that these status rewards in the organization are actually available.

On the other hand, although the top careerists in the IRS today more nearly resemble the conventional view of the organization man, there are many forces at work, both inside and outside the agency, which point toward the development of a professional managerial staff. One such outside force is found in formal management training in the business schools and schools of public administration, which considers the management corps of large organizations as a specialized functional professional group. Forces within the agency pointing in the same direction, some dating back to the 1952 reorganization, include the structuring of the organization along highly functional lines, the participation of field and national office officials in planning with the national office Planning and Research divisions, the use of the task force device in the handling of specific problems, and the concern of management officials in their public pronouncements with ethical considerations in tax administration.

To the foregoing trends toward professionalization can be added the dynamic effects of recent developments in information technology, the resulting pressures for innovation, and applications of the computer to the solution of management problems. Some of the effects of the computer have already been described: improved statistical reporting with emphasis on the development of management statistical and data control systems, the reorganization of the IRS Collection Division, the establishment of a separate data processing office, the increasing importance of the Planning and Research divisions, and the expansion of the federal-state audit program through the exchange of computer tapes.

These changes and trends, however, will create critical

problems for IRS managers in the years ahead, problems of organizational design and structure, problems related to the cost and the pace of implementing technological advances, and problems in the design and management control of work-flow systems. Most important to innovation and change—to the extent to which the new technology and other changes can be built into the IRS organizational structure—will be the manner in which the agency managers handle the human element in the organization. For example, as statistical reporting becomes more sophisticated and as mechanized controls over work loads improve, the danger increases that production goals and reporting will be interpreted by front-line workers, supervisors, lower-echelon managers, and the public as personal quotas. Further, the very tempo of future innovations and changes suggest innumerable problems in overcoming the built-in resistance to change inherent in any large organization. In other words, the need here is the one facing most large organizations in the electronic age, the need to build into the "task model" (the members' shared notion of the organization's task) the very dynamics of change.

Problems equal in importance to the social aspects of organization membership will have to be faced by IRS managers in introducing innovations and changes in tax administration to the public and its representatives in Congress. Basic tax equity, as well as effective tax administration, rests in large measure on the willingness of the American taxpayer to meet his tax obligations on a voluntary basis. Although voluntary reporting is fortified by a withholding system on most salary and wage payments and by a return audit examination system, IRS managers fully appreciate the precarious foundations of the voluntary system. They are particularly aware of the danger if the taxpaying public should come to the conclusion that enforcement is so limited that other taxpayers are not meeting their fair share of the tax burden. And it is indeed questionable whether the new information technology will be able to meet this future challenge with today's level of audit coverage. Should public revolt appear imminent, there are no assurances that the public will draw a rational distinction between inequities resulting from underenforcement and those attributable to rules enacted by Congress, which, for one policy reason or another, provide special tax preferences for certain taxpaying groups.

The dilemma of the Internal Revenue Service is obvious. On the one hand, the agency faces the future with resources sufficient to examine less than 3 per cent of the returns it receives; yet, at the same time, it is charged with the enforcement of complex and sometimes unintelligible rules, based on laws enacted by Congress that often reflect policy decisions based on political considerations unrelated to tax fairness. On the other hand, the IRS is faced with the necessity of explaining to the public that the federal tax system treats the public fairly, but at the same time it remains in the position of being unable to explain that much of the unfairness is attributable to the failure of Congress to provide sufficient resources for effective enforcement and to political forces at work in a democratic society. It is apparent that the present rules of the game just do not permit either the Internal Revenue Service or the Department of the Treasury to take these issues directly to the American public.

Perhaps even this will change. Permanence, after all, is a myth. Nothing stands still.

Appendix A

Letter from N. P. Langford, U.S. Collector for the Territory of Montana, to J. W. Taylor, May 20, 1866

"In our local matters, we were completely under the rebel rules:—the rule of what is familiarly known here as the left wing of Price's [Confederate] Army; that is the wing that left his army."

So wrote N. P. Langford, United States Collector for the Territory of Montana, in reporting to his Washington superior on May 20, 1866. This "ace" collector took flour riots, gold-rush stampedes, the Blood Indians, and vigilante law in his stride. He innovated, cajoled, and made summary arrests. In the end, he had his district "thoroughly organized" and his taxpayers convinced that "Montana was in the United States, instead of Secessia."

Matters were indeed different in Langford's time—at Virginia City, Blackfoot, and Jeff Davis Gulch—than they are today. But, if they were any easier, this classic document in the history of tax administration does not reveal it.

Virginia City, Mon[tana]
May 20th 1866

J. W. Taylor, Esq.

Dear Sir:

I have often been minded to write to you, giving you some idea of what I have been doing in Montana:—the difficulties I have had to contend with, and annoyances to bear with, in organizing this Collection District:—and while I do not claim any undue credit for what I have accomplished,—for I have done no more than faithfully discharge my official duties.—I nevertheless feel a pride in the fact, that a greater success has been attained, than the most sanguine could have anticipated:—and I am convinced that few men would have undertaken what I have, in such a community as this—and I am equally well satisfied that I owe much of my success in enforcing the revenue law, to my previous acquaintance with men and manners in Montana, as well as the knowledge, by those with whom I came in contact, that their threats of personal violence would not prevent me from doing my duty. . . .

Considerations such as these determined me to give up all thought of anything else, and devote myself solely to the duties of my office, ignoring all political prospects, so far as they related to myself, although they were flattering:—probably more so than those of any union man in Montana:—for reasons connected solely with law and order:—to maintain which I ran many risks of life. The "History of the Vigilantes" details these facts fully and I need not further refer to them.

When I first entered upon the duties of my office, I had neither blanks nor a copy of the Rev. Law:—the only book of service to me being Boutwells Manual.

The Assessor had a copy of the law, but lived 65 miles away. My knowledge of the law, therefore, was confined to what I remembered of it, after having read it one day in Washington. After the lapse of six weeks I borrowed a copy of the law from a "pilgrim." Then I had no blanks. Twenty (20) blank licenses were received from the Department and these were all. I borrowed four hundred of the Collector of Utah:—but with economy in their use issuing but one blank for several occupations, these were not sufficient, and I was forced to get blanks printed here or suspend Collections.

Upon receiving my first list, I gave notice in our city paper of the time when the duties would be due:—and posted about two hundred notices in this county. Within two or three days after posting these notices some twelve or fifteen men came into my office to talk with me about the collection revenue. They generally went over about the same ground:—said they were "loyal and believed in paying their taxes" but there were many who didn't believe in it, and wouldn't pay. They wanted to know what would be done with delinquents:—if I'd try to enforce the law:—if I thought I could do it without the aid of a Regiment of soldiers and other such questions. I told them that I should enforce the law, after giving full notice to all persons, and that I didn't think that I'd need any military force, but if I did I'd get it. They advised me not to "press the matter" on the start, for fear of trouble. They came they said, "to advise with me as friends." These men did not all come together, but in parties two or three at a time, and at first I thought nothing of it:—but the questions asked by different parties were so similar, my suspicions were aroused, and I plainly saw that it was a preconcerted plan. Sometimes a man was more violent than the others, and would say that he owed no allegiance to any government, but that of Jeff Davis, and that I need not expect to collect a tax from him, for he wouldn't pay it.

Well, the advertised time passed, and there were over 100 delinquents. I immediately gave each one a personal notice, (as I had no department blanks for that purpose) that I'd seize and distrain within 10 days, if the duties were not paid. This brought in about fifty more, and at the expiration of ten days, I issued warrants for the remainder and seized property. But many of the warrants were returned unsatisfied, although I knew the parties had money.

I then gave public notice that every delinquent would be indicted at the next term of the court (U.S.). This produced no effect, but loud talking and threats, and some of my friends advised me, for fear of trouble, to let the Collection of duties pass by "for this time."

I told them all, that all who violated the law inadvertently would be favored more than the law required me to favor them, but that wilfull offenders should be punished:—that I was sent here to Collect U.S. Taxes, and I'd do it or resign.

As the time for the sitting of the Court drew near, I had some stormy times in my office:—and to tell the truth, I was not without anxiety, at times [*sic*], concerning the results. I was in a Territory more disloyal as a whole, than Tennessee or Kentucky ever were. Four-fifths of our citizens were *openly declared* Secessionists. Virginia City, was first called *Varina* in honor of Mrs. Jeff Davis. Then we had Jeff Davis Gulch, and Confederate Gulch, "Straws show" &c &c.

At Bannock, I had seen a Secesh flag flying, and men standing near by with revolvers, daring any bystander to say that he didn't like to see that flag, or that he didn't support Jeff Davis. Only two months before these assessments were made, our Delegate in Congress McLane, discussed the issues of the campaign under a *white* flag, on which was embroidered an olive branch.

In our local matters, we were completely under the rebel rules:—the rule of what is familiarly known here as "the *left wing* of Prices Army":—that is the wing that left his army. So you see that I had not the support of one-fourth of our people, and threats of Violence were the rule, and not the exception.

I often thought of your counsel while I was east:—that it was not expected by the Department that I would place myself in jeopardy in the discharge of my duties. But I determined that I would at once settle the question whether I should yield to them, or they to the law:—and at the session of the Court, I had every delinquent indicted:—60 or 70 in all. This really astonished them, and they concluded that Montana was in the United States, instead of Secessia.

I deemed it to be a matter of the most imperative necessity, that an example should be made of these wilful offenders, and that the supremacy of the law should be maintained; and having shown them that I would enforce the law, I asked the Judge to fine them but five cents and costs. This satisfied them that I did not care for the moiety of fines, (which I might have had put at $100.00 each), but only that the law should be observed.

Two only were abusive:—and after bearing all I could from them, I stepped in front of my counter, and told them not to speak another word in my office, or I'd thrash them as they had never been thrashed before. This quieted them, and they soon left.

"Let no man despise thee" is the advise of St. Paul to Titus, and the time may come, when forbearance ceases to be even a

Christian virtue. The rebels may hate me, but they will not despise me. I will have their respect, even if I have to flog it out of them.

In April 1865, occurred the flour riots. The miners of Nevada City to the number of several hundred, came up to Virginia City, and for two days had everything their own way. They took all the flour in the City and distributed it among themselves, paying the prices ruling before the scarcity. The mob was well organized and swept everything before it. They expected to have found a large quantity of flour secreted, but there was none to find:—and in their disappointment, they threatened to "confiscate" what money they could find in the Banks and Collectors office:—but hearing of this, I cashed my collections.

About a week after the riots, I caught a man tearing down one of my official posters, and arrested him and brought him into Court, and he was fined for hindering a Revenue Officer.

He turned out to be a Captain of 100 of the rioters:—very brave at their head, and believing himself to be equally brave when alone by himself, but he was terribly frightened on being brought into Court.

But no more annoyances occurred till the first of May 1865. During the month of April many "stampedes" had taken place, and rumors of thriving towns coming into existence, reached us from all directions. These "stampedes" are to an inexperienced man, singular affairs. A few prospectors discover a rich Gulch, and after securing claims for themselves and their friends, they give the alarm, and within an hour, perhaps five hundred miners "stampede" to the new Gulch, and thousand more are on the ground in a few days. The Gulch is perhaps rich enough to furnish employment to 2000 miners, and, of course, merchants flock in and build a town. . . .

The amendment of March 3, 1865, imposing a license duty of Ten Dollars on Miners, went into effect the first day of May, and the miners were notified to comply with this provision of the law. Miners are the most independent class of people in the world:— extremely jealous of the privileges they have always enjoyed— and they looked upon this requirement of the law as an aggression upon their privileges.

I was told that the miners in the lower part of the gulch would refuse to take license. I posted notices in the gulch setting forth the requirements of the law, and a few days thereafter, five gentlemen came into my office, and told me that they were a committee appointed to inform me that the miners did not believe it was right to be required to take licenses, and that it would lead to bloodshed if I persisted.

I told them that it was useless to talk of resistance:—that the law must be enforced and that I would enforce it. They urged me to consider it well, before acting &c. Our conversation occupied about an hour during which not an angry or excitable word was spoken on either side. They were gentlemen:—Secesh of course: —and I really feared the result of the advice of these men, more than the threats of a hundred loud talkers. It was just a few days after we had received the intelligence of Lee's surrender:—and as the Committee rose to go, one of them said—"I am in favor of paying these duties, but was put on the committee and had to act." I replied that I supposed that he was forced into it by his neighbors, as Gen. Lee was into the rebellion. He said "I suppose so." I responded, "I don't think you can hope for greater success in resisting the law, than Gen'l Lee attained." The conference ended here, and they went their way:—and the miners came up and took licenses a few days later.

I was also notified that a miners meeting had been held at German Gulch at which it was resolved that no taxes should be collected from miners. At the next term of the U.S. Court, in the second judicial district, I went over and had a large number indicted. They made many threats especially against Mr. Cross, the Asst. Assessor, and myself, and they so thoroughly frightened Mr. Cross, that he resigned. One of the delinquents was so abusive that the U.S. Marshall handcuffed him, and sent him over to Madison Co. Jail, 75 miles. For want of newspapers, I had posted several hundred notices in the mining gulches, setting forth the requirements of the law:—but these notices were for the most part torn down or defaced, yet I couldn't find out who did it, such was the disposition, to screen each other, and oppose the law. At "Last Chance" gulch, a large number were indicted.

In Confederate Gulch, the Revenue officers were threatened with personal violence if they came there:—and the U.S. Marshal

(Pinney) who was there at the time, advised me not to go there alone, on account of those threats:—but I'd have gone, and been glad to have done so, if I'd had the time to spare, but it was 165 miles from my office, and I could not well go over:—so I notified them that if they didn't come to Helena, and get their licenses of my deputy, (Helena being in the same Division) I'd have them all indicted. They "saw the point," and came over. . . .

The District of Montana is one of the largest in the United States:—that portion of it containing settlements, and over which I have repeatedly traveled, and which my Deputies occupy, being as large as the state of New York. The circuit of the mining camps at the present time, is about 1400 miles, of which about 300 may be traveled by coach, the balance 1100 miles on horseback, and this distance cannot be travelled over, at best, in less time than 15 days, for a constant ride, day after day, of 75 miles each day, is all a man can bear. To organize this vast District, was no easy task, and I ran the risk of losing my scalp on two different occasions. One of my first Deputies, Frank Angevine, formerly in the Collectors Office in Colorado, was killed at Ophir by the Blood Indians. His death necessitated a journey by me to his Division, which I did not especially desire to take in view of the continued hostility of the Bloods. Mr. Angevine had made no collections, as he was just entering upon his duties, yet he would have made a most efficient officer. I lost $40 Revenue Stamps that I had given him.

It has been necessary that I should have thorough, and brave men as Deputies:—men who can take care of themselves if trouble arises.

In the States a Collector advertises that he will be at A—— on Monday, at B—— on Tuesday, and so on. Now suppose that I were to adopt this course here:—that I were to notify the public that I'd be at Blackfoot on the 10th and at Hell Gate, on the 12th of May, to receive taxes. Such an advertisement would be a notice to all the "Road Agents" (highwaymen) in the country that a man with some money would be travelling the road from Blackfoot to Hell Gate on May 11th, and it is not probable that the Collector would ever get to Hell Gate. Deputy Collectors cannot be found, who will take such risks. Neither is it practicable here, to pursue the old round about system of making returns, adopted in the States. There Assistant Assessors make their returns to the Assessor,—the Assessor to the Collector—and the Collector to his Deputies in the various Divisions. To do this here would involve a delay of from four to eight weeks:—for that time would elapse after the assessments, before Deputy Collectors would receive the lists, and in the mean time, many of the assessed persons would have "stampeded."

In Montana, each assistant Assessor delivers to the Deputy Collector of that Division *daily,* a list of assessments, and the Deputy makes immediate demand. I think the same plan might be advantageously pursued in the States also. My experience is, that a large share of taxpayers, are as ready to pay when first assessed, as a month later:—and a courteous suggestion that a Deputy Collector was ready to receive the tax at the time of assessment, would ensure the payment of a large portion of the tax at least a month before an imperative demand could be legally made. . . .

My district is now thoroughly organized, and it is not without a feeling of satisfaction that I look upon the result of what has been the severest labor of my life. At times, I have been almost discouraged, as it seemed as if everything was working against me, but for a determination to do thoroughly what I set about doing, I'd have given up my position long ago. I can get the same salary ($4,000) in occupations carrying with them no such responsibilities as those which attach to my office; but I have the vanity to believe that I can collect 10 percent more revenue in Montana than any one else can. I have collected, under all my difficulties, 96 percent, of the assessments. The remaining 4 percent, for peculiar reasons existing here,—as they do not in the States,—is not collectible. Thus:—a laboring man has earned $6.00 per day for 300 days; total $1,800. His family has expended every cent of it, and he has not a dollar in the world; for a laboring man earning six dollars per day here is no better off than he who earns $1.25 per day in the States. This man makes an honest return of an income of $1,800,—of which $1,200 is taxable. His tax is $60, but it can never be collected. If it were not for these peculiar cases I'd collect 98 percent, of all the assessments.

There is still much opposition to the law, and to its enforcement;—but the refractory have learned from experience, that I will not be trifled with. Still they improve every opportunity to find fault, or escape the payment of duties. . . .

The Vigilantes are the main stay of this Country, and we all trust in that body for safety. The only murderer ever tried by a Court in Montana was sentenced to 4 years imprisonment for manslaughter. Genl. Meagher, acting as Governor, reprieved (?) him until the will of the President could be made known; and ordered him set at liberty. The U.S. Judge ordered him to be re-arrested;—but before that could be done the criminal returned to Helena where the murder was committed, and was immediately taken by the Vigilantes and hung. If it were not for the Vigilantes no man's life would be secure. Even with them, it is far better to "keep a close mouth" and not express an opinion concerning the character of the men we meet here. . . .

In the report of the Hon. Commissioner of Internal Revenue for 1865, the population of Montana is estimated at 30,000. This estimate is much too large. There were 6,230 votes cast last fall for Delegate to Congress. Over two thirds of our entire population are voters, and last fall the voting was very general. Our population cannot exceed 18,000 persons. . . .

With this basis of population, the Revenue returns of Montana are creditable to her;—and in the future will be much increased. My District is now well organized,—our citizens are becoming familiarized with the operations of the law, and to feel that the surest method of reducing the present high rates of taxation is to require every man to pay his just dues, that none by making false returns, or through negligence of duty in officials may throw upon their neighbors the share of the burden which they themselves ought to bear.

When I think of the labors of the past 18 months, and the annoyances I have had to submit to, I have reason to congratulate myself that the affairs of this District are in so prosperous a condition. My labors have been most severe, and the compensation, ($4,000 per Annum) no more than I can obtain in positions of much less responsibility than this:—but I have felt a pride in demonstrating that the establishment of this District was desirable

—and having done this, I have less desire to hold the position now, than I have ever had before. It is an unpopular position at best, and no where more so than here;—and the salary affords me no more than a decent support. I sometimes resolve to give up the office, and may do so the coming summer. This will depend upon whether my official expenses will be allowed, or not, my duties are now sufficiently laborious, even with the payment of all my expenses. If these expenses are not allowed as I have incurred them, I cannot hold the office with credit to the Government, without loss to myself;—and I shall then give it up. . . .

I have endeavored to give you some idea of the situation of affairs here, as I found them, and as they now are. Perhaps it may interest you. In this Godless country, this country of lawlessness, highway robberies, and Vigilance Committees,—this country where nearly 200 murders have been committed but no man convicted by the Courts,—this country where a U.S. Grand Jury, recommended that the court turn over all criminal business into the hands of the Vigilantes,—this country where every man takes his life into his own hands wherever he goes,—it is but a record of a common experience;—very tame in comparison with my experience during the two previous years, when for upholding law, and publicly denouncing a gang of desperadoes, with our sheriff, their secret Chief, a price was set by them upon my head. . . .

But these scenes of violence, and threatened violence, are fast passing away. The millennium is dawning. The reign of Peace is drawing nigh;—and without fertile agricultural vallies, and rich resources in mineral wealth, when throughout our Territory shall rise those twin-pioneers of civilization, the Church and the School House, this land will be the fairest of the fair.

Sincerely yours,
N. P. LANGFORD

Appendix B
Charts and Graphs

Charts and graphs sometimes provide insights that would otherwise remain buried in the printed word. This is the case in any effort to trace the twistings and turnings of federal tax administration over a period of almost two hundred years.

The charts and graphs on the next few pages are intended to complement the kaleidoscopic account of the history of the Internal Revenue Service outlined in Chapter I, which concludes with an attempt to illustrate the dual concern of the IRS today—with volume and with complexity. Charts B1, B2, and B3 portray the changes and growth of federal tax administration in terms of the types of tax levies and the revenue they provided the federal government from 1792 to 1969. Charts B4 and B5 provide a view of the IRS today both in terms of its work load and in terms of the sources and eventual distribution of the federal budget.

CHART B1

U.S. Government Receipts and Population, Customs Duties Era, Selected Years, 1792–1862. Total receipts include negligible amounts of internal revenue excise taxes for 1792–1840, none for 1850 and 1862. (Source: *Statistical Abstract of the United States,* 1968)

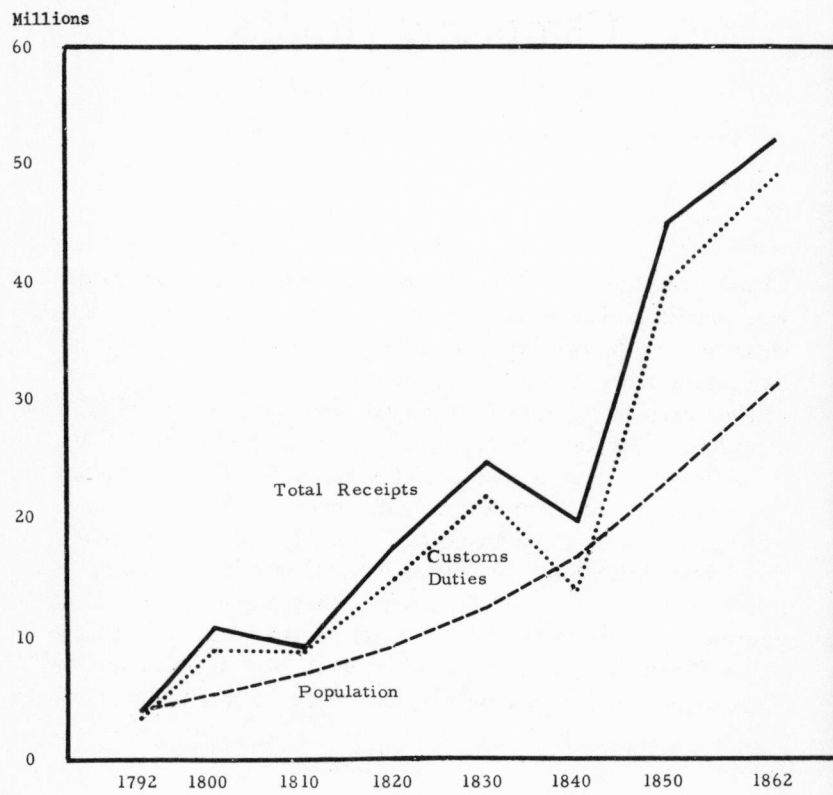

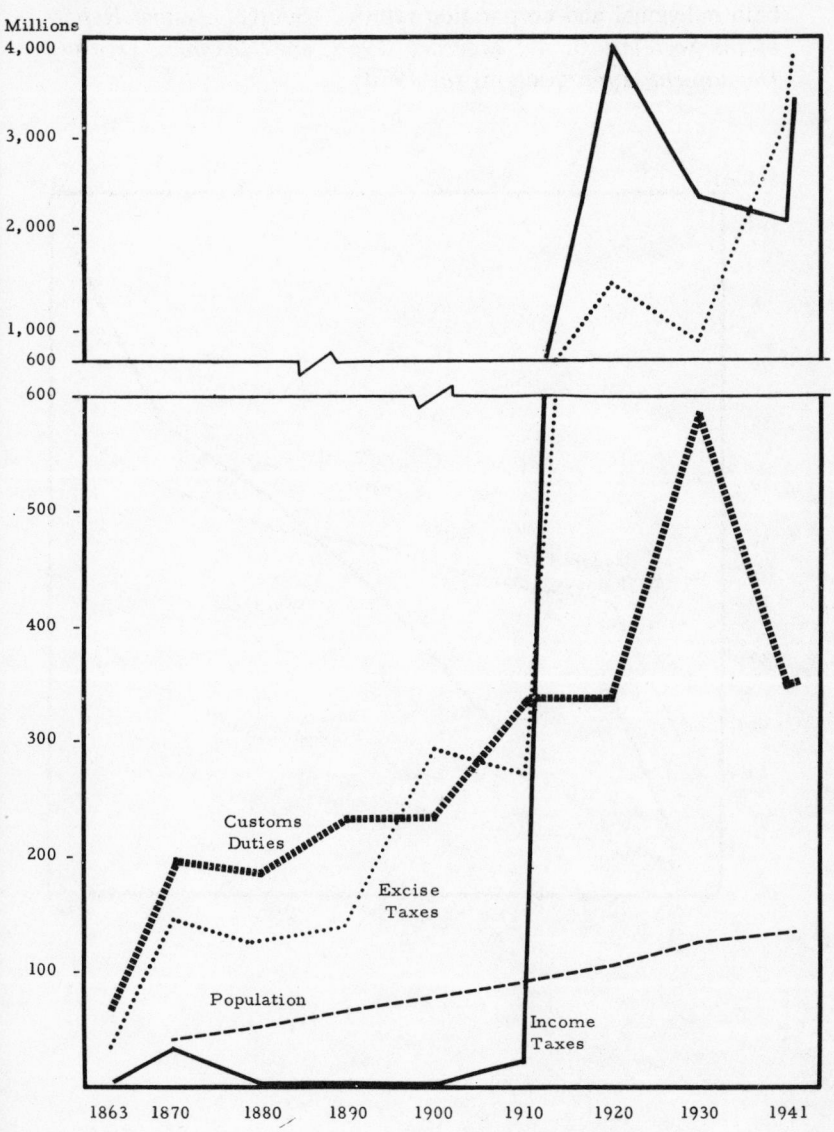

CHART B2

U.S. Government Tax Revenue and Population, Internal Revenue Era, Selected Years, 1863–1941. (Source: *Statistical Abstract of the United States,* 1968)

Millions

Customs Duties

Excise Taxes

Population

Income Taxes

CHART B3

U.S. Government Internal Revenue and Income Tax Returns, Age of the Income Tax, Selected Years, 1942–69. Excise taxes include employment taxes. Income tax returns, given in millions, include both individual and corporation returns. (Source: *Annual Report of the Secretary of the Treasury, 1966,* and *Hearings, Treasury Department Appropriations for 1970*)

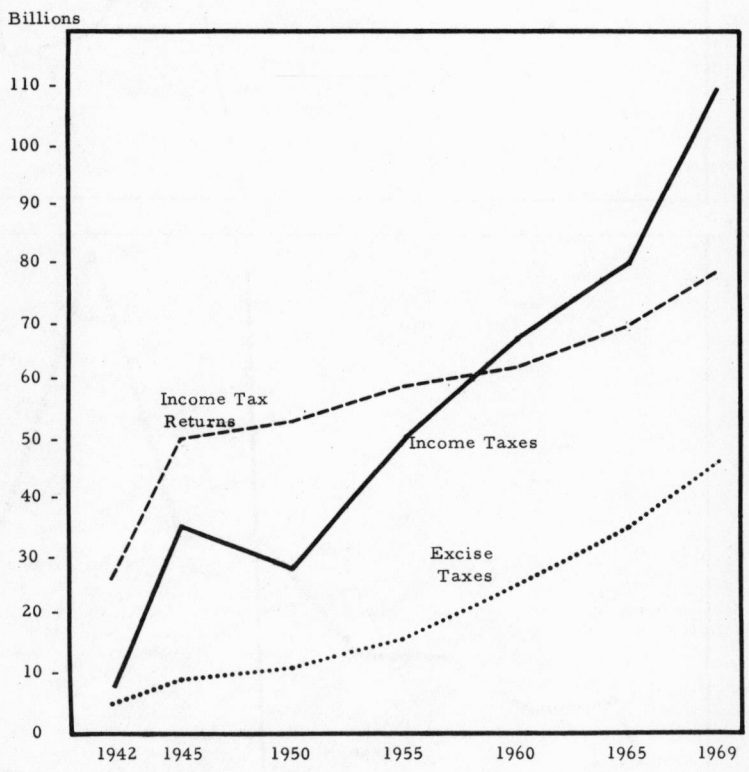

CHART B4

Income, Estate, and Gift Tax Work Load, Internal Revenue Service and the Courts, 1968. Total tax returns for 1968 were 107.6 million. (Source: *Annual Report of the Commissioner of Internal Revenue,* 1968)

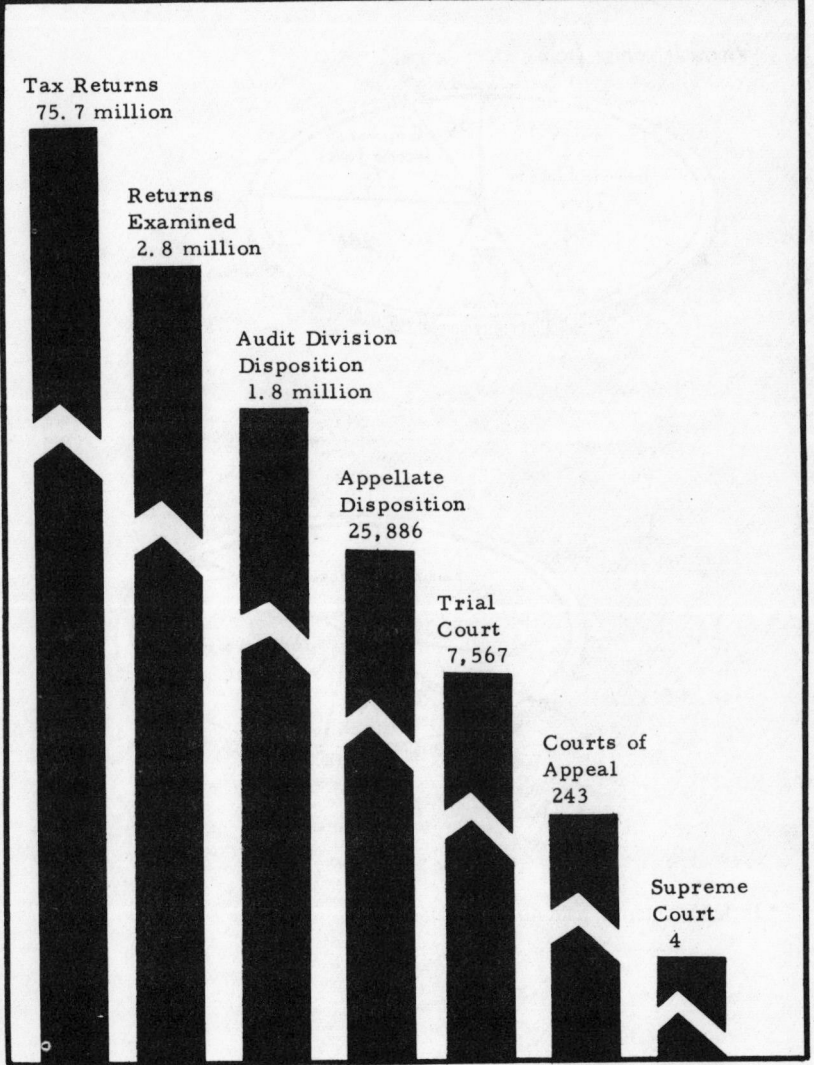

Tax Returns
75. 7 million

Returns
Examined
2. 8 million

Audit Division
Disposition
1. 8 million

Appellate
Disposition
25,886

Trial
Court
7,567

Courts of
Appeal
243

Supreme
Court
4

CHART B5
The Budget Dollar: Estimates for Fiscal Year 1971

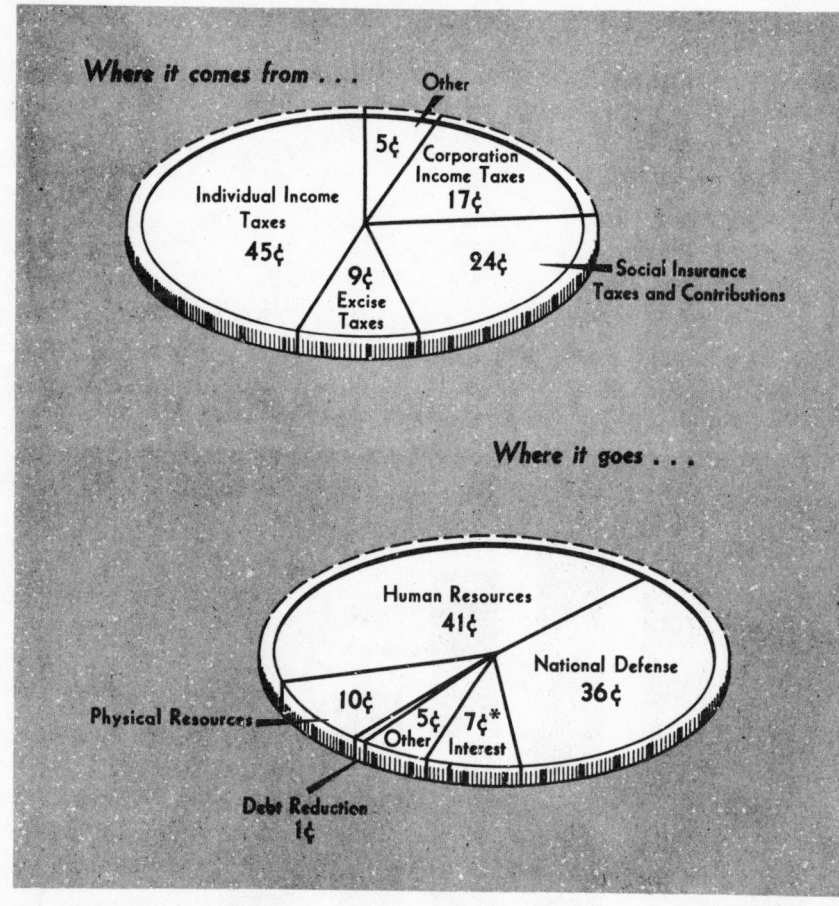

Where it comes from . . .

Other

5¢

Corporation Income Taxes 17¢

Individual Income Taxes 45¢

9¢ Excise Taxes

24¢

Social Insurance Taxes and Contributions

Where it goes . . .

Human Resources 41¢

National Defense 36¢

Physical Resources

10¢

5¢ Other

7¢* Interest

Debt Reduction 1¢

* Includes interest paid to trust funds.

Bibliography

Books and Pamphlets

BITTKER, BORIS I. *Federal Income, Estate and Gift Taxation.* Boston: Little, Brown, 1964.

Calvert Distillers Company. *An American Tradition.* 1965.

CHOMMIE, JOHN C. *Federal Income Taxation.* St. Paul, Minn.: West Publishing Co., 1968.

DORIS, LILLIAN, ed. *The American Way in Taxation: Internal Revenue, 1862–1962.* Englewood Cliffs, N.J.: Prentice-Hall, 1963.

FLOWER, LENORE E. *Visit of President George Washington to Carlisle, 1794.* Carlisle, Pa.: Hamilton Library and Cumberland County Historical Society, 1932.

Joint Tax Program. *Problems of Tax Administration in Latin America.* Baltimore: John Hopkins Press, 1965.

Licensed Beverage Industries, Inc. *Annual Reports on The Moonshine Industry.* New York: 1961–68.

MELLON, ANDREW W. *Taxation: The People's Business.* New York: Macmillan, 1924.

MERTENS, JACOB, JR. *The Law of Federal Income Taxation.* Vol. 9. Mundelein, Ill.: Callaghan, 1965.

MESSICK, HANK. *Secret File.* New York: Putnam's, 1969.

OLDMAN, OLIVER, et al. *Manual of Income Tax Administration.* Harvard Law School International Program in Taxation. Cambridge: 1967 (mimeo).

PAUL, RANDOLPH E. *Taxation in the United States.* Boston: Little, Brown, 1954.

RATNER, SIDNEY. *Taxation and Democracy in America.* New York: Wiley, 1967.

SURFACE, WILLIAM. *Inside Internal Revenue.* New York: Coward-McCann, 1967.

SURREY, STANLEY S., and WILLIAM C. WARREN. *Federal Income Taxation, Cases and Materials.* Brooklyn: Foundation Press, 1962.

ARTICLES

ACREE, VERNON D. "From the Thoughtful Tax Man." *Taxes,* 40:73 (1962).

AUBRY, ARTHUR S., JR. "The Alcohol and Tobacco Tax Division." *Police,* Jan.–Feb., 1968.

BACON, DONALD W. "Ethical Considerations in Federal Tax Administration." *Taxes,* 41:74, (1963).

———. "Internal Revenue Service Policy Concerning Reopening of Closed Cases." *Tax Lawyer,* 22:659, (1969).

———. "Taxing Foreign Income of United States Taxpayers." *Taxes,* 43:362 (1965).

———. "The New Changes Taking Place in the Office of International Operations." *J. Taxation,* 24:361 (1965).

BALTER, HARRY G. "How the Office of International Operations Enforces U.S. Taxes in Foreign Countries." *J. Taxation,* 24:356 (1965).

BARRON, DEAN J. "How We Audit from Magnetic Tapes." *Taxes,* 40:83 (1962).

———. "The Processing Cycle: What Happens from Filing Date to Action Date." *J. Taxation,* 24:306 (1966).

BARRON, JOHN. "The Tragic Case of John J. Hafer and the IRS." *Reader's Digest,* Jan., 1969.

———. "Time for Reform in the IRS." *Reader's Digest,* Sept., 1968.

———. "Tyranny in the Internal Revenue Service." *Reader's Digest,* Aug., 1967.

BELZ, SAUL C. "Federal Tax Rulings: Procedure and Policy." *Vanderbilt Law Review,* 21:78 (1967).

BLUM, WALTER J. "Nonagression Revisited in a Nutshell—A Satirical View of Mr. Wormser's Plea." *J. Taxation,* 20:186 (1964).

BRAZILL, CLARENCE P., JR. "The Audit Trail." *New York Univ. Tax Inst.,* 21:1217 (1963).

CAPLIN, MORTIMER M. "The Commissioner's Reply: Reasonable Tax Administration and Current Policies of IRS." *J. Taxation,* 20:110 (1964).

CHAMBERLIN, HOPE. "The IRS Information Program." *National Public Accountant,* April, 1965.

CHRISTENSON, REO M. "Report on the *Reader's Digest.*" *Columbia Journalism Review,* Winter, 1965.

COHEN, SHELDON S. "Latin American Tax Improvement." *Accounting Forum,* May, 1968.

COLLIE, MARVIN K., and THOMAS P. MARINIS, JR. "Ethical Considerations on Discovery of Error in Tax Returns." *Tax Lawyer*, 22:455 (1969).

CONLON, CHARLES F. "Administration of the State Income Tax." *1962 Proceedings National Tax Assn.*, 1963, p. 404.

EICHEL, CLAUDE L. "Administrative Aspects of the Prevention and Control of International Tax Evasion." *Miami Law Review*, 20:25 (1965).

ESCEW, ANNE E., *et al.* "Lead Poisoning Resulting from Illicit Alcohol Consumption." *J. Forensic Sciences*, 6:337 (1961).

FARIOLETTI, MARIUS. "Statistical Records for the Management and Control of Tax Administration." In *Problems of Tax Administration in Latin America*, Baltimore: John Hopkins Press, 1965, p. 112.

FOX, C. I. "Office of International Operations: What It Does and How It Functions." *J. Taxation*, 24:162 (1965).

GOULD, STEPHEN. "A Case Study in Effective Recruitment." *Personnel Administration*, 25:31 (1962).

GRANT, IRVING M. "The Sierra Club: The Procedural Aspects of the Revocation of Its Tax Exemption." *UCLA Law Review*, 15:200 (1967).

HABERSTROH, CHADARCK J. "The Impact of Electronic Data Processing on Administrative Organizations." *National Tax J.*, 14:258 (1961).

HUSTON, LUTHER A. "IRS Leans on Press to Assist Taxpayers." *Editor and Publisher*, April 22, 1967.

JACK, ROBERT L. "ADP—An Analysis of Its Operations and Results." *New York Univ. Tax Inst.*, 24:99 (1966).

———. "Man v. Machine: Routine Correspondence Now Carried on by IRS Computer." *J. Taxation*, 24:307 (1966).

KLOTZ, ARTHUR H. "Administrative Appeals—Avoiding Litigation." *Tax Executive*, 19:188 (1967).

KRAGEN, ADRIAN A. "The Private Ruling: An Anomaly of Our Internal Revenue System." *Taxes*, 45:331 (1967).

LEHRFELD, WILLIAM J., and GEORGE D. WEBSTER. "Administration by the IRS of Non-Profit Organization Tax Matters." *Tax Lawyer*, 21:591 (1968).

LINK, DAVID T. "RIRA—A Legal Information System in the Internal Revenue Service." *Taxes*, 43:231 (1965).

MACHIZ, IRVING. "How the Internal Revenue Performs Its Review of the Revenue Agent's Report." *Taxation for Accountants*, 1:201 (1966).

MARRS, AUBREY R. "The Constitutional Power of Congress over the Administration of Federal Taxation." *Taxes*, 31:503 (1953).

MILLER, REAM V. "A Tax Representative's Appraisal of Tax Simplification and Uniform Tax Administration." *Tax Executive*, 17:7 (1964).

MILLER, RICHARD S. "Administrative Agency Intelligence-Gathering: An Appraisal of the Investigative Powers of the Internal Revenue

Service." *Boston College Industrial & Commercial Law Review*, 6:657 (1965).

MILLER, ROBERT N. "The Reorganization of the Bureau of Internal Revenue—An Appraisal." *Taxes*, 30:967 (1952).

MONTAGUE, EDWIN N. "Internal Revenue Service Training Program for Tax Men." *1959 Proceedings National Tax Assn*, 1960, p. 124.

MOSS, HAROLD. "Experience Under the U.S. Foreign Tax Assistance Program." *1967 Proceedings National Tax Assn*, 1968, p. 392.

PACKOWSKI, GEORGE W. "Alcoholic Beverages, Distilled." In Kirk-Othmer, *Encyclopedia of Chemical Technology*, Vol. 1, New York: Wiley, 1963.

PENNIMAN, CLARA. "Reorganization and the Internal Revenue Service." *Public Administration Review*, 21:121 (1961).

———. "Selected Problems in State Income Tax Administration." *1955 Proceedings National Tax Assn*, 1956.

PLUMB, ROBERT C. "Report of Survey of Federal Audit Practices." *Tax Executive*, 16:214 (1964).

RITHOLZ, JULES. "The Commissioner's Inquisitorial Powers." *Taxes*, 45:331 (1967).

RIVERS, CARYL. "IRS: They're Usually Honest With Newsmen." *Editor and Publisher*, April, 1964.

ROBERTSON, JOSEPH M. "Recent Developments in Federal-State Co-operation." *1958 Proceedings National Tax Assn*, 1959, p. 483.

ROGOVIN, MITCHELL. "The Four R's: Regulations, Rulings, Reliance and Retroactivity." *Taxes*, 43:756 (1965).

ROSAPEPE, JOSEPH S. "How to Collect $155—Billion." *Public Relations Journal*, April, 1968.

SEGHERS, PAUL D. "Federal Tax Reform: The Practitioner's Viewpoint." *1963 Proceedings National Tax Assn*, 1964, p. 71.

SEMLING, HAROLD V., JR. "Data Processing at the Internal Revenue Service." *Modern Data Systems*, Feb., 1968.

SMITH, DAN THROOP. "The Function of Tax Treaties." *National Tax J.*, 12:317 (1959).

SMITH, WILLIAM H. "Developing a New Technique in Selecting Returns For Audit." *J. Accountancy*, 123:22 (1967).

———. "Disciplinary Problems of the Service." *Tax Lawyer*, 22:255 (1969).

———. "Electronic Data Processing in the Internal Revenue Service." *National Tax J.*, 14:210 (1961).

STILLMAN, DON. "Attack on the Taxman." *Columbia Journalism Review*, Winter, 1967–68.

STOCK, LEON O. "From the Thoughtful Tax Man." *Taxes* 42:403 (1964).

SURREY, STANLEY S. "Computer Technology and Federal Tax Policy." *National Tax J.*, 19:248 (1966).

TREUSCH, PAUL E. "Chief Counsel's Office: A Dynamic View of Its

Organization and Procedures: The 'Hows' and Something of the 'Whys.' " *So. Calif. Tax Inst..* 12:19 (1960).

TURNER, JAMES R. "Federal-State Cooperation in Tax Administration." *William & Mary Law Review,* 9:958 (1968).

URETZ, LESTER R. "Settlement of Tax Controversies." *Taxes,* 44:794 (1966).

VOLPONE, STEPHEN C. "How a Tax Controversy Is Handled at the Appellate Division Level." *J. Taxation,* 23:178 (1965).

WORMSER, RENE A. "To the Commissioner of Internal Revenue: A Plea for 'Nonagression.' " *J. Taxation,* 20:108 (1964).

U.S. GOVERNMENT PRINTING OFFICE PUBLICATIONS

Department of the Treasury. *Income Taxes 1862–1962: A History of the Internal Revenue Service,* 1962.

———. *Report of the Secretary of the Treasury.* Annual.

House Committee on Appropriations. Subcommittee on Treasury, Post Office, and Executive Office. *Annual Hearings.* Part 2, Treasury Department.

House Committee on Government Operations. *Federal Effort Against Organized Crime: Report of Agency Operations,* 1968.

House Committee on Ways and Means. *Treasury Department Report on Private Foundations,* 1965.

———. Subcommittee on Internal Revenue Taxation. *Progress Report,* 1957.

NOTE: The *Hearings* of both the House Ways and Means Committee and the Senate Committee on Finance frequently contain material on tax administration.

Internal Revenue Service. *Alcohol and Tobacco Tax Division.* Publication 425, 1966.

———. *Commissioner's Report to the Secretary of the Treasury.* Annual.

———. *Detection and Investigation of Attempted Criminal Violations of Tax Laws.* Document 5490, 1967.

———. *Dimensions of Personnel Management,* 1967.

———. *Distilled Spirits: History of Taxation and Law Enforcement.* Document 5574, 1966.

———. *IRS Answers* Reader's Digest *Article; Gives Facts on Tax Cases Made Public.* Document 5958, 1967.

———. "Statement of Organization and Functions." *Federal Register,* 34:1657, 1969.

Senate Committee on Judiciary. Subcommittee on Administrative Practice and Procedure. *Hearings on Invasions of Privacy,* Parts 3, 4, and 5, 1965–66.

Index